P9-AFC-698

DATE DUE

AP 14 '8	E 16 '8		
SE 28 '84	E 25	E 19 '0	
OC 10 '8	Y 15 '8		
NO 14 '8	OC 16 '87		
R	M 8 '88		
	MY 12 89		
OC 16 81			
A	AG 18 94		
E 26 '0	E 16 '94		
MY 28 8	FE 18 9		

NK
2115.5
I55K76
1978

Kron, Joan.

High-tech

RIVERSIDE CITY COLLEGE

LIBRARY

Riverside, California

MAR   1980

HIGH-TECH

HIGH-TECH

THE INDUSTRIAL STYLE AND SOURCE BOOK FOR THE HOME

BY JOAN KRON AND SUZANNE SLESIN
FOREWORD BY EMILIO AMBASZ
DESIGNED BY WALTER BERNARD
RESEARCH ASSOCIATE: NANCY KLEIN

Clarkson N. Potter, Inc./Publishers
DISTRIBUTED BY CROWN PUBLISHERS, INC., NEW YORK

Riverside Community College
Library
4800 Magnolia Avenue
Riverside, CA 92506

NK2115.5.I55 K76 1978
Kron, Joan.
High-tech : the industrial
style and source book for
the home

To our mothers, Rose and Niuta

Copyright © 1978 by Joan Kron and Suzanne Slesin

All rights reserved. No part of this book may be
reproduced or transmitted in any form or by any
means, electronic or mechanical, including
photocopying, recording or by any information
storage and retrieval system, without permission
in writing from the Publisher.

Inquiries should be addressed to
Clarkson N. Potter, Inc., One Park Avenue,
New York, N.Y. 10016.

Second Printing, November 1978
Produced by Chanticleer Press, New York
Printed by Amilcare Pizzi, S.p.A., Milan, Italy

Library of Congress Cataloging in Publication Data

Kron, Joan.
  High-tech: the industrial style and source book
for the home.

  Includes index.
  1. Industrial equipment in interior decoration.
I. Slesin, Suzanne, joint author. II. Title.
NK2115.5.I55K76 1978 747.883   78-9433
ISBN 0-517-53262-X

Half-title photograph by Peter M. Fine

ACKNOWLEDGMENTS

The making of *High-Tech* has been a year-and-a-half-long adventure that was sometimes exhausting but always fascinating. We did not make this trip alone. While we are willing to accept the blame for whatever, God forbid, may be wrong, whatever is right is certainly because of the help of hundreds of people who shared their knowledge, talents, experience, often secret sources, or encouragement along the way. We'd like to mention a number of them here.

Our thanks:

to all those people who live in the homes illustrated in this book and to the designers and architects, credited throughout, who helped shape many of the environments. We didn't invent high-tech or the industrial style—they did;

to the numerous photographers, credited individually on each page, whose marvelous pictures allow us to "visit" other peoples' homes without intruding. But special kudos to Raeanne Giovanni and Peter M. Fine, who took the largest number of commissioned photos in the book, and to Dan Wynn, who came back from Paris sooner than he would have liked to, just to keep a crucial shooting date; and to Lynn Karlin, Charles Nesbit, Peter Aaron, Tom Yee, David Riley, and Daniel Miles Kron, who took a lot of photographs under difficult circumstances;

to Columbia University's Avery Library, which allowed us to photograph (and publish) a rare Crystal Palace chromolithograph from its original two-volume set titled *Great Exhibition of the Works of Industry of All Nations, 1851*. Thanks also to Herbert Mitchell of the Avery Library, who personally held the book while we took pictures;

to Kenneth Frampton, who helped us contact Michael Carapetian in Iran. Mr. Carapetian provided us with the rare photos of the Maison de Verre on pages 12 through 15;

to the design editors of *New York* magazine, *Philadelphia* magazine, *Gentlemen's Quarterly, House & Garden, Esquire Fortnightly, Family Circle, New York Times, House Beautiful, Abitare,* and *Domus,* among others (in which some of our pictures and ideas originally appeared) for their foresight in recognizing the industrial trend as far back as ten years ago;

to Family Circle and Condé Nast Publications for permission to use their copyrighted photographs (credited on pages 118, 86, and 155.

to the Library of Congress, New York Public Library, and numerous manufacturers, credited throughout, for lending photos;

to the Thomas Publishing Co., who gave us a complete set of the Thomas Register of American Manufacturers and the Thomas Catalogue File—invaluable source books; to the McGraw-Hill Information Systems Co., which loaned us a much coveted thirty-one volume set of Sweet's Catalogue File (we don't want to give it back);

to the many experts who patiently answered our questions, offered advice and direction (and often the names of their sources), including Emilio Ambasz, J. Stewart Johnson, Christopher Wilk, Ada Louise Huxtable, Alan Buchsbaum, Paul Marantz, Kenneth Walker, Barton Myers, Yann Weymouth, Peter Coan, John Young, Richard Rogers, Norman Foster, Ward Bennett, Robert Bray, Michael Schaible, Joseph Paul D'Urso, Richard Penney, William Lacey, William Grover, Tharon Musser, Sonia Cicero, George Fred Keck, Robert Mayers, John Schiff, William P. Bruder, Richard Oliver, Terence Conran, Lewis Davis, Paige Rense, Ben Benedict, Carl Pucci, William Conklin, James Rossant, Chad Floyd, Jeff Riley, Paul Segal, Henry Smith-Miller, Karen Daroff, Robert Patino, Vincent Wolf, John Saladino, Robin Drake, Philip Ferrato, Anne Gilbar, Lee Ryder, Richard Knapple, Peter Carlsen, Liz Whiting, Steven Rogin, Michael Jantzen, Marianne Lorenz of *Domus,* Silvia Latis of *Abitare,* Deda and Giotto Stoppino, John Prizeman, Alain Mertens, Patrick Jacob, Herwin Schaefer, Erving Goffman, Antonio Morello, and Donald Savoie; Andy Colquoun, Stafford Cliff, and Tina Ellis of Conran Assoc.; Murray Gelberg.

to a number of manufacturers, wholesalers, and retailers for their cooperation, advice and, often, loans of merchandise; these include Victor Potamkin of Potamkin Cadillac; Joel Golden of the Metalstand Co.; Jeff Liss of A. Liss and Co.; Jack O'Brien of American Racing; Julia McFarlane and Judith Kress of Manhattan Ad Hoc Housewares; Elsy Menashe of Jason Ind.; Mara Levy of The Professional Kitchen; Joan Burgasser of Thonet; Neil Schwartzberg of Dallek, Inc.; Milton Kamenstein and Kenneth Davis of Rennert; Bruno and Jacqueline Danese, Ludovico Acerbis, and Bernard Featherman of Bernard Franklin Co.; John Domalewski of the Arthur H. Thomas Co.; Campbell McCarthy of Up-Right Scaffolds; Thypin Steel; Shure Manufacturing Corp.; Lakeside Manufacturing, Inc.; L. L. Bean; Brookstone; Charles Gabbour of Mondo Rubber; Pirelli Rubber; Bloomingdale's; Daniel Woodhead Company; Garret Vandermolen of Vandermolen Corp.; Fiorucci; L & B Products Corp.; Air France; Morton Quality Products; Holland Shade Co.; Simplex Ceiling Corp.; Etalage Fabrics, Inc.; Aquino Sailcloth, Inc.; Adam Metal Supply; Robert Finkelstein of Cook's Supply Corp.; United Textiles Corp.; L. W. Sleepwell; Art et Industrie; Charette Corp.; Tedruth Plastics Corp.; Tepromark International; Childcraft Center; Julian Tomchin of Wamsutta Mills; J. P. Stevens; Springs Mills; Grayarc Co., Inc.; Bretford Manufacturing, Inc.; Roblan Manufacturing; Kathleen Gonden Davis; Marvin Gelman of Lighting Services; Chuck Levy of Century Strand Lighting; General Electric Lighting Institute; Illuminating Engineering Society of North America; Smithsonian Institution; Division of Electricity; Maggie Heaney; Louis Brennan of American Olean Tile Co.; James Goslee; the Material Handling Institute;

to Lucy Kroll, who was much more to us than an agent, a special thanks. She had faith, found us the wherewithal, championed us, protected us, held our hands, suggested titles, and cheered us on to the finish line; to James Howe; to Stanley Rothenberg, who made it legal, to Patricia Golbitz, Robert Ginna, Narcisse Chamberlain, Carol Baron, and Peter Mayer for encouragement and advice before the fact; to Jane West, our publisher, for her unwavering faith in us and in the idea and for her total support; to Carolyn Hart and Nancy Novogrod, our editors, for their thoroughness and patience; to Michael Fragnito, who miraculously shepherded this book through production despite our inability to meet his deadlines; and Jean Rodriguez, who assisted him;

to Nancy Newhouse and James L. Greenfield of the *New York Times* and to Clay Felker of *Esquire Fortnightly* for easing our respective workloads at appropriate times;

to Nancy Klein, our research associate, who gave this project continuity while we tried to keep our jobs. She was an indefatigable photo and product researcher, fact finder, scout, sleuth, typist, exchecquer, organizational genius, good-will ambassador, terrific right arm, and good friend;

to Deborah Harkins and Dorothy Seiberling, who advised us on special editing problems;

to Ruth Miller Fitzgibbons, who collated our directory in record time; to Pat Parmalee, who typed it, among other things; to Judy Migliaccio; to Judy Wright, who looked after us;

to Walter Bernard, the brilliant designer of *High-Tech*, who brought to this project not only his taste, creative ability, judgment, mediation powers, and unflappability but also a firm commitment through the unpredictably long haul;

to Joan Dworkin, assistant designer, and Eloise Vega, who contributed much more than layouts; to the art staff—Toby Rosser, JoAnne Seador, Barbara Kraus and Stephen Doyle—all of whom contributed beyond the call;

to Rudy Hoglund, Lily Hou, Anthony J. Libardi, Frank Nigra, Muriel Maher, Chas B Slackman, Jay Harper, Lynn Milnes, Rita Wynn, Stanley Feldman, and Orbit Messenger Service for special artistic and technical assistance; and to Milton Glaser special thanks for the use of his studio facilities and for his continual encouragement;

to our nearest and dearest ones, Jerry Marder and Michael Steinberg, as well as to Harold Klein and Bina Bernard, for their unflagging support and encouragement and for fending for themselves nights and weekends through too many seasons; in addition, a special thanks to Jerry Marder for ignoring the fact that a Xerox machine, boxes upon boxes of catalogs, typing tables, charts, layouts, coworkers, guest towels, and the ever-present tuna fish salad had progressively taken over his living-room, dining room, bathroom, and refrigerator. In spite of these multiple inconveniences, he was a proficient copy editor to the end.

Joan Kron
Suzanne Slesin
May 31, 1978

CONTENTS

FOREWORD
The Alternative Artifact

As the natural landscape replaced the divine milieu in becoming Renaissance man's primary area of concern, so a newly emerging man-made landscape has become the all-pervading framework of contemporary man's thought and imagery.

For the most part this man-made landscape is populated by innumerable varieties of industrial products, reproducing themselves at an extraordinary rate like flowers of an instant, only to disappear a moment later. Like the first chair-maker, who used the wood of surrounding trees, we are now beginning to use the objects and processes—and sometimes the memories—surrounding us.

The reutilization of industrial artifacts has a young but noble tradition. (It should not be confused with a much older one, nowadays loosely called *recycling*, which has seen the marbles and stones of Greek temples and Roman villas removed from their original setting to become part of fences or the whole of peasant dwellings.) The industrial object *reutilized*, that is to say, made to operate in a different context while retaining most of its original functions, was granted resounding professional legitimacy in 1851 when, for the International Exhibition in London, Joseph Paxton built the Crystal Palace using industrial products such as steel and glass and building techniques first developed for the production of prefabricated greenhouses.

The industrial object *rebaptized* (or, in mythological terms, reborn) was granted aesthetic value and assigned philosophic meaning during this century's teens when Marcel Duchamp proclaimed his *ready-mades* (urinals, bicycle wheels, bottle-drying racks) to be art objects, and when Picasso transformed *found objects* into icons—assembling, for instance, a bicycle seat and handlebars into a representation of a bull's head. Although apparently similar, both these artistic operations were, in essence, diametrically opposed: the former stands for Image, the latter for Idea.

Duchamp's action was polemical—a protest against the prevailing idea that a work of art is an object rather than the idea it embodies. Thus in Duchamp's work the object represents an idea whose ultimate physical embodiment is still absent; the object we see is but a surrogate for that which is yet to arrive. Picasso's was an aesthetic act—formal modification of an object to make it resemble another.

In such opposition of complementaries, which at once binds found objects to and separates them from ready-mades, lies the constantly shifting contradiction we shall see also underlying the present reutilization of industrial objects. On the one hand, industrial objects stand as surrogates with which we try to "make do," while on the other, these same objects would prove themselves inadequate were we to seek through them the enactment of an alternative mode of existence. Therefore, each of today's alternative artifacts can be seen at once as both found object and ready-made. A laboratory flask, for instance, is a found object when we choose it to hold flowers at home. But by not accepting available containers to hold flowers, the flask can also be seen as a ready-made—not only is it a surrogate for that well-designed and well-priced container that is not yet available but, more important, it stands as a sign of our having reached a level of awareness—a realization that the core of our problem is finding a solution to the process of containing rather than finding the tasteful flower vase.

Nowhere can this ambiguity be seen more clearly than in what is rightly recognized as the greatest contemporary accomplishment of the "doctrine of alternative reutilization": Charles Eames's own house, built in 1949 in Santa Monica, California. In this very influential design—a veritable compendium of found objects and ready-mades—Eames utilized mass-produced materials, such as doors and windows, steel columns and open-web joists, normally used in the construction of factories. Eames's house came, at that time, to stand as a surrogate for that new and better type of

At left, an alternative artifact—a detection mirror used as a dressing table mirror in an interior designed by Joseph Paul D'Urso.

housing that prefabrication was to bring. It was a mythopoetic creation, a joyful act of optimism, where objects removed from one domain were used to represent a supposedly richer way of life yet to come. The Santa Monica house has remained as that unique instant when both the found object and the ready-made were symbolically and functionally fused: a formal paradigm of the modern movement's belief in the aesthetics of prefabrication as well as the ideological demonstration of the social benefits to accrue from good design and industrialized building.

Eames's optimism of 1949 was by no means unique. After all, it had been a long-standing assumption of the modern movement that if all man's products were well designed, harmony and joy would emerge eternally triumphant. It is only in the last quarter of this century that conflicting signs from different sources have made it evident that although good design is a necessary condition, it is not by itself sufficient. Consequently, today, many architects and designers, and, what is more important, a growing number of consumers, are expanding their traditional concern for the aesthetic of the uses to which the object will be put. Thus, the object is no longer perceived as an isolated entity, sufficient unto itself, but rather as an integral part of the larger natural and sociocultural environment.

But the desanctification of design is not a recent phenomenon. Already in the 1950s, and all during the 1960s, the brilliant Castiglione brothers design team (especially the late Pier Giacomo) had sensed that the cultural premises once giving rise to the modern movement in product design had lost their value. Inspired by Duchamp's antiaestheticism, they set aside many of design's accepted academic scaffoldings and claimed that "finding" and "choosing" were also the object-maker's rightful tools. The Castigliones' own working method was mainly assemblage, and their designs were arrived at by utilizing found objects usually recovered from the surrounding industrial landscape. Going one step further, they utilized irony to make comments on the social values assigned to objects in our society. Such was the case, for example, when they designed the "Mezzadro" stool in 1955, juxtaposing a humble tractor seat with an elegantly polished steel and wood base. The found object was turned into a ready-made. Another example of this approach is their 1962 design of the "Toio" lamp, where they utilized an automobile headlight perched on top of what looked like a fishing rod. For their assemblage method as well as for their early use of a repertoire of available industrial elements, they should be recognized as one of this book's intellectual antecedents and as the forefathers of many of the projects herein illustrated.

While many of the environments pictured in this book were created by architects and designers, the book's underlying premise, and hope, is that the users may, themselves, eventually engage in design and management as a means of transforming everyday existence. One way of doing so is to explore the man-made landscape and choose from the large repertoire of its "flora and fauna." Many industrial objects (flasks, wheels, scaffolding, lockers) are noble pieces of anonymous design, unencumbered by the artificial need to reflect status. Created outside the realm of the consumer society, they are straightforward and honest in their ability to render good service (often with a minimum of cost to our personal economy and to that of the ecological environment). If not always handsome, they are usually wholesome, and perhaps because of that, they are touchingly lovable. They can be used to satisfy the necessity people have for creating their own habitat according to their own needs, desires, and images of themselves. They may also be used to express our wish not to follow social patterns imposed by those who manipulate culture, invent desires, and shape fashions.

However, there is always the risk these products will

become the new fashion of a subculture that will assign these industrial objects pseudoliberating powers. This may in turn lead to the same consumption-inducing mechanisms this group was trying to escape from. To counteract such risks we must develop a high level of consciousness and keep in mind that we are using industrial objects in an alternative manner as a form of moral protest. Should this be forgotten, we may run the peril that those industrial objects we have selected, because in some way they could be assigned the role of representing a future yet to come, may, in turn, be the same ones that distract us from reaching our ultimate purpose: that of achieving an environment designed by ourselves.

Nonetheless we should now welcome this book for what it honestly wishes to be and very capably accomplishes. It is a very good road map, one of the first "botanical and zoological guides" to the man-made landscape. It is a most useful guide to the difficult tasks we must set for ourselves if we are ever to learn how to effectively live in and act upon our man-made landscape, distinguishing the noxious and damaging species of products from those which are necessary to support an environment conducive to the highest enjoyment of the senses and the mind.

—*Emilio Ambasz*

Emilio Ambasz, a prize-winning architect and designer, was Curator of Design at the Museum of Modern Art from 1970 to 1976. He is the author of, among other works, The Architecture of Luis Barragan, *and* The Taxi Project, *and the editor of* Italy: The New Domestic Landscape.

INTRODUCTION

Something is happening in home furnishings: instead of velvet, movers' pads are being used as upholstery; instead of crystal chandeliers, white-enameled factory dome lights are hanging over dining tables; in place of teak wall units and brass étagères, steel warehouse shelving is holding the books in smart living rooms; and in the bathroom, where gold-plated swans or chrome nuggets once reigned supreme, hospital faucets are adding new cachet.

Some people call this phenomenon "the industrial style," but we call it "high-tech." High-tech, a play on the words *high-style* and *technology*, is a term currently used in architectural circles to describe buildings incorporating prefabricated, or "off-the-rack," building components.

For instance, when a residence sports open-web steel joists, corrugated aluminum siding, roll-up loading-dock doors, and/or steel mezzanines—components more commonly used in the construction of factories, warehouses, and schools—it's called high-tech.

High-tech is also used to describe buildings with a technological look: the Centre Georges Pompidou in Paris, a cultural center that has been likened to an oil refinery; the new Sainsbury Centre in Norwich, England, a cultural center that has been compared to an airplane hangar; and the Occupational Health Center in Columbus, Indiana, that has been described as looking like a boiler room.

This book moves "high-tech" one step beyond this architectural nuts-and-bolts definition. Taking license, we have expanded its meaning to describe the parallel trend in interior design: the use of utilitarian industrial equipment and materials, out of context, as home furnishings.

While those who bury their heads in fringed and flowered throw pillows might consider it a fad or a farce, we see this appropriation of products originally created for use in warehouses, factories, battleships, hospitals, and offices—products that some people would no more consider using in their homes than they would wearing sneakers with a tuxedo—as a major trend.

Engineered rather than designed, the myriad items of commercial and industrial equipment turning up in homes today were produced originally for utilitarian purposes, often with no thought given to style. Form followed function, not for aesthetic reasons but for efficiency, economy, and safety.

The quilted movers' pads prevented damage to goods and claims against the company; factory light fixtures were designed for performance, not looks—a flickering light on the assembly line could result in a hand being cut off; fireproof metal shelving was developed to support the large inventories of a burgeoning consumer economy; and the distinctive shape of a hospital faucet handle was the result of new antiseptic procedures.

But today architects and designers are looking at these functional objects with new appreciation. They see virtue in the fact that many of these products are well designed, although unintentionally, having evolved through a process of invention, modification, and improvements, and that they are readily available. In addition, many of these objects and materials are cheaper than comparable merchandise available through decorator sources or custom-made. And when they are not cheaper, they are usually more durable.

This *ad hoc* appropriation of utilitarian equipment and materials is not limited to home furnishings. A society that once hewed to the work ethic is now embracing the work aesthetic—all across the cultural board.

In fashion we see the adoption of work clothes—blue jeans, overalls, army-navy gear, hiking boots, lab coats, aviator glasses—as everyday apparel. The work-clothes movement may have started as counterculture fashion, but today it's over-the-counter fashion in establishment stores worldwide.

In personal transportation we are seeing people who

At left, Municipal Bank of Buenos Aires, Condor Branch, designed by architects Manteola, Sánchez Gómez, Santos, Solsona, Viñoly.

1

could afford Mercedes or Cadillacs trading down to vans and pickup trucks. Among the fastest moving properties in real estate are the industrial lofts vacated by light manufacturing companies that are now being converted to living spaces.

In retail merchandising, one of the newest phenomena is the emporium specializing in restaurant kitchen equipment. Even department stores are beginning to sell professional cooking equipment. And in the kitchen appliance market, the restaurant range, although not cheaper, has replaced the built-in double oven as the status appliance.

Simultaneously, in the design concept of boutiques and restaurants (an early warning system alerting us to what will be selling next year for rumpus rooms) the latest "nostalgia" theme, which supersedes Art Nouveau, Art Deco, and the Casablanca look, is what might be called "George Meany modern." The visual symbols of this decorating style are construction site scaffolding, yellow warning lights, Men At Work signs, and a hard hat on a hook.

The Sandwich Construction Company, an eatery in North Carolina, is one example of this pop-tech version of the industrial vernacular. It features factory lights, drop cloths, plants in tin pails, and menus done up like blueprints.

But high-tech can also be more black turtleneck than blue collar. One group of New York interior designers places "equipment" against pared-down, multileveled backgrounds covered in battleship gray "industrial" carpeting. In their hands, detection mirrors, restaurant table bases, drafting lamps, and lab carts and chairs take on a pristine elegance, totally devoid of sentiment or pop overtones.

Why, you might ask, is the paraphernalia of industry (that was never intended for residential use) being used as home furnishings? There are numerous explanations: you could call it the nostalgia of a postindustrial society (electronic technology turning the machine into an art form as Marshall McLuhan hypothesized); a throwback to the Bauhaus (a German academy of the arts, founded in 1919, dedicated to making well-designed furnishings for mass production); the fulfillment of Le Corbusier's edict in the 1920s that the house should be a machine for living furnished with equipment; the pragmatic solution to the high cost of custom craftsmanship; the logical follow-up to such things as the antimaterialism of the 1960s and the do-it-yourself and back-to-nature movements; or you could call it industrial chic—and there are those who will; or all of the above.

Certainly high-tech has its roots in industrialization and prefabrication—the first important example of which was the Crystal Palace, built in London in 1851.

Next had to come an appreciation of utilitarian objects; they were despised in the nineteenth century but we learned to love them in the twentieth century. A series of exhibitions—1906 in Dresden, 1925 in Paris, 1928 in New York, and others in between—helped foster a new taste for equipment and machine-made products. This movement was finally canonized in 1934 when the Museum of Modern Art staged a Machine Art show and founded its influential design collection, a shrine to the appreciation of product design.

But now that what was once avant garde has finally become establishment—the radical bent tubular Breuer chairs designed at the Bauhaus (they were the symbols of a better life through mass production) are the status symbols of the elite living room; the "good design" Eames chair is copied and sold at countless stores—it is time for us to discover the more humble and more anonymous designs of the machine age.

However, even if you are ready for this stuff, where do you find it? We are limited by what stores and manufacturers offer us. Many manufacturers have two catalogs, one for industrial users and one for consumers. Often the only difference between the products in these catalogs is that the consumer version is jazzed up while the industrial version is simple and straightforward.

Inevitably, as designers and consumers become aware that there can be more (or less, depending on how you look at it) to bathroom fixtures than pink, blue, and desert tan, industrial lines will find their way to the marketplace through existing channels or through new ones. When this happens, high-tech will be more than just an avant-garde trend—it will be a bona fide major style.

We have tried to accomplish *three* things in this book: First, we wanted to report and record the new industrial aesthetic in design that we think is one of the most important design trends today.

Second, we wanted to illustrate a cross section of industrial products that have residential potential, while at the same time showing their blue-collar origins. These items have untapped marketing possibilities and offer innumerable options for the consumer.

Third, we didn't want our book to just sit there on the coffee table looking pretty. To that end we have tried to demystify the industrial landscape with our directory of sources; no matter where you live it can serve as a guide to sources of supply and an inspiration to finding more sources on your own.

For those with motivation, imagination, and occasionally the required powers of persuasion to convince a company that sells by the gross to sell just *one* of something, there is a whole world of exotic, underemployed industrial equipment, materials, and supplies that could moonlight residentially. And there are sources for them in or near every community in the country—in fact, in the world. The Midwest is a treasure trove of manufacturers. For rare antiques you may have to go to London, Paris, and New York; but for the tools of the trade—the pallets and skids, rolling ladders, laboratory glass, mezzanines—you can

shop in many cities or by mail. Every city has a material handling equipment outlet and hospital, restaurant, janitorial, and auto supply stores nearby. Only marine hardware stores are scarce inland.

How do you find these sources? Many industrial purchasing agents use the Thomas Register, a comprehensive directory of American manufacturers published once a year by the Thomas Publishing Company, One Penn Plaza, New York, New York 10001. This twelve-volume directory, which sells for about $70, lists more than 100,000 manufacturers and has more than one million classified product listings. But take heart, it's available in many libraries.

Architects use the Sweet's Catalogue File published annually by McGraw-Hill. Sweet's includes the actual catalog pages of thousands of manufacturers of building products and furnishings. Sweet's cannot be bought, however. It is distributed only to designers and architects who purchase a certain minimum quantity of products per year, but it too is available in libraries.

The consumer's next best guide to buried treasure in any city is the telephone company's Yellow Pages. If you don't live in a large city, the phone company, for a small charge, will supply you with the Yellow Pages of any city you request.

But asking questions can sometimes reveal as much as these directories. If you see a bookcase or a table base or a doughnut tray in a public place, ask the proprietor where it comes from. It took a few phone calls, but Consolidated Edison graciously shared with us the source for its manhole barriers pictured on page 180.

In the back of this book you'll find the *High-Tech* directory listing almost 2,000 industrial sources, which are organized according to the chapter headings of this book: Structural, Systems, Storage, Furniture, Materials, Lighting, The Works, and Finishing Touches. In this directory you will find the addresses of the manufacturers and distributors of all the products illustrated in the book, as well as hundreds of additional sources, national and worldwide. We have tried to give at least one source for every product category. But, obviously, 2,000 sources are only the tip of the iceberg.

Buying commercial and industrial products is not as easy as buying a cake of soap in the supermarket, but it still can be done. We have indicated whether a source is a manufacturer, wholesaler/dealer, retailer, or mail-order house. Since it is a fairly new phenomenon for consumers to buy industrial goods, there were not many retail stores we could list. Manufacturers, for the most part, will not sell directly to a consumer, but they will send catalogs and product information and refer potential customers to dealers in their areas.

In a number of cases we have listed the manufacturer as well as the manufacturer's distributor. But some manufacturers have so many distributors they prefer that readers write to them directly for a dealer referral. And some manufacturers, like Amelco, for instance, which sells double-glazed windows with venetian blinds inside, told us they would sell directly to anyone. Eliason Door Co., a firm that sells supermarket and hospital doors, also told us it would sell directly to anyone.

What about the price tag on all this? It depends. Illustrated in this book are items costing from about $1 for disposable salt and pepper shakers to $10,000 for a revolving electric filing cabinet. There is a tendency for the uninitiated to equate industrial with cheap. While some industrial products, such as chemical glass and restaurant china, are considerably less expensive than consumer products sold for the same purposes, other industrial items have hefty price tags; however, they can still be less expensive than so-called decorator furniture.

We have quoted prices wherever possible, but they are to be used only as a guide, not as firm quotations. Prices can vary significantly depending on quantity, finish, size, increases in steel prices after we have gone to press, which dealer you buy from, and in which part of the country you're located. In every case, shipping is extra. Also, as they say in industry, prices are subject to change without notice.

Reporting a trend, as this book does, will inevitably accelerate the trend. As demand for some of these products increases, they may become available to the general public through conventional retail outlets. Unfortunately, each time another source comes between the manufacturer and the user, the price will probably go up.

In the final analysis, this book is about resources and resourcefulness. It could alter your ideas about what is and is not appropriate for use in the home. We will consider it a success if, when you pass a manhole barrier, when you see an interesting table base in a restaurant, or when you see a bumper guard or an automatic door that could work in your home, you say to yourself, I wonder where I can get that?

At right, the waiting room of the high-tech Occupational Health Center in Columbus, Indiana, designed by architects Hardy Holzman Pfeiffer Associates.

NORMAN McGRATH

HIGH-TECH

THE INDUSTRIAL AESTHETIC

DANIEL MILES KRON   COURTESY OF AVERY LIBRARY, COLUMBIA UNIV.

PETER M. FINE

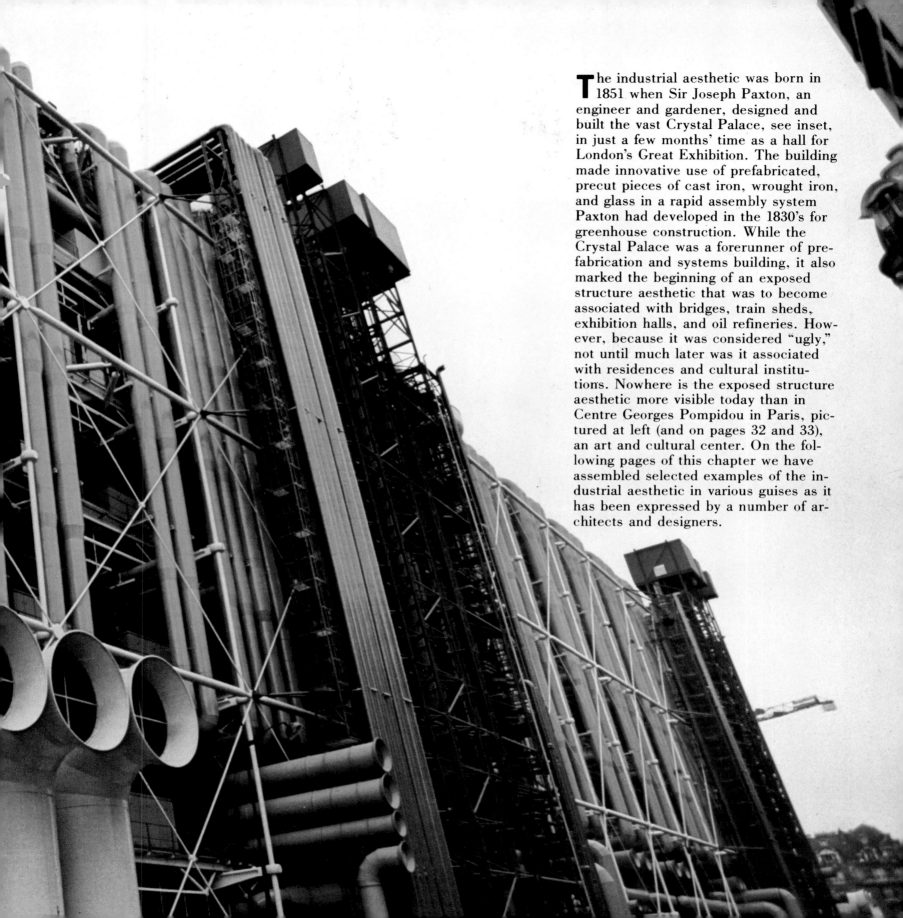

The industrial aesthetic was born in 1851 when Sir Joseph Paxton, an engineer and gardener, designed and built the vast Crystal Palace, see inset, in just a few months' time as a hall for London's Great Exhibition. The building made innovative use of prefabricated, precut pieces of cast iron, wrought iron, and glass in a rapid assembly system Paxton had developed in the 1830's for greenhouse construction. While the Crystal Palace was a forerunner of prefabrication and systems building, it also marked the beginning of an exposed structure aesthetic that was to become associated with bridges, train sheds, exhibition halls, and oil refineries. However, because it was considered "ugly," not until much later was it associated with residences and cultural institutions. Nowhere is the exposed structure aesthetic more visible today than in Centre Georges Pompidou in Paris, pictured at left (and on pages 32 and 33), an art and cultural center. On the following pages of this chapter we have assembled selected examples of the industrial aesthetic in various guises as it has been expressed by a number of architects and designers.

PETER M. FINE

FRENCH GOVERNMENT TOURIST OFFICE

The Eiffel Tower, built in Paris for the 1889 Centennial Exposition, is the embodiment of the industrial aesthetic. During its construction it generated scores of outraged letters from prominent citizens. Later hailed as the right kind of architecture for the twentieth century, the 984-foot-high tower designed by engineer Alexandre-Gustave Eiffel was more than just an aesthetic statement; it was a demonstration of the possibilities of prefabrication. Built of precut wrought-iron trusses, it was completed in a few months, for modest cost, with a small labor force.

HEDRICH-BLESSING

The Crystal House, above, was built in 1934 for Chicago's Century of Progress exhibit by George Fred Keck. Now in his eighties, Keck was one of the first American architects to explore the industrial landscape for concepts that could be applied to residential construction. Sheathed in glass, the Crystal House was supported by an exterior framework of steel trusses reminiscent of scaffolding, bridges, train sheds, and its namesake, the Crystal Palace.

MICHAEL CARAPETIAN

The Maison de Verre—the glass house—designed in 1928 by Pierre Chareau (an engineer and interior designer) with Bernard Bijoet, and completed in 1932, was probably the first major residential demonstration of the industrial aesthetic. According to architect and historian Kenneth Frampton, "it was redolent with industrial potential although the [custom-made] methods of realization were far from industrial." The steel and glass-block house and office combination, built for a physician, Dr. Dalsace, and his wife, is still privately owned. It is being maintained by an organization established to preserve it. Although it was considered utopian when it was built, designers today are rediscovering it— fascinated with its sensuous use of light and space and its mechanistic furnishings, including remote-controlled steel louvers, adjustable mirrors, retractable steel shop ladders, revolving closets, and metal bookcases.

The main salon of the Maison de Verre, shown on the previous two pages, can be seen here at far right, above, from a different angle. As Kenneth Frampton pointed out in an article in *Perspecta 12*, the Yale architectural journal, mobility is the recurring motif in this amazing house. Among the movable parts are the rolling library ladder of the salon; boldly scaled louvers, above, which bring air into the salon; revolving closets in the bedrooms; adjustable mirrors in the bathrooms (one is shown far right, below); and in the same photograph, one of the earliest adjustable track lights.

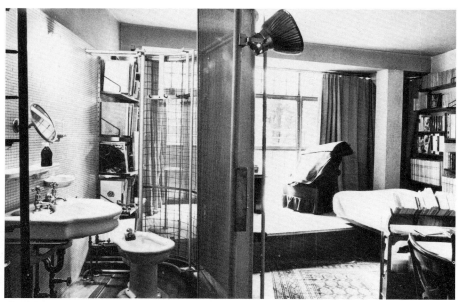

PHOTOGRAPHS BY MICHAEL CARAPETIAN

15

ORLANDO R. CABANBAN

Rust was encouraged, not resented, in this vacation
retreat designed by Chicago architects Harry Weese &
Associates. "Shadow Cliff," built in Green Bay, Wisconsin,
in 1969, is constructed of Cor-Ten self-weathering
steel, which forms a natural dark brown protective rust.

In 1949, when designers Charles and
Ray Eames built their landmark Santa
Monica home-cum-studio, it was revolutionary to assemble, as they did, a
house from so-called off-the-peg industrial parts commonly used to build factories. The house, a demonstration project, incorporated exposed open-webbed
steel joists, prefab steel decking, and
factory-style windows, most of it ordered
out of catalogs. If this house—which
lacked all the romantic visual symbols of
home—did not capture the hearts of
Middle America, it did create a climate
for experimentation with industrial materials used out of context.

CHARLES EAMES

GERHARD CHRIST

This flat-roofed steel and glass house built in the early 1970s in Wiesbaden-Sonnenberg, Germany, by German architects Christ + Christ is a simple rectangle with rounded corners. Materials such as the corrugated steel facade panels, cross bracing, and two-story-high jalousie windows—more commonly associated with commercial buildings—give the house its high-tech image. Inside the two-story-high steel "container," the spiral steel staircase leading up to the bedroom study and the oval-shaped doorways remininscent of ships' passageways further emphasize the industrial appearance of the house.

With the exception of the igloo, the dome has traditionally been associated with important public buildings or mosques, and more recently with grain silos and astronomy labs. But just as the factory "look" has been co-opted for residences, the symbolic dome has been appropriated too. The corrugated-steel-clad solar house pictured at left, designed and built by nonarchitects Michael and Ellen Jantzen of Carlyle, Illinois, uses one half of a prefabricated silo dome for a roof.

PHILIP TURNER

The metal and glass house pictured above is not your typical suburban Chicago house. It was designed for a family of five by Stanley Tigerman & Associates, a Chicago firm, and completed in 1975. Its industrial look is the sum of its exterior parts—a number of prefabricated elements such as an astronomy dome, modified roll-up garage doors, Alcoa's aluminum facade panels, and zipper-gasketed windows.

ometimes mistaken for a
filling station, architect
Michael Hopkins's award-
winning home, built in 1975 in
Hampstead, England, is made
of steel framing and decking
used in large-scale factory
construction. Storage is industrial bins on warehouse shelving; bathroom floors are covered in plastic duckboards.

PHOTOGRAPHS BY TIM STREET-PORTER/ELIZABETH WHITING & ASSOCIATES

PHOTOGRAPHS BY HELMUT SCHULITZ

In 1977 German architect Helmut Schulitz built a prototype house for himself on a 40-degree cliff site in Coldwater Canyon, California, that was thought to be unusable. The building's steel frame was erected in two days, and only those components that fitted into his modular grid were selected. "I wanted to minimize on-site labor by maximizing the use of precut, prefinished parts," said Schulitz. The windows, open-web joists, aluminum panels of the facade, steel stair treads, steel decking used for ceilings, kitchen cabinets, and the fireplace are some of the prefabricated components incorporated into what has been described as an "erector set" house. Working also as the house's contractor, Schulitz built the 2,500-square-foot house for $76,000—$28 per square foot. His plan is to apply this method of construction— and this aesthetic—to larger developments. "In the future," he said, "all buildings will be built like this."

23

NORMAN McGRATH

Another house in the high-tech style is the de Bretteville-Simon house, a two-family house built in 1977 by architect Peter de Bretteville in Laurel Canyon, Los Angeles. The two residences are united behind a continuous 124-foot wall of corrugated asbestos and fiber-glass panels, which has been notched in the middle for the two entrances. A descendant of the Eames house (pages 16-17), the de Bretteville-Simon house is

NORMAN McGRATH

also similar to the Schulitz house, shown on the preceding pages, in its use of prefabricated industrial components, including railings, paneling, decking, and open-web joists. Two balconies run the length of the house: an inside one for circulation and an outside one that is covered to shield the house from the sun. Inside the de Bretteville house, beams and yellow foam-block-furniture play off against a pink stair rail.

PHOTOGRAPHS BY RAEANNE GIOVANNI

Ward Bennett, left, sitting in an old dentist's chair and talking on a phone that rests on a rusty I beam, is the mentor of, and inspiration to, designers working in the industrial style. Before becoming a prominent furniture and interior designer (his work includes the CBS offices and many private homes), Mr. Bennett was a sculptor, fashion designer, and painter. Working against the fashion of the early 1960s, he stripped

PETER M FINE

his interiors to their bare essentials and explored the industrial reservoir, rediscovering such things as factory lamps, marine hardware, warehouse shelving, laboratory glass, and hospital hardware. His much-publicized Long Island home and his New York apartment (shown on these pages), filled with such things as a table made from a 1937 Buick wheel hub, top left, continue to be his design laboratories.

PHOTOGRAPHS BY PETER AARON

Cyclone fencing, a rotating cleaner's rack, a surgeon's sink, a detection mirror, restaurant food-storage drawers, slotted-angle shelving, a doctor's scale, hospital doors—these are some of the "high-tech" furnishings used by designer Joseph Paul D'Urso, reflected above, in the New York apartments shown on these and the next two pages. "The best design work in this country is in the industrial sector," says D'Urso, whose subtle handling of industrial elements has brought recognition to and respect for the "industrial style." He admires products created for transportation and hospitals because of their quality, because the materials are easy to maintain, and because no attempt is made to satisfy anyone's sentimental preoccupations. D'Urso always takes "the logical approach." People have called it style. "I prefer to think of it as an attitude, a vocabulary. For me, design is problem solving. The objects don't mean anything in and of themselves. They only take on importance in the way they are combined in an interior."

MICHAEL DATOLI

But even when he uses industrial elements, as on the previous two pages, D'Urso's style remains minimalist. At left, one of D'Urso's pared-down spaces with the gray-carpeted floors and glossy white walls that have become his trademark. "I don't make decisions to amuse myself," he says. "I use commercial carpeting in dark gray because it's easy to clean, nice to sit on, doesn't show dirt, is a unifying element, and is the most logical material to cover floors in New York apartments." D'Urso also likes to keep the walls bare—to use them as material to complete the visual experience—juxtaposing the surfaces and volumes created by the "split" hospital door, the geometric fireplace, the arched wall. "I want to create spaces that are serene and easy to live in," he says. "If being labeled a minimalist means achieving complexity and richness through restraint and economy, I accept it."

PHOTOGRAPHS BY PATRICK JACOB

Parisians today complain as much about their Centre National d'Art et de Culture Georges Pompidou as their grandparents did about the Eiffel Tower when it was erected in 1889. Designed by English architect Richard Rogers and his Italian partner Renzo Piano, the Centre Pompidou—now nicknamed the Beaubourg—that rises dramatically out of the surrounding area of Les Halles is a building turned inside out. With its exposed heating and cooling ducts, exterior escalators, electrical conduits, and water pipes (the elements of a building that are usually hidden on the inside are visible here on the outside), the museum is the ultimate embodiment

of the industrial aesthetic. The smokestacks, water towers, and scaffoldlike facade have prompted fans and critics to liken the Centre Pompidou to an ocean liner, oil refinery, distillery, launching pad, and factory. Paradoxically, although the building looks very much like a free-form assembly of standardized parts, almost every piece of hardware, every component, has been custom-designed, engineered, and fabricated. With its polychromed facade—blue for air conditioning, green for water, red for elevator machinery—the Centre Pompidou is a joyful, playful example of the visual possibilities of the factory aesthetic.

For two and a half years Ted Bakewell, III, right, a St. Louis architectural designer and a real estate developer, camped out in a warehouse that he furnished with industrial discards. "It was an experiment in low-energy, low-cost living," said Mr. Bakewell, who admits he is strongly influenced by space technology. His industrial campsite brought a new perspective to every conventional artifact of daily life: the front door (a slit to save heat loss), seating (made of foam discards inspired by the foam pits Bakewell used to land in when he was a pole-vaulter), the bed (recycled scaffolding), and the bed's canopy (an army surplus parachute) among other things. Bakewell's only regret is not having videotaped guests arriving for the first time. "Some people keep their homes nostalgic as a buffer against future shock," he observed. "Those types were horrified. But others," he said, "loved this space." His current project is making a mobile home into a solar home.

PHOTOGRAPHS BY KRISTEN PETERSON AND KIM ELOCK

STRUCTURAL ELEMENTS

40 WINDOWS AND GREENHOUSES

Expand the house or raise the roof with an easily available factory-fabricated greenhouse or skylight—or consider overhead garage doors for windows.

44 DOORS

When stripped of their wood-grain veneers, the swinging aluminum doors found in hospitals, hotels, and restaurants are very handsome and economical too.

46 STAIRCASES

The circular steel staircase was one of the first industrial items to be accepted in homes. It looks better than ever today.

48 MEZZANINES

Mezzanines made of standard parts are quick solutions to adding a second story in high-ceilinged spaces, and you can take them with you when you move. Most steel shelving manufacturers offer them.

50 RAILINGS

Pipe is a many splendored thing, especially when used as railing. Ships' hardware and tennis nets can keep you from going overboard too.

OVERLEAF *Greenhouse photo, courtesy Roper IBG; inset, Lord & Burnham "Greenhouse" extension designed by Bray-Schaible Designs, photo, Raeanne Giovanni.*

The old stereotype of the architect—like the hero of Ayn Rand's novel *The Fountainhead,* sitting at his drafting table sketching chimerical buildings and Utopian communities—may have to be replaced with a new scenario: the architect sitting at his or her desk leafing through catalogs looking for compatible factory-fabricated components out of which to assemble buildings.

While the custom-built house, the unique work of art, couture clothes, and custom-built cars à la James Bond are deeply ingrained in our fantasy lives, the fact is that in the past 150 years we have moved from a custom-made world to a mass-produced and interchangeable-parts world—a component society. Do-it-yourself products, mix-and-match sportswear, hi-fi, and high tech are all part of the same twentieth century phenomenon—the components approach to home improvement, dressing, audio equipment, and building construction. However, like bad lip sync in a film, our awareness of them lags a little behind the reality. The promise of prefabricated housing, once thought to be the wave of the future, has never been fulfilled. Since the 1950s there have been numerous attempts at a systems approach to building, most of which have resulted in the fast erection of schools. The buzz words of prefabrication are "open systems" and "closed systems." In a closed system only parts of the same system can be used. In an open system, just as the speakers from one stereo manufacturer can be used with the amplifier from another, or the jacket of one designer can be used with the pants and skirt of another's, parts from many systems can be interchanged.

But while total prefabrication of buildings falters, the art of assembling a building from factory-fabricated and standardized elements is on the rise. Even if you are not building a house from scratch, we have unearthed in this chapter a number of prefabricated elements that would be suitable to use in a renovation. One of the first factory-fabricated elements to gain a foothold in the home was the factory-made steel staircase, a nostalgic backstage prop familiar in Broadway melody-type movies of the 1930s and 1940s. After years of exposure in home furnishings magazines, the spiral steel staircase has taken on a romantic aura that belies its origins in theatres, ships, and firehouses.

Commercial and industrial doors made for supermarkets, hospitals, and gas stations have residential potential as well. But perhaps the most underappreciated industrial structural element is the mezzanine. With more and more people moving into high-ceilinged lofts and formerly commercial spaces, building a mezzanine is a simple way to double the usable space. In fact, mezzanines were invented to take advantage of the wasted overhead space in warehouses; that's why they are not listed in most Yellow Pages under Mezzanines but under Steel Shelving Manufacturers, who make and sell them.

However, the one structural element that is the most symbolic of the industrial revolution in building is the greenhouse, which can be prefabricated in the factory to your measurements and installed in record time. With it you can make any add-on room a miniature Crystal Palace.

ENLARGED KITCHEN *Lord & Burnham glass-to-ground lean-to greenhouse (from $1,500) used by designer Michael Kalil.*

WINDOWS AND GREENHOUSES

Prefabricated windows, greenhouses, and skylights, originally designed for commercial installations, offer a wealth of residential possibilities. The greenhouse as we know it—a skeleton of metal with glass sinew—dates back to the early nineteenth century, when glass became cheap and abundant. Iron and glass skylight construction was used thereafter for all sorts of public buildings, from conservatories to railway stations to exhibition halls.

Today you can expand a house or raise a roof with an easily available prefab greenhouse. Less romantic but just as adaptable for home use are industrial sashes—the neat gridwork of factory windows—portholes, overhead garage doors with windows, and doublepane windows that have fully adjustable venetian blinds built in. Check the Yellow Pages under Windows-Metal, Greenhouse Builders, Doors-Garage, Hardware-Marine, and Glass.

RAISED ROOF *Architects Edward S. Knowles and John Immitt used a Lord & Burnham greenhouse* (right) *to remodel a stable for artist Lowell Nesbitt.*

NORMAN McGRATH

BRECHT-ENZIG LIMITED

UP AND AWAY *A Hillaldam Coburn overhead garage door like those used in firehouses is London architect George Wolton's window solution.*

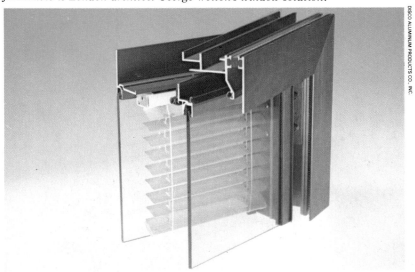

DISCO ALUMINUM PRODUCTS CO. INC.

WINDOW PLUS *A venetian blind is built in between a sandwich of glass in Disco's T-2001 thermal window ($300 and up); another source, Amelco.*

JOSEPH W. MOLITOR

FIXTURE WINDOW *The steel "industrial" sash, above, from the Roblin Architectural Products Company was chosen by architects Bohlin and Powell for large windows in a Connecticut home. They like the way the factory windows "break down the scale."*

ON SHORE *In the office of architects Paul Segal Associates, an old brass porthole, right, works as a reception window.*

PETER M. FINE

IN STOCK *A standard Ickes-Braun Sunhouse (fiber-glass greenhouse) roof was the solution of architects A. J. Diamond and Barton Myers for a courtyard roof, above, in Mr. Myers's Toronto house.*

SOFT EDGE *Round-cornered windows, such as the ones at right used by architects Piano + Rogers in an English factory, are custom-made, but resourceful people can buy similar ones from automobile sun roof manufacturers such as Young Windows.*

YUKIO FUTAGAWA

NORMAN McGRATH

PATRICK JACOB

ANDREW HOLMES

RECYCLED *Architect Ulrich Franzen, above, reassembled a 55-year-old lean-to greenhouse in order to enclose the terrace of his city apartment. Secondhand greenhouses can be bought from greenhouse builders.*

SHADY *Rolling outdoor shutters, such as the ones at left at the Pompidou Center in Paris, are standard in Europe for light control. In the United States, rolling metal doors are used on counters and for service doors. One source is the Overhead Door Company.*

DOORS

From the revolving doors of hotels and department stores, to automatically opened supermarket doors, roll-up hangar doors, roll-down protective grills, aluminum hospital swinging doors, and tambour doors—industrial doors are a lot more interesting to contemplate than the Spanish and Mediterranean-style paneled doors available at the lumberyard. We looked, without success, for someone who had tried the clear plastic loading dock "curtains"—used to keep heat in where there are constant comings and goings—that resemble overlapping strips of cellophane. Perhaps in our next book. However, aluminum swinging supermarket doors abound residentially. Robert Bray and Michael Schaible of Bray-Schaible Design, and Joseph Paul D'Urso, who all use these doors regularly, say that compared to custom-made doors, which are costly to fabricate and hang, Eliason Easy Swing doors—which come complete with patented pivot hinges—are a simple solution to the high cost of labor today. These doors are available for openings 22-inches to 88-inches wide and up to eight feet high. They come in satin aluminum finish or can be veneered with plastic laminates. They can even be perforated or made with windows as shown here.

MOTEL DOORS *Bray-Schaible specified all the doors on this page. Above, two Eliason aluminum doors ($130 each) are in a bedroom.*

DOWN *Exterior tambour shades by Amrol conceal a bookcase indoors.*

RESTAURANT STYLE *Another pair of Eliason doors used by the same designers—these doors have mirrors instead of windows.*

UP *Here is the rolling door, pictured above, in the up position.*

DOCKING *Overhead Door Co. loading-dock doors, right, are used as garage doors by Connecticut architects BumpZoid.*

44

PETER M. FINE

AMERICAN ORNAMENTAL METAL CO.

STAIRCASES

Spiral metal staircases, dating back to the nineteenth century, when they were used in boiler rooms, firehouses, and backstage, are becoming household fixtures. The graceful cantilevered spiral stair tread—a tread not connected to adjoining steps—was patented in 1917 by Pierre Duvinage, a French ironworker who opened a foundry in Baltimore at the turn of the century. Until 1950 almost all spiral stairs produced were for industrial and commercial use. But today about half of these stairs are sold for residential use. Although you can buy spiral stairs in do-it-yourself prefabricated kits, for about $350, one custom-made to your requirements can start at about $375 plus installation. Galvanized steel stairs fare better in salt air or damp climate. Aluminum stairs are lighter. Each tread should be no more than 8¼ inches above the previous one. Since stairs are often priced by height, some manufacturers cut costs by spacing treads too far apart, resulting in a hard-to-climb stair.

HOLDS BARRED *Safety experts would frown on Ward Bennett's checker-plate stairs without balusters, but he likes the look.*

CHARLES NESBIT

GREAT ENTRANCE *Designer Robert Currie likes the bare-bones look of the Equipto-type steel stair leading to his loft bed.*

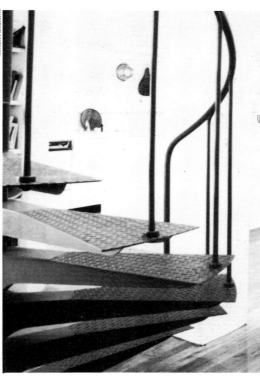

NORMAN McGRATH

UNDERCOVER *In a Soho loft renovation, architect Alan Buchsbaum used a shop-finished green Duvinage stair.*

PETER M. FINE

DOUBLE LANDING *Architect Donald Mallow used a Duvinage custom spiral stair in Milton and Shirley Glaser's New York apartment.*

CHARLES WIESEHAHN

FOOTED *The industrial spiral stair used by Arthur Scott and Mark Sephton is the footed kind. Treads are checker plate.*

IAN SAMPSON

STRAIGHT AND NARROW *The stair in architect Barton Myers's Toronto home is made from off-the-shelf metals stocked by Abel Metal Co.*

TIM STREET-PORTER ELIZABETH WHITING & ASSOCIATES

DOTTED LINE *London architect Michael Hopkins adapted a standard spiral stair using perforated risers and checker-plate steel sheeting.*

SECOND STORY *Dress designer Alice Blaine wanted a balcony in her high-ceilinged loft. She looked up Shelving in the New York Yellow Pages and called a company which for $10,000 built her a prefab mezzanine in one day (see the flooring, stair, and rail details below).*

MEZZANINES

At the end of World War II there was an acute shortage of warehouse space in Europe. The solution was the steel mezzanine—a way to double storage space by building up instead of out. Today most major shelving manufacturers offer a prefabricated system of stairs, decking, and upper-floor supports that are an integral part of their shelving system. (See page 80.) Available are freestanding and cantilevered mezzanines, catwalks between shelving units, and "layovers" that create a second floor on top of shelf units. Mezzanines can often be built in a day's time from prefabricated parts and can be two to four stories high.

CLOSE-UP *The mezzanine includes prefab steel decking, rail, and steps.*

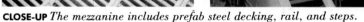

PREFABS *Most steel shelving companies sell prefab mezzanines. Penco's freestanding mezzanine, left, 10'6" x 12', sells for about $1,800 plus installation; from A. Liss.*

DARING YOUNG MAN *Michael Jantzen of Illinois, designed and made the hillside mezzanine at right using industrial steel grating for flooring and nylon nets for seating.*

BRIDGING THE GAP *Across her living room Italian architect Gae Aulenti put a catwalk with a steel-grating floor.*

OFF THE RACK *Architect Peter de Bretteville used factory-fabricated steel decking modules for a library balcony in his California home.*

CARLA DE BENEDETTI

NORMAN McGRATH

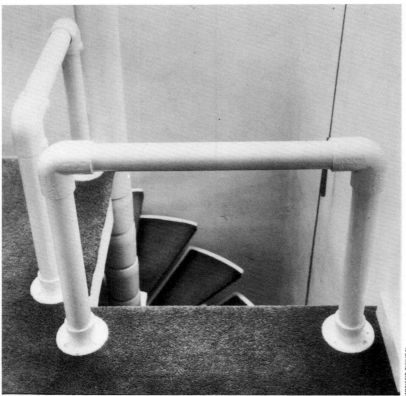

PLUMB LINE *Architect Christopher Smallwood used plumber's pipe to make the two low railings in the London apartment of art dealer Alain Mertens.*

RAILINGS

From the decks of the great passenger ships to the revolutionary simplicity of Le Corbusier's housing to the cliff-hanging white houses by contemporary architect Richard Meier, there is hardly a more versatile architectural element than railings. Gleaming and painted in white, they warn, protect, and provide visual architectural unity. De-signed now for safety, prefab-ricated metal railings must meet industry standards, thanks to union efforts to eliminate safety hazards. Pre-fabricated railings are obtain-able from "material handling equipment" companies such as Equipto and from pipe-systems manufacturers such as Kee Klamp. Or look in the Yellow Pages under Railings.

CLASSICS *Painted pipe railings are coupled with glass block in the stair-well, right, of this apartment house.*

SEAFARER *Designer Joseph Paul D'Urso chose turnbuckles and cables from a marine hardware source for this residential landing.*

SHIPSHAPE *Nautical pipe railings were specified by architect Leslie Armstrong of Armstrong/Childs for harpsichordist Albert Fuller's living room.*

TENNIS ANYONE? *Manteola, Sánchez Gómez, Santos, Solsona, Viñoly, a Buenos Aires architectural firm, added tennis netting to this pipe railing.*

SEPARATE TABLES *Designer Philip Tusa laced red canvas to pipe railings, nautically, to define areas in New York's Left Bank restaurant.*

51

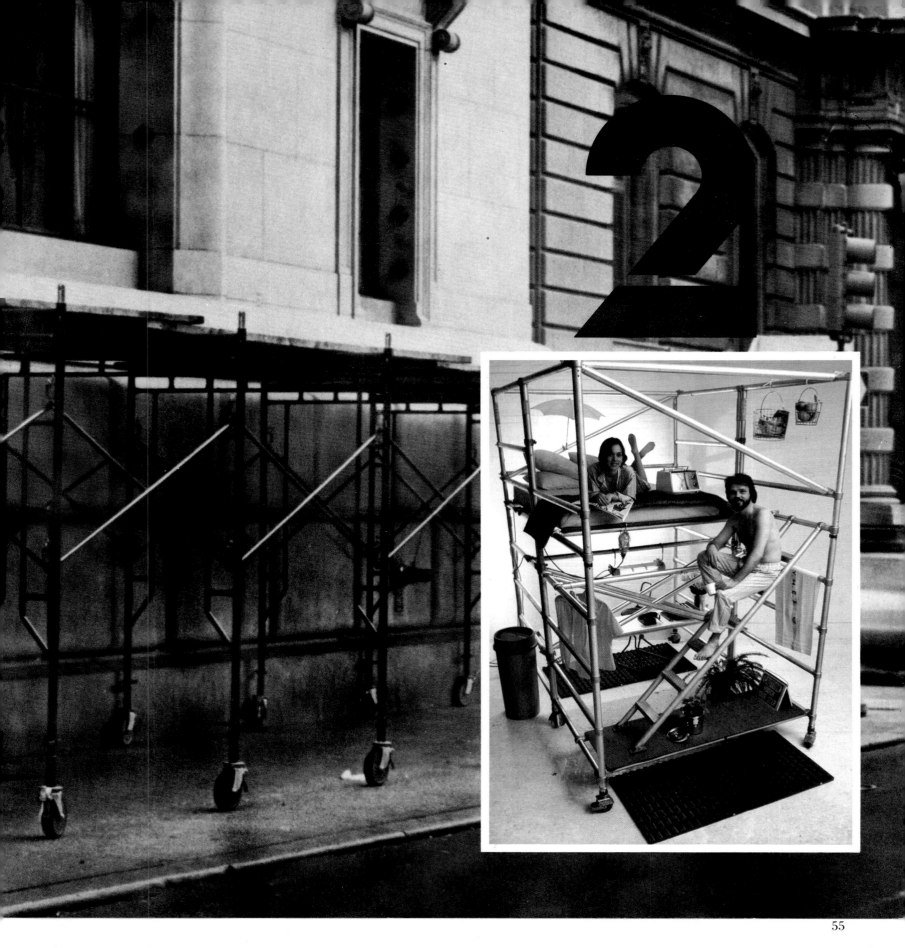

DAN WYNN

HIGH & MIGHTY *The loft bed, above, conceived by Morsa, the design team, was made of about $1,700 worth of standard Up-Right Aluminum Span Scaffold parts. Sheets are from J.P. Stevens; quilt from Art et Industrie; accessories from Manhattan Ad Hoc; lights from Daniel Woodhead Co.; Tepromark mats are $130 for six.*

SCAFFOLDING AND PIPES

Steel scaffolding has been around for at least seventy years; aluminum scaffolding is more recent. Although scaffold structures are more commonly used by maintenance crews in office buildings or in the aircraft and construction industries, reusable, dismantleable scaffold elements (that can be assembled by one person) could certainly be put to work at home. To demonstrate this point we asked Morsa, the New York design team of Antonio Morello and architect Donald Savoie, to design a loft bed of standard scaffolding parts. They chose Up-Right

Scaffolds's Aluminum Span Scaffold, which the company's delivery person erected, by himself, in twenty minutes. The only improvement we would make for home use would be to add a plywood deck to cover the raw planking that is supplied. If $1,700, the estimated price for this structure, sounds like too much money, you can construct your own "scaffolding" using plumber's pipe and one of the many pipe-coupling systems listed in the Yellow Pages under Pipe Fittings. Three brands that have come to our attention are the Kee Klamp made by Gascoigne Industrial

Products of Buffalo, New York; the Rota-Lock made by Up-Right Scaffolds (both of which are available through C & H Distributors); and the Nu-Rail clamps made by the Hollaender Manufacturing Co. of Cincinnati, Ohio. Architect James Rossant was so impressed with the Nu-Rail clamps when he built a loft bed (pictured on the next page) for his son, that he called the company to rave. Soon after that he and his partner, William Conklin, were flown out to Cincinnati and hired as consultants; and prepackaged loft kits are currently in the works.

UP-RIGHT SCAFFOLDS, INC.

CARLA DE BENEDETTI

SCAFFOLDING AND PIPES

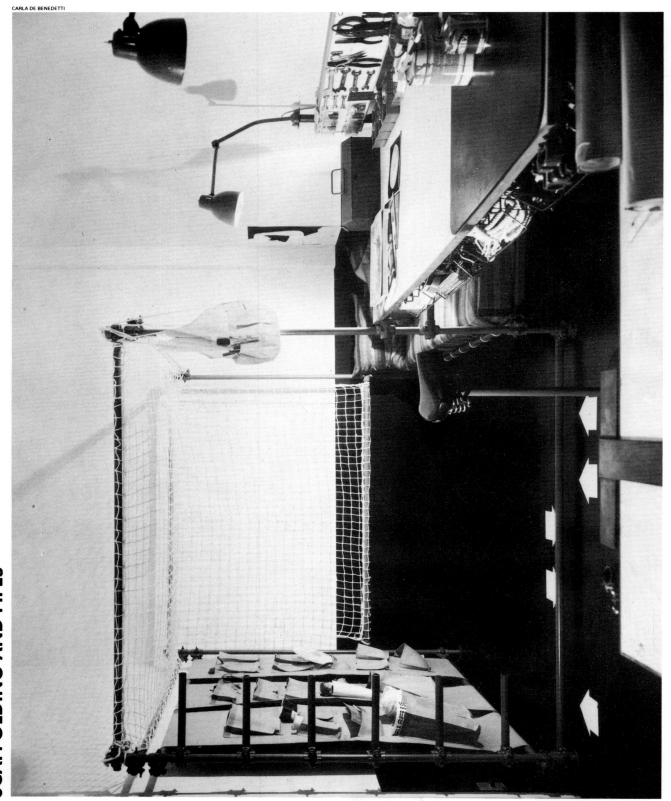

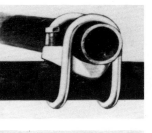

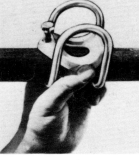

PIPED *Milan architects Gigi and Adriana Moretti built a bed environment, above, of turquoise-painted pipe; the desk chair is a bike seat.*

MOD COUPLER *Up-Right Scaffolds's Rota-Lock ($4 to $7 depending on size) claims an 8,000-pound grip. Available through C & H.*

PIERRE BOTSCHI

NORMAN McGRATH

RED CLAMPS *Architect James Rossant built a loft bed/study, above, for his son with plumbing pipe and Nu-Rail clamps (about $5 each). He liked them so much his firm, Conklin & Rossant, is designing pipe kits for Hollaender Mfg. Co.*

STRUCTURED *In his London home designer Pierre Bötschi built a cozy study, left, out of steel scaffolding.*

THE KEE *Depending on size and configuration, the Kee Klamp, a pipe coupler, below, sells from about $2 to $10 through C & H Distributors, a mail-order supply house.*

METRO SYSTEM

The Metro wire system that has been turning up as bookshelves, beds, tables, and rolling carts in some of the handsomest living rooms was developed in 1955 by Louis Maslow. Maslow founded the Metropolitan Wire Corp., which produced a variety of food-preparation utensils, in 1930. Mr. Maslow himself developed all the machinery for making his Erecta and Super Erecta shelving, systems that can be put together without tools. Metro was accepted readily by the food-service industry because, unlike industrial steel shelving, the wire shelves were ideal for use in refrigerators or in dark storerooms where light and air could filter through. Today Metro sells $30 million worth of its Erecta and Super Erecta shelving and accessories per year, and it has five imitators. There are Metro plants in Canada; California; Wilkes-Barre, Pennsylvania; and Japan; and 6,000 "distributors" worldwide including Macy's and Sid Diamond.

METROPOLITAN WIRE CORP

RAEANNE GIOVANNI

JAIME ARDILES-ARCE

CARTS *Metro can be used in many ways; above, designer Juan Montoya used the system to make a rolling cart in a small New York kitchen.*

WALL SHELVES *Metro can also be used to build cantilevered wall shelves as shown at left in a closet storage area designed by Patino Wolf.*

BEDPOSTS *Juan Montoya designed a canopy bed for photographer Jaime Ardiles-Arce with panels from Metro's Tran-Stor material handling system.*

METRO

TANA HOBAN

TABLES TOO Sid Diamond, a Metro dealer in New York, makes furniture out of Metro; this table sells for $61.

POLES Super Erecta is Metro's latest innovation. At left, this pole system is used on wheels by Patino/Wolf.

KITCHENWARE Morsa, the design team, used Metro wall shelves as over-the-counter storage in the loft of New York photographer Tana Hoban.

BOOKCASE Designer Ivan Chermayeff used the Erecta panel system to build a storage wall, right. Shelves can easily be rearranged or disassembled.

62

RAEANNE GIOVANNI

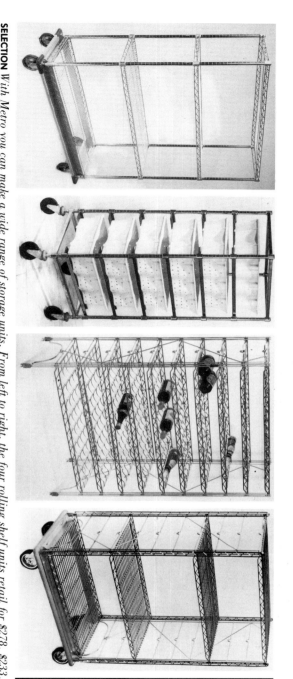

SELECTION *With Metro you can make a wide range of storage units. From left to right, the four rolling shelf units retail for $278, $233, $263 (for the wine rack), and $169, at Manhattan Ad Hoc. Solid and perforated shelves are available in addition to wire ones.*

RAEANNE GIOVANNI

SLOTTED ANGLE

Slotted angle is an inexpensive system of steel L-shaped strips perforated with a pattern of horizontal and vertical oval-shaped slots that reminds one of an erector set. It's ideal for building beds, shelves, tables, and partitions. It was, originally made in England just after World War II. A similar product became available in the United States in the 1950s. Usually sold by weight, slotted angle comes in boxes or bundles of ten pieces either 10 or 12 feet long, ranging from about $45 to $80 a bundle, complete with nuts and hexhead bolts. The pieces can be cut with a hacksaw or power tool, but the easiest and most accurate way is with an angle cutter, which costs about $90 or can be rented by the day from a local industrial shelving supplier. Slotted angle comes in a variety of gauges, and although the galvanized steel and gray baked-enamel finishes are standard, some manufacturers also carry green and white elements.

HARD EDGE Architects Yann Weymouth and Peter Coan of Redroof Design used $100 worth of slotted-angle elements to build a romantic four-poster bed (the netting is cheesecloth) and TV stand in a New York loft. One advantage of this system, besides its low cost, is that two straight pieces can form a joint without a connector.

SSI FIX EQPT. LTD

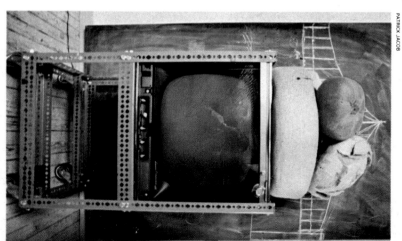

PATRICK JACOB

LYON METAL PRODUCTS, INC.

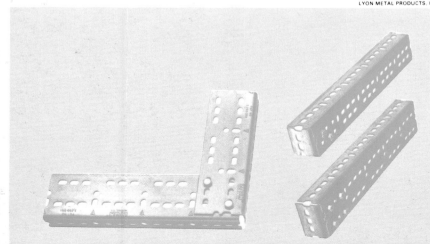

OPTO INC.

CARLA DE BENEDETTI

DISPLAY SYSTEMS

For over a hundred years there has been a fascination with folding, telescoping furnishings with easily combinable parts. Recombinability is the principle of most of today's display systems, which date back to the 1950s when the traveling exhibition (bringing art to middle America) and the trade show (which brought buyers to the goods instead of goods to the buyers, spelling death to the traveling salesman) became big business. The booth, erected by unskilled labor, had to go up and come down easily and travel small. Architects and designers were quick to see the possibilities of many of these systems—which were also used in retailing for quick-change displays—and appropriated them for the home. Just a few of the many systems that could work at home are Abstracta, Unicube, Opto, Converta, Click, Alka, Apton, and Foba.

KITCHEN DISPLAY *Milanese architect Claudio Dini constructed kitchen shelving, left, with the tubular steel Abstracta system.*

CARLA DE BENEDETTI

EXHIBITIONISTIC *The Apton display system of one-inch-square tubing used by Rome architect Pierluigi Pizzi is available in kits.*

SHOWCASE *With the various Click systems you can build everything from furniture to shelving for displays or audio equipment.*

UNICUBE *Each system has its own special coupling device; Unicube, above, has two-to-six-pronged ones.*

OPTO *Opto's connector, above right, latches on from the outside and tightens with a special lever.*

STEVE MYERS

ALKA *The Alka system, right, is based on a series of pressed aluminum extrusions, patent joints, and clamp-type locks.*

OUTER ACCESS *Opto claims its system, sold in parts, is the only one with a coupling device that joins tubing from the outside.*

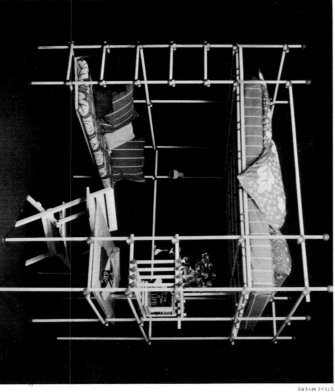

STEVE MYERS

STORAGE

72 LOCKERS
Have closets, will travel: lockers are fairly inexpensive pieces of storage equipment that are easily transported.

76 CABINETS AND DRAWERS
File cabinets, plan files, and shop drawers have all been drafted into domestic service.

80 OPEN SHELVING
Steel shelving, the basic industrial storage system, has come to the attention of designers. Its possibilities are just beginning to be recognized.

86 REVOLVING STORAGE
Industrial users have found revolving bins store more in less space. There is a certain charm to them as well.

88 CONVEYORS
The electric revolving dry cleaner's rack is the ultimate closet accessory. Revolving file cabinets have possibilities too.

90 WIRE STORAGE
Ease of installation has endeared wire closet systems to builders; now that these wire shelves and bins are attractively vinyl coated, they will also appeal to consumers.

92 PICK RACKS
Pick racks are the spice racks of the automotive industry. They can be used for spices, buttons, love letters, or any other small-parts storage.

94 BASKETS, BOXES, AND BINS
Industry makes baskets for pickling, plating, and straining. Take them home and do what you will with them.

98 ROLLING STORAGE
Industrial storage is often mobile. Big wheels make sense for short hauls too.

OVERLEAF Locker photo, courtesy Penco Products, Inc.; inset, Lyon Metal Products locker wall designed by Mayers & Schiff, photo, Harold Krieger.

ou are what you keep and what you keep it in is the universal problem. In the beginning there was only one storage system, the carved wooden chest. But today there are more storage options than there are lockers in Grand Central Station, and lockers are just one of the many nontraditional options. To some people lockers are inappropriate for anything except a gym or an airline terminal, but to a diligent storage forager no resource, no matter how esoteric, is considered off limits, from an ammunition case to a pick rack for nuts and bolts.

So, as you sit there contemplating your possessions that need housing—boxes of books, stereo and hi-fi equipment, skis, sneakers, shell collection—do not reach for the nearest chrome étagère, or shovel it all into a Fibber McGee closet, instead pretend you're a material handling equipment engineer.

Even if you don't have to grapple with the logistics of storing and retrieving 100 rolls of carpet, 1,000 spare tires, and 10,000 small parts, there are some similarities between domestic and industrial storage problems: industrial customers also require strong, durable, economic, and fire-resistant systems. They often need a combination of storage types—open shelving, bins, racks, drawers, cupboards—plus easier access to items used frequently and out-of-the-way storage for others. The industrial user can usually find all these functions in a single steel shelving system.

Steel shelving is the Cinderella product of the industrial revolution. A staple in almost every industry that keeps inventory, it began to replace wood shelving in the 1920s when the metal was heralded as being hygienic as well as fireproof. Steel shelving comes in a variety of depths—36 inches deep for the dress manufacturer, 18 inches for the hardware store—and in varying heights and widths. The less expensive models are assembled with nuts and bolts, other models with clips. It usually costs more if you buy it already assembled. Most of the 25 major (and 450 lesser) steel shelving manufacturers in the country offer accessories—bins, boxes, drawers, shelf dividers—that can be easily attached to their shelves which have perforations for this purpose.

It doesn't seem fair that, despite its versatility and good design, this basic steel shelving system has, until recently, had the least status. In the Museum of Modern Art's design-collection office, for example, ordinary steel shelving, bolted together and painted black (and not without style) holds the collection's books. But this functional product has never been singled out for recognition in the collection. Likewise, in department stores, which are ever responsive to the design preferences and prejudices of their customers, hundreds of thousands of dollars' worth of basic steel shelving holds inventory behind the scenes (comparable to the homeowners' basement) while on the selling floor (in the living room) display fixtures, for better or for worse, often sport expensive "styling."

In the department store and in the home, however, that may all be changing. "Designed" equipment is growing more expensive, and due to the slowness of deliveries, some designers are looking at commonplace steel shelving and seeing new possibilities in it. When painted and properly scaled, these simple, anonymous units can transcend their humble origins.

Besides ordinary steel shelving, there are dozens of other industrial storage products ripe for making the transition from factory or office to home: consider electric conveyors, parts bins, or doughnut trays. Some of the more expensive systems like the Ferris wheel-revolving file cabinet by Sperry Univac may not make it into the average home because of the price, but if you ever stumble on one secondhand, you'll know what to do with it.

Manufacturers of major systems are listed in the directory in the back of this book along with selected dealers across the country and abroad. If there is no dealer in your area, write to the manufacturer.

PENCO PRODUCTS, INC.

LOCKERS

The first self-service metal lockers were installed in a California bus terminal in 1909, but it wasn't until the 1920s that the metal locker business took off. Today lockers are ubiquitous—you'll find them in schools, gymnasiums, factories, hospitals, barracks, terminals, and offices. And now that the prejudice against metal furniture is waning, lockers are turning up in homes. Most lockers offer either vertical storage space suitable for hanging clothing or box or cubbyhole types of space. Some units offer a combination of the two. There are also lockers made out of expanded metal mesh for better ventilation and lockers with adjustable shelves. Write to manufacturers listed in our directory for distributors in your area or check the Yellow Pages under Lockers. Used lockers can be a good buy.

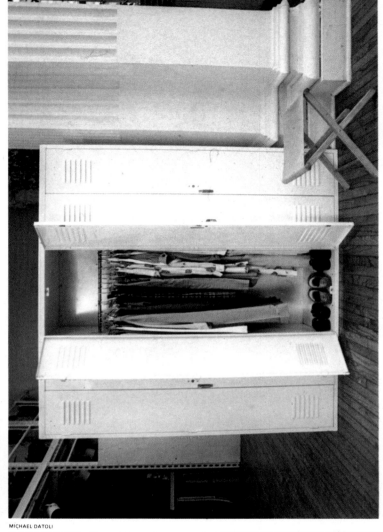

RAEANNE GIOVANNI

WIDE OPEN *Unusual double-door lockers, above, allow for easy access to hanging clothes and shoes in fashion designer Alice Blaine's New York showroom.*

FREESTANDING *Sample clothes are stored in back-to-back lockers in the Alice Blaine showroom, right. Similarly, in a home, lockers could be used to divide space.*

DAVID MASSEY

FRENCH SCHOOL *Artist François Arnal stores clothes in his Paris bathroom in recycled school lockers. The units are fitted with rods and shelves.*

MICHAEL DATOLI

KID STUFF *Designer Joseph Paul D'Urso chose open mesh multiple-tier lockers painted red, left, to hold toys and clothes in a child's playroom.*

72

HOSPITAL TREATMENT *Herman Miller Inc.'s Co/Struc, above, is a hospital system with interchangeable components that could be adapted to home use.*

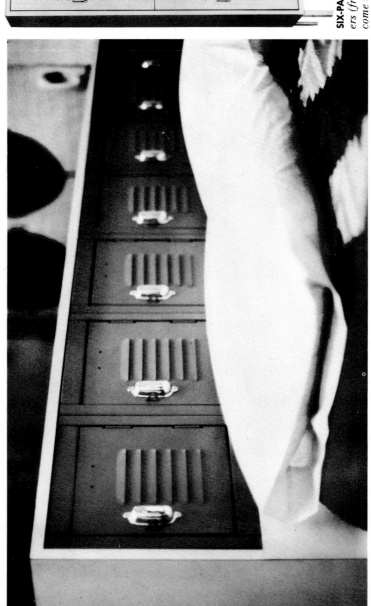

HEAD START *Custom-made, 1-foot-square, gray enamel lockers with chrome pulls, below, serve as graphic designer Kenneth Cooke's headboard.*

SIX-PACK *Penco double-tier lockers (from $120) in basic gray come with hooks and louvers.*

PHIL KOENIG

74

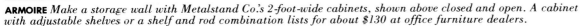

ARMOIRE *Make a storage wall with Metalstand Co.'s 2-foot-wide cabinets, shown above closed and open. A cabinet with adjustable shelves or a shelf and rod combination lists for about $130 at office furniture dealers.*

SHELF LIFE *Lyon Metal Products' gray locker has eight shelves ($190).*

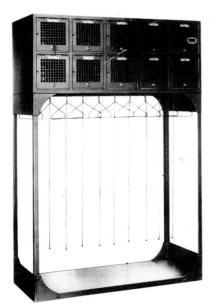

OVERHEAD *Lyon Metal Products' storage unit has ten hinged compartments, ten hangers, and a raised base ($342).*

TEAM SPIRIT *Twenty-four-inch-wide locker from Lyon is $250.*

SEE THROUGH *Swimming pool basket rack on casters from Lyon Metal Products ($328).*

UP AND AROUND *There are sixteen separate compartments in this Lyon Metal Products locker and rack unit ($310).*

75

LYON METAL PRODUCTS, INC

CABINETS AND DRAWERS

Document cabinets date back to fifteenth-century Germany; unit furniture, which can be arranged side by side in series, is supposed to be a nineteenth-century American innovation. Put them together and you have the contemporary office with its walls of file cabinets. But as more and more offices switch to electronic storage and retrieval of information, today's office cabinets may be tomorrow's antiques. Whether it's prescience or resourcefulness, many people are already finding filing cabinets and office-type cabinets handy for stowing clothing and household effects which could never be put in a computer. Other commercial and industrial storage facilities ripe for domestication are factory small-parts cabinets, plan files, machine shop tool chests, dental cabinets, luncheonette cake cabinets, institutional washroom medicine cabinets, sheet-music chests, and cassette racks.

NORMAN McGRATH

COUNTERCULTURE *Architect Peter de Bretteville used a luncheonette overhead cabinet as a kitchen cabinet in his California home. Buy similar ones secondhand or new from restaurant supply stores.*

TOM WEIR

FOREMAN FUNCTION *Shure Manufacturing Co. offers red stacking workshop drawers, 7 inches high ($41 each).*

MICHEL TCHEREVKOFF

PILLBOX *Locker-room cabinet by Charles Parker Co. ($175) even stores liquid soap.*

CHARLES NESBIT

HOLDING PATTERN *Oak flat files from Sam Flax, used by designers Robert Patino and Vincent Wolf, could hold silver and linens.*

RAEANNE GIOVANNI

PETER M. FINE

OTHER PLANS *Low plan files (available from Sam Flax or Charette) were used by designer John Saladino for a window-seat base.*

TOP DRAWER *File the records in a computer and put the shirts in the file cabinet—this one an Olivetti ($350) from Inter/Graph.*

CABINETS AND DRAWERS

FILE FOLDED *Take your work furniture home. Olivetti file cabinet can solve haberdashery storage problems with its shallow and deep drawers.*

HOLD THE SINK *Designer David Barrett's stainless steel night tables were fabricated by American Metal Restaurant Equipment Company.*

MORLEY BAER

RAEANNE GIOVANNI

PETER M. FINE

RAE-ANNE GIOVANNI

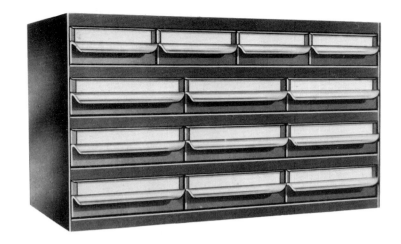

CACHE AND CARRY *The functional steamer trunk is still a handy storage chest. Find others at secondhand luggage or antique shops.*

LONG AND SHORT *Equipto stacking steel drawers, right, ($165) are made to order from A. Liss.*

IN DEPTH *Lyon Metal Products' 11-inch-deep units ($110) come in other depths too, from A. Liss.*

TOOLING UP *Lyon Metal Products' four-drawer shop chest, above, is finished in gray enamel ($210).*

OPEN-AND-SHUT CASE *Equipto's open cubbies and steel drawers, right, come in various configurations.*

BOX STORAGE *Ordinary mailboxes were a budget storage solution by architects MLTW/Moore, Lyndon, Turnbull, Whitaker at northern California's Sea Ranch Swim and Tennis Club, left.*

MULTIPURPOSE *Red, white, blue, or yellow—fourteen 2-inch-deep drawers; the 37-inch-high chest sells for $125 at Sam Flax.*

79

NORMAN McGRATH

RERUN *Artist Jack Ceglic paid $250 for 60 feet of secondhand shelving from A A Steel Shelving that he painted white.*

UNIVERSAL *Cantilevered units like those in the Italian home above are sold in Design Research ($140 per unit).*

OPEN SHELVING

If it weren't for steel shelving, the gross national product would be sitting on the floor. This ubiquitous piece of equipment is available in depths from 12 to 36 inches, in heights from 3 feet to 10 or more feet, and in widths of from 18 to 48 inches. Steel shelving dates back to about 1920, when it replaced wood shelving and was readily accepted because it was more fireproof. Another benefit was its perforated shelves, to which dividers and acces-sories could be easily attached for special storage problems. Today there are almost 450 steel shelving manufacturers in this country. There is a great similarity of product. Units are available with open or closed sides, all sorts of accessories, optional drawers, and bins. Some manufactur-ers offer clip-on shelves that require no bolts. Remember, the bolted-shelf system needs to be assembled on the floor, so allow for headroom. If there is none, get clip shelving.

EQUIPTO

80

CARLA DE BENEDETTI
RAEANNE GIOVANNI

COOP *Poultry nester, below, from Sears Farm Catalogue ($35.50) is storage unit in Armen Kachaturian's kitchen. Idea, Peter Price. Designer, Harry Fischman.*

NUTS AND BOLTS *Michael Schaible's Able Steel shelves, above, have clamp-on book dividers.*

A LA MODE *Kenneth Cooke made a $35 used pie case, below, into a medicine chest.*

ARMEN KACHATURIAN
PHIL KOENIG

OPEN SHELVING

EX-LIBRE *Republic Steel's library shelving with dividers can be wall-hung or floor-based (about $170).*

POSTED *Hodges' Post Master system — modular adjustable shelving based on posts ($110 to $175 per section).*

NO SWEAT *Moving shelves is easy with Lyon Metal Products' shelving ($143 from A. Liss).*

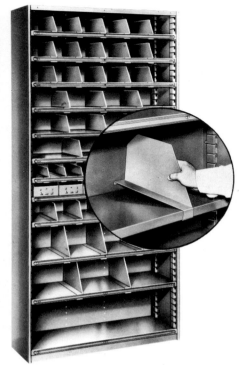

SECTIONAL *Most metal shelving manufacturers have dividers like Lyon Metal's unit ($148 from A. Liss).*

UPSTANDING *Books won't fall with boltless dividers. Lyon Metal's unit ($200 from A. Liss).*

SAFEKEEPING *One hundred and eight boxes fit on Lyon Metal's shelf unit ($560 from C & H).*

MAGAZINES *Art et Industrie sells newsstand racks for $75 and $90.*

NEWSY *Daroff Design detailed New York's Cafe Fanny's paper rack. Claridge makes similar ready-mades.*

COLD STORAGE *Various wire-shelf systems for food plants are made by Metro (page 60), Amco, and Hodges.*

JESSICA STRANG

A NATURAL *Some industries use nonconductive wood shelving for inventory. The Lundia prefabricated wood shelving system in heights up to 9 feet can be put together without tools. It's available with optional accessories such as drawers, clothing rods, bin dividers, and edge guards, and can be double-decked with catwalks. Sold through the Workbench.*

COMBINE *Sculptor Kenneth Snelson combined two depths of ordinary bolted-together steel shelving for a storage wall—12 inches deep for books and an 18-inch-deep section which he had fitted with plastic laminated doors by a local carpenter.*

PETER M. FINE

NORMAN McGRATH

BRACED *Seventy feet of Hallowell steel shelving and enclosed storage, painted black, unify a loft designed by Marlys Hann, who used the unusual X-shaped structural braces of this system as a design element.*

THROUGH A GLASS *Architect Christine Bevington searched hard to find these glass-door bookcases, left, from F. E. Hale Manufacturing Co. Today few firms make this type of case except on special order from the government. Look for used ones in secondhand office furniture outlets.*

TORKIL GUDNASON

85

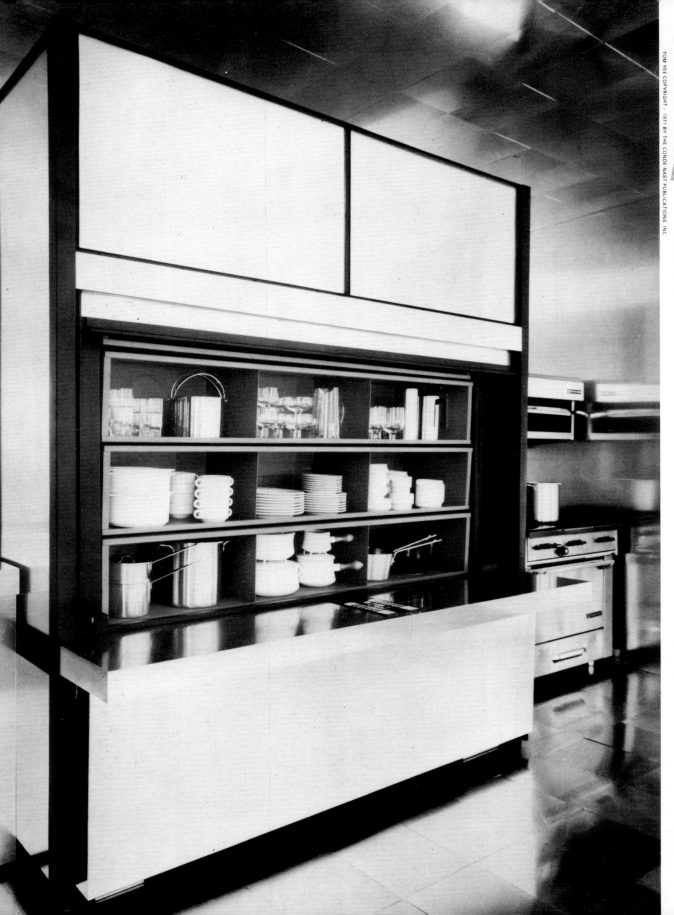

TOM YEE COPYRIGHT · 1971 BY THE CONDE NAST PUBLICATIONS, INC.

FRICK-GALLAGHER MFG. CO.

REVOLVING STORAGE

In the beginning there was the wheel. In the sixteenth century Agostino Ramelli designed a Ferris wheel-like revolving bookcase. In the nineteenth century, bookcases revolved on a horizontal axis as well. The revolving steel parts bin was born in the 1920s in response to automobile manufacturers' needs. In 1933 the Frick-Gallagher Mfg. Co. introduced the patented Rotabin, shown at right, which is still available in a variety of styles and sizes from 17 to 58 inches in diameter. Lyon Metal Products Company makes a similar product but with fewer choices. Meanwhile, the sixteenth-century Ferris wheel-type bookcase was reincarnated in the 1960s as Sperry Univac's electric storage and retrieval cabinet—the residential possibilities of this cabinet were explored by *House & Garden* some years back—but it has yet to become a household fixture.

CHOCK FULL *Sperry Univac's Lektriever, left, is an electric revolving file cabinet ($6,000 to $10,000) that supplies 117 lineal feet of storage in a 4-by-8-foot floor space.*

HAROLD KRIEGER

LYNN KARLIN

TALL AND SPIN *Frick-Gallagher's eight-tier Rotabin, left, retails for about $750 from A. Liss. White paint and freight are extra.*

CERTAIN SIMILARITIES *Manhattan Ad Hoc Housewares sells Lyon Metal's 34-inch-diameter revolving bin, above ($650 including white finish).*

CLOSET CASE *Frick-Gallagher's 34-inch-diameter Rotabin with overhead storage (about $530) would work well in a closet; from C & H.*

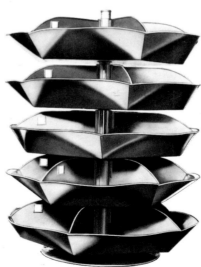

C & H DISTRIBUTORS

SUPERDUPER *Frick-Gallagher's 44-inch-diameter Rotabin, above, is for extra-heavy bulk storage.*

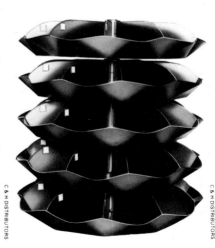

C & H DISTRIBUTORS

ALTERNATIVE *Another Rotabin, 56 inches high, 44 inches in diameter, has ten compartments on each level.*

CONVEYORS

The railroad inspired all types of industrial conveyor systems, including the overhead conveyors of the Cincinnati slaughterhouses, circa 1850, which are the mechanical antecedents of the dry cleaners' electric revolving conveyor clothing rack. From the late nineteenth to the mid-twentieth century a number of revolving coatrack systems were patented. But it wasn't until after World War II, when Americans increased their clothing consumption dramatically and the dry cleaning business increased commensurately, that such systems filled a need. In the early 1960s Abe and Sam Rutkovsky, brothers and partners in a clothing rack business, patented the space-saving Railex system—an electric revolving clothes rack that, by eliminating the need for aisles, could increase storage space dramatically. Soon, the "dry cleaners' rack" became the ultimate closet accessory, despite the $800 and up price. The minimum space required is 5 feet square. In addition to Railex, both Amsco and White also manufacture revolving conveyors.

EX-CHECK ROOM *A ceiling-hung Railex revolving clothes rack was used in a showroom, at left, designed by Joseph Paul D'Urso, who also uses such systems in homes.*

CONTROLLER *The low-voltage Railex revolving conveyor system can be had with a foot control, this hand control, above, or an automatic dialer.*

ROUNDABOUT *The White Carousel Storage Conveyor, above, can be fitted out to hold files, books, clothing, or bulky items. Prices start at $1,411.*

WIRED FOR ACTION *Air can circulate through Elfa's colorful vinyl-coated steel wire bins installed in this Italian model kitchen.*

CARLA DE BENEDETTI

WIRE STORAGE

Vinyl-coated-wire storage bins and closet systems fall into a category called builders' hardware—meaning that it is the builders not the tenants who usually install them in private residences, condominiums, or housing developments. These systems are not generally available through ordinary consumer outlets. Sweden's thirty-year-old Elfa system, consisting of various-sized baskets that can be installed on runners in closets and under counters, has recently become available here through specialty shops (listed in our directory). The Closet Maid system has to be ordered through the dealer (although the Sani-Shelf System made by the Schulte Corporation that looks similar to Closet Maid's is sold in selected hardware stores). Closet Maid uses a coated-steel-wire shelf and rod system that can work as effectively inside clothes closets or in kitchens, wall-hung, as it does in food processing plants in walk-in freezers.

CLOSET MAID CORP.

90

KITCHEN AIDE *Designer Michael Schaible used the Closet Maid shelves in his own kitchen. He likes them because they never need dusting.*

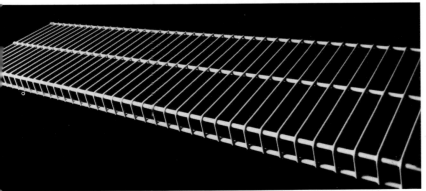

WIRE WORKS *Closet Maid is a closet storage system made of wall-mounted coated wire racks and rods; $12 for a 4-foot shelf.*

CLOSETED *In the photo above, you can see how the Closet Maid shelf doubles as a clothes rod; tilted shoe racks are available too.*

OPEN AIR *Elfa system plastic-coated bins in many sizes list from $6.50 to $15; frames list from about $23.50 to $73.50. Write Admac International for local sources.*

SCHAFER SYSTEMS INTERNATIONAL - SYSTEME FIX

PICK RACKS

Just as chests of little wooden drawers bring to mind the nineteenth-century apothecary, steel pick racks call to mind the automotive industry, which was built on a system of replaceable parts. You don't have to build Fords to need small-parts storage today. Pick racks and small-bin systems are the mainstay of hundreds of businesses. Repair people who make house calls use wall-mounted bins inside their panel trucks. One bin brand favored by designers and architects is Dexion, a well-designed system originated in England, which offers both steel and colorful plastic bins that either stack or hook onto wall panels. The Dexion Co. was acquired a few years ago by Interlake, which makes an identical product. Akro-Mils makes a similar system. Less contemporary-looking but just as useful are pick racks made by most steel shelving companies. Check the Yellow Pages under Materials Handling Equipment and our directory under Pick racks.

AS YOU LIKE IT *Dexion plastic bins can be used on shelves in a home office, above left; under Yann Weymouth's bathroom sink, above right; or clipped to a louvered backplate as in Kenneth Walker's office, far right.*

OFF THE WALL *Steel clip-on bins, above, as well as plastic ones are available in the Dexion system. Panel stand retails for about $235; bins from $18 and up.*

TAKE YOUR PICK *Twenty-one drawers come and go easily from Equipto's pick rack, right (about $267).*

92

ROBERT PERRON

FRENCH GOVERNMENT TOURIST OFFICE

BASKETS, BOXES, AND BINS

Containers are the litmus test of a society. Future anthropologists will have their work cut out for them analyzing the baskets, boxes, and bins of the industrial society: litter baskets and letter baskets, frying and foundry baskets, baskets for pickling, plating, clamming, dipping, straining, and toting; bins for everything from grain storage to concrete mixing, laundry storage to inventory control. These containers come in every conceivable material from cardboard to fiberboard, canvas, plastic, wire, steel, and wood. They come in sizes small enough for 1,000 buttons or large enough to mix concrete. Since industrial containers can cost $1.29, $129, or $1,029, the size of your pocketbook can help determine your selection. For every choice we've made, there are a hundred others ripe for domestication.

TIN CAN ALLEY *Silverware holders, left, at New York's Eat & Drink cafeteria designed by Harper and George are made of paint cans.*

TEN-PACK *Swing-arm wall unit, above, holds stationery items; Horchow Collection ($11).*

CARRY ON *Swedish fiberboard boxes, bright green, can hold checks, records, or even clothing. The Horchow Collection sells them mail order; large size, $9; small, two for $8.50.*

94

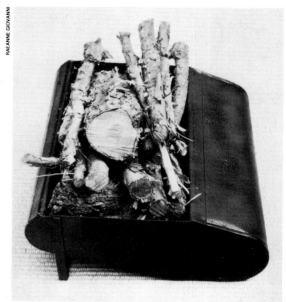

HARDWARE STORY *Designer Ward Bennett converted a paint dipper, above, normally used with a roller, into a bin for kindling to sit next to his fireplace.*

BEAUTY AND THE BINS *Basic wood crates are turned on end, left, to make arty and serviceable firewood storage units.*

GOOD BUY *Stacking cardboard totes; $1.39 to $2.99 by mail order from Fidelity. Cheaper by the hundred.*

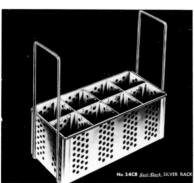

SILVER STAR *Store the stainless flatware in a stainless steel silver holder; Metropolitan Wire Corp.*

TEST-TUBE BASKET *Four compartment, 10-inch-diameter basket ($9.55); from Arthur H. Thomas Co.*

CLEAN SWEEP *Consider nylon-coated wire sterilizing baskets (about $27), Metropolitan Wire Corp.*

CINDERELLA *Lakeside's 14-by-21-inch stainless steel dishpan can hold mail or magazines.*

BIN AROUND *Lakeside's stainless steel waste boxes can hold more than trash. Why not umbrellas?*

SHOP RIGHT *Lyon Metal Products' gray enameled stacking shop boxes measure 12-by-18-by-6-inches.*

NEST *Fiber totes from Ikelheimer-Ernst, Inc., have steel corners; 10-by-16-inches, $105 per dozen.*

RAEANNE GIOVANNI

BREADBASKET *Architect Rita Bormioli, working with Joseph Lembo, specified a Metropolitan Wire Corp. doughnut tray as a magazine bin in a client's living room. Manhattan Ad Hoc Housewares sells three sizes, all 2 inches deep, for $9, $11, and $13.*

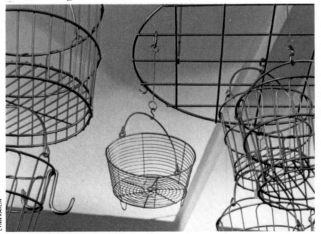

LYNN KARLIN

EGGED ON *At Manhattan Ad Hoc Housewares the egg baskets come in two sizes that sell for $10 and $15 respectively.*

PHIL KOENIG

POST OP *Designer Kenneth Cooke's mailbox is a medical chart holder from Peter Pepper Products.*

LYNN KARLIN

HOUSEKEEPER *Rubber-bumpered maid's basket holds glasses ($12.50); at Manhattan Ad Hoc.*

DANIEL MILES KRON

RECYCLED *Philadelphia designer Dian Boone hung bicycle baskets on her kitchen wall to hold vegetables, drinks, and gadgets.*

NORMAN McGRATH

ON TRACK *Architect William Conklin had curved plastic bins fabricated to order and fitted with Garcy hardware to hang on wall track.*

LYNN KARLIN

SOLID HOLD *Oversized heavy aluminum pan with lid from Bloomfield Industries ($150); at Manhattan Ad Hoc.*

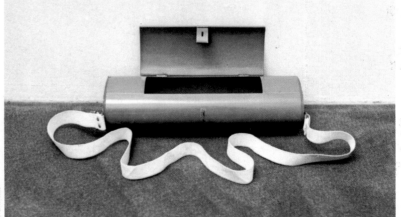

PETER M. FINE

STRAPPED *Bright green enamel European specimen-collecting box with a carrying strap is used by designer Ward Bennett as a desk catchall.*

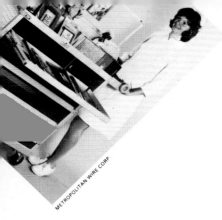

METROPOLITAN WIRE CORP

ROLLING STORAGE

Americans move a lot but their furniture is more stationary. Until recently the only furniture wheels you saw on residential floors were the ones on brass bar carts or wooden tea wagons. But wheels on storage and shelving, not just on carts, show signs of becoming the next breakthrough in residential furnishings. Casters are the lace-up work boots of rolling stock—the things that can turn any piece of furniture into "equipment." They are the exact antithesis of the discrete wheels found on elegant nineteenth-century tables, chairs, and pianos. Hospital wagons, linen carts, restau-

rant tray racks—all on heavy-duty casters—are becoming important components of the industrial-style interior. While some heavy-duty industrial carts might be considered overqualified for home employment, their substantiality gives them an edge over the frankly tinny carts that have heretofore been offered to the consumer. If you need rolling storage, look for hand trucks, supermarket carts, art supply, or library carts. Major manufacturers of rolling storage include Harloff Manufacturing Co., Interroyal Corp., Rubbermaid Commercial Products, and United Hospital Supply Corp., among others.

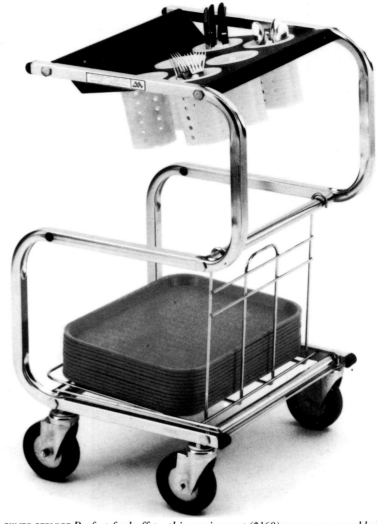

SILVER SERVICE *Perfect for buffets, this service cart ($160) comes unassembled. Order through Metropolitan Wire Corp. dealers.*

OUT OF WORK *Multipurpose stainless steel cart is from Market Forge.*

BIEFFE

CLASSIC *Joe Colombo's BoBy cart, $116 to $259; Inter/Graph, Sam Flax.*

BIN TOP *Lakeside Manufacturing's self-service cart sells for $185.*

ARNOLD ROSENBERG

SUPERMART *Samuel Underberg sells shopping carts from $40 up.*

FOREIGN OFFICE *Helit's storage cart has removable stacking drawers.*

POSSIBILITIES *Homak's stacking tool chests could hold other things too; through C & H.*

MOBILE MEDIA *Architect Peter de Bretteville uses a restaurant kitchen rack for hi-fi storage.*

BASIC *You can add extra shelves to Lakeside's basic steel cart.*

HOLDING ACTION *Canvas liner is optional with Harloff Manufacturing Co.'s perforated steel hamper.*

BEEN AROUND *A six-bushel laundry basket ($59) from Steele Canvas Basket Co. has potential.*

FURNITURE

104 TABLE BASES
After a decade-long love affair with the chrome table base, a new object of designers' affection is the humble restaurant pedestal table base.

106 WORKTABLES
With two sawhorses and a few planks the paperhanger is in business; so is the do-it-yourselfer. Sawhorses from the art supply store and a selection of factory shop tables are a few of the industrial tables you might choose to work on at home.

108 SITTING UP
Chairs reveal their job descriptions as do the uniforms of our city workers. Just because some chairs are made for other purposes doesn't mean they have no place in the home. In fact, these days the work credentials of counter stools, drafting stools, luncheonette booths, and secretarial chairs make them even more desirable.

112 SITTING DOWN
There isn't too much sitting around in factories, but mass transit, movies, dentists, and desk jobs keep us in our seats for many hours in the day. If some people would term theatre, canoe, and auto seats *ad hoc* solutions, rather than "high-tech" ones, we won't quarrel.

114 ROLLING TABLES
Rolling tables are the pack mules of the industrial environment; however, their serviceability doesn't end there.

116 BEDS AND LINENS
Hospitals—design labs for bedding ideas—introduced the functional, decoration-free crib and the adjustable bed. Camping trips and military campaigns spawned the folding cot. Resorts and motels popularized monogrammed linens—even if your name isn't Holiday Inn or Y.M.C.A. you might like them.

118 OUTDOOR FURNITURE
Parks, playgrounds, outdoor cafés, bazaars, and marketplaces have a furniture vernacular all their own.

120 CONVERSIONS
There are no hubcap wall arrangements in this book, but we want to call attention to some automotive parts that could go places at home. And then we want to explain about pallets.

OVERLEAF *Diner photo, courtesy New York Public Library Picture Collection; inset, Alan Buchsbaum's loft, photo, Charles Nesbit.*

ontemporary design historians see the history of chairs over the last two hundred years as a gradual progression toward ever more modern construction techniques—from the eighteenth-century tongue-and-groove to nineteenth-century bentwood, early twentieth-century bent metal tubing, 1940s molded plywood, and 1950s molded plastic.

But there is another way to look at the industrial revolution's impact on seating design. It can be seen as having spawned a whole new set of furniture types shaped by new ways of life, new modes of travel, and new types of job categories. The machine age gave us the typist's chair and the sewing machine chair, adjustable stools for factory workers and draftsmen, chairs with writing arms for students, and a whole pecking order of office chairs now defined as executive, managerial, and operational that are being designed ergonomically—according to human engineering principles—as well as hierarchically—the executives get the headrests and the rank and file do without arms. Other by-products of the machine age are institutional chairs, which can be hooked together in tandem to make an instant auditorium or stacked to make room for a dance floor; folding bleachers for instant gymnasiums; and hide-in-the-wall benches and tables for instant dining rooms. There are bolted-to-the-floor stools for easier cleaning in restaurants and swivels on the stools to facilitate faster exits from fast food counters. There are reclining chairs for around-the-world flights, stand-up chairs to lean on in factories—demanded by German unions—and all-steel swivel chairs that give a laboratory-clean look to rooms.

Many of these chairs could work well at home—an idea which was unthinkable fifty years ago when Le Corbusier, the Swiss architect, first suggested that this equipment would be the ideal home furnishing. One of his uncompleted projects was to adapt the secretarial chair to the living room. Why not, we say today, forgetting how class-conscious drawing rooms used to be about chairs as well as guests?

The chair has been a status symbol since the Middle Ages when only nobles sat on chairs and everyone else used the floor or a three-legged stool. In the early twentieth century, when work was still looked down upon, status-conscious people did not use office chairs, work chairs, and chairs from public places in the front reception rooms of the home where one was expected to "put the best chair forward." But ruling taste is giving way to good taste, and in today's society the work chair and the public chair are welcome—their functionalism and visual appearance are all that matter—not their lineage. The taste for the modern office chair is bringing with it a taste for 100 years of commercial and industrial classics from the tractor seat to the bentwood chair (which started out in cafés), the bent tubular metal chair (which spent its early years in doctor's offices), the old wooden office chair (seen in jury boxes, libraries, and banks), the factory worker's chair, the bucket seat, and today's high-tech five-legged pedestal secretarial chair.

And there has been a commensurate open-mindedness about other categories of furniture. Worktables—the artist's drafting table, the office desk, factory tables—are inching into the residential landscape too. From the hospital we have borrowed the adjustable bed, from the sportsman the folding cot, from the playground its equipment. This is the industrial revolution in furniture.

TABLE BASES

In 1953, when Eero Saarinen designed his now classic pedestal table, he asserted that he was doing away with the tyranny of table legs, but in fact pedestal bases had been widely used before that in cafes and restaurants. In the last few years designers have begun to appreciate the simplicity and durability of some of these tables, and they are turning up in a number of residential dining rooms, often topped with surfaces too elegant to hide under tablecloths. Simple restaurant table bases, usually made in three parts—a baseplate, metal column, and "spider" that supports the top—are comparatively inexpensive and can be had round, square, or double; built into the floor, as on boats; in dull or shiny finishes; in special colors; or embossed. "Restaurant" tabletops can be ordered in your choice of plastic laminate or butcher block and with optional vinyl impact edges. They can even expand from square to round with hinged flip-up wings. Purchases can be made through local restaurant equipment dealers, or write manufacturers such as Falcon, Johnson Industries, and L & B for local outlets.

CEMENTED *Sculptor Kenneth Snelson cemented two pipes into the floor. The plastic laminate top flips over—it's white on one side, black on the other.*

BASIC BLACK *Bray-Schaible Design coupled a round black matte restaurant pedestal with a shiny black top for a side table in this Chicago residence.*

SCULPTURED *Bruce Scott and Paul Kramer designed this pewter-finished base for Thonet. $175 list.*

HOBNAILED *Ilmari Tapiovaara's oxidized-iron restaurant base lists for $217, from I.C.F.*

EMBOSSED *Boiler-plate design on the 18-inch-diameter table base is made by Johnson Industries ($166).*

SUPPORTING ROLE *In designer Ward Bennett's apartment, the floor-mounted column used as a table base contrasts with the smooth wood tabletop.*

WEIGHTED *Based on a cast iron flange, the table in this London kitchen has industrial airs. Kenneth Lynch and Sons sell stanchions and flanges.*

STOVE TOP *For a New York client's dining room, Bray-Schaible Design specified four black restaurant pedestals and a Chinese red porcelainized top.*

WASTE NOT *The desk/table rigged up by Ward Bennett in his summer house is a large top suspended between two of the house's structural columns.*

LEG WORK *New York interior designers Ned Marshall and Harry Schule bought a gray enamel steel shop table which they use both for working and dining.*

MEAT SPECIAL *Butcher block is $198 at The Professional Kitchen.*

WORKTABLES

Butcher blocks, sawhorse tables, and factory workbenches are all candidates for home use. Important to keep in mind when ordering them, however, is that industrial worktables often come in a choice of two heights: 34 to 36 inches high or 28 to 30 inches high (the latter is the standard for desk and dining). Be sure to get the lower height if you don't want to use high stools. Oak sawhorses can be purchased ready-made in art supply shops such as Charette for about $50 apiece. Do-it-yourself sawhorse hardware costs about $5 per base in these stores (you supply the wood). Factory shop legs cost about $18 each.

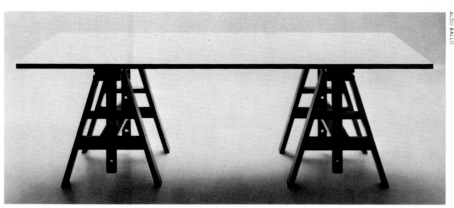

ARTIST'S PROOF *Elegant, adjustable, and beautifully detailed draftsman table by the Italian manufacturer Zanotta retails for $462 for 30 x 60 size at Abitare.*

SEESAW *Two simple sawhorses, available in most lumberyards, are used as support for this functional worktable that can be easily disassembled.*

WORK SURFACES *From top to bottom, just three of Lyon Metal's many steel workbench/table configurations, which sell for $150, $120, and $140.*

PAPER WORK *Designer Ward Bennett adopted an Italian wallpaper hanger's worktable as a desk and painted it black matte.*

LAUNDRY *Canvas work-top table/bench, 18 inches high, from Steele Canvas Basket Company. Retails for $13 at A. Liss.*

SITTING UP

Chairs are the bread and butter of the contract furniture industry, which is ripe for residential harvesting. In the past century most of the production and design innovation in seating has come out of the commercial environment or found acceptance there first: the tilt and swivel chair on casters in the office, the stacking chair in institutions, the snack bar stool in fast-food establishments. It took 100 years for the Thonet bentwood chair of the 1850s—the first mass-produced machine-age chair—to find its way out of cafes and restaurants, where it started its career, into residential dining rooms. Today chairs are engineered for worker efficiency as much as for ease of production. The renewed interest in the worker's chair is accompanied by a taste for the classics of the commercial seating vernacular: the Bank of England chair, the draftsman's stool, the computer operator's work chair. Why not use them at the dining table?

DRAFTED *Work stool with hardwood seat and steel legs comes in eight colors; height adjusts from 24" to 33"; $29.75 from Charette.*

DRIVERS' SEATS *Architect Russell Childs used the last of International Harvester's metal tractor seats for seating in this Connecticut kitchen.. But the swiveling bases and platform to which they are anchored were made to order.*

BANK NOTE *Harper & George, designers, furnished New York's Eat & Drink restaurant with reproduction Bank of England chairs. These office classics are made by Jasper Seating Co. ($139 through office furniture dealers).*

OUT OF CONTEXT *In a dining room designed by Patino/Wolf Associates, six Designcraft secretarial chairs surround a stainless steel dining surface made by A & E Manufacturing Co., fabricators of restaurant kitchen counters. Table legs are prefab parts of the Unicube display system used in stores.*

NO TIPPING *L & B's bolt-to-the-floor counter stool retails for about $125 through dealers.*

MEDIC *Stainless steel medical stool from Preston ($100), in a kitchen by Bray-Schaible Design.*

ART SUPPLY *Charette's drafting stools, with back ($60) and without ($30), are designers' favorites.*

LABOR VOTE *Stand-up seats like this one by H. W. Dreyer ($70) are required in German factories.*

CHARLES NESBIT

DINING IN *Architect Alan Buchsbaum liked the way these stools looked when he bought them on the Bowery, New York's restaurant equipment row. He ordered matching bases to hold up the counter.*

OUT OF PRISON *GF Business Equipment's 40/4 chair is $53 at R&G; dolly is $1100.*

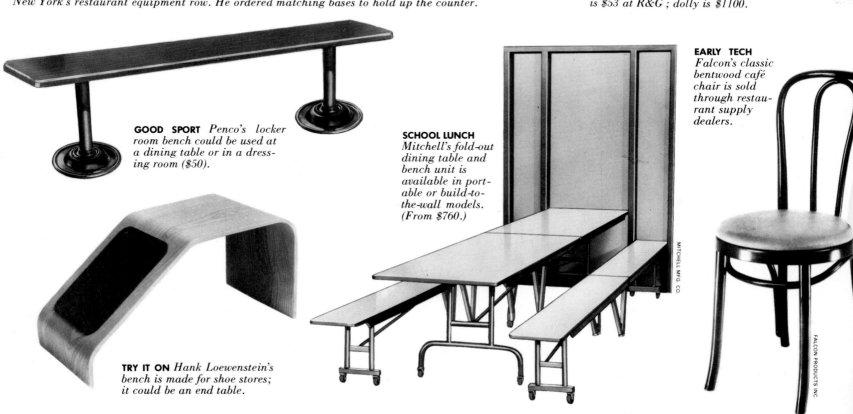

GOOD SPORT *Penco's locker room bench could be used at a dining table or in a dressing room ($50).*

TRY IT ON *Hank Loewenstein's bench is made for shoe stores; it could be an end table.*

SCHOOL LUNCH *Mitchell's fold-out dining table and bench unit is available in portable or build-to-the-wall models. (From $760.)*

EARLY TECH *Falcon's classic bentwood café chair is sold through restaurant supply dealers.*

MITCHELL MFG. CO

FALCON PRODUCTS INC.

PETER M. FINE

CHURCH SUPPER *Folding chair with perforated star seat ($12); from Cosco Business Furniture.*

COFFEE SHOPPING *The tuftless restaurant booth by Falcon Products sells for $150 for a single-sided, 45-inch-long seat and $240 for the double-sided section through local restaurant equipment dealers.*

VERDICT *Jasper's Bank of England chair, left, is used on a pedestal base for juries ($215).*

KEEPING BOOKS *Jasper's wooden steno chair, below, swivels ($130).*

RIGHT ARM *Jasper's classic school chair, right, is still available ($65).*

EAT OUT *Hank Loewenstein's Duna chair, left, is used in restaurants ($80).*

MR. CLEAN *Ajusto's all stainless steel swivel chair ($57) is made for laboratory "clean" rooms.*

111

SITTING DOWN

DANIEL MILES KRON

Comfort and travel have been synonymous in America since the 1860s, when George M. Pullman put luxury into railroad cars and reclining chairs into our design vocabulary. Barber, dentist, and steamer chairs followed. Today planes, sports cars, and movie theatres are all equipped with adjustable seats, although Pullman's footrest has vanished along with adequate leg room. New and used automotive seating can be found at stores listed in the Yellow Pages under Automobile Parts and Supplies or under Auto Scrap Dealers. In the High-Tech Directory under Furniture you will also find a list of manufacturers of airline seats, barber and beauty chairs, folding canoe seats, resort chaise lounges, and industrial foam. If you said these were all *ad hoc* solutions rather than high-tech ones, we wouldn't argue with you. So what is a high-tech solution to sitting down? The high-backed executive swivel-and-tilt chair on casters. If you don't rate one at the office, have one at home (see pages 20 and 21).

USED CAR *Interior designer Philip Haight uses a Mercedes-Benz leather upholstered bucket seat, left, as a lounge chair in his home.*

BOAT RIDE *Ash canoe seat, right, with caned back and seat folds for easy storage ($47); from L. L. Bean.*

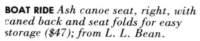

FOUR ON THE AISLE *Mark Ravitz found and repainted four theatre seats, left, and put them into the waiting room of Jules Fisher and Paul Marantz.*

BUILDING BLOCKS *Display designer Charles Hughes bought black spray-painted industrial foam blocks to use as seating in his apartment, above.*

OPERATING ROOM *Designer Bruce Bierman's friends are unnerved when they learn his bar cart is an operating table; from Institutional Industries.*

ROLLING TABLES

FRENCH GOVERNMENT TOURIST OFFICE

The latest thing in industrial rolling carts is the robot that wends its way down office corridors following an invisible magnetically marked path, delivering and picking up mail. But not all industrial carts are automated. There are a number of less sophisticated ones that could lighten the home work-load. Mobile tables manufactured for use in hospitals, factories, restaurants, and institutions are made to stand up to hard wear. They are available with adjustable shelves; adjustable-height tops; locking casters; plexiglass domes for food, display, and service; electric receptacles built in that make them ideal for use as slide and movie projection tables; and even clip-on bins and baskets. All material handling equipment catalogs include rolling tables, as do catalogs for medical supplies, rehabilitation equipment, office supplies, and beauty parlor equipment. Of course, restaurant supply dealers also sell these tables. Now about the robot—it's called the "Mailmobile," and it's made by Lear Ziegler, Incorporated/ Automated Systems of Zeeland, Michigan. This handy assistant sells for $10,000 to $12,000—which includes a one-year warranty and "introductory assistance."

LYNN KARLIN

EQUIPMENT STAND *TV stands don't have to be rickety. Lakeside's is stainless steel.*

PETER M. FINE

FACTORY MODEL *Harry Schule and Ned Marshall's bar is an ordinary rolling shop cart.*

PETER M. FINE

IT'S OK *Designer David Barrett uses a hospital cart as a TV stand in his elegant bedroom.*

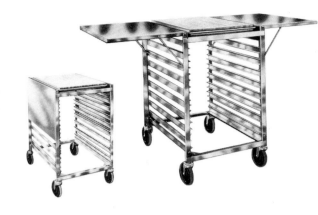

FOOD PREP *Lakeside's stainless steel drop-leaf table has pan and tray racks underneath.*

KITCHEN HELPER *Lakeside also makes a mobile food preparation center, 48 by 27 by 34 inches high.*

LYNN KARLIN

MEDICAL *Bloomfield Industries' utility table, above, is $187 from Manhattan Ad Hoc.*

RAE-ANNE GIOVANNI

CUISINE ART *Bray-Schaible used a French restaurant cart, right, in a client's kitchen.*

CHEMISTRY *Adjustable-height lab cart is from Arthur H. Thomas Co., $525, mail order.*

115

SPORT TECH *You won't lose any sleep over the price ($13.25) of L. L. Bean's folding camp cot, right. The quilt is $45; from Art et Industrie.*

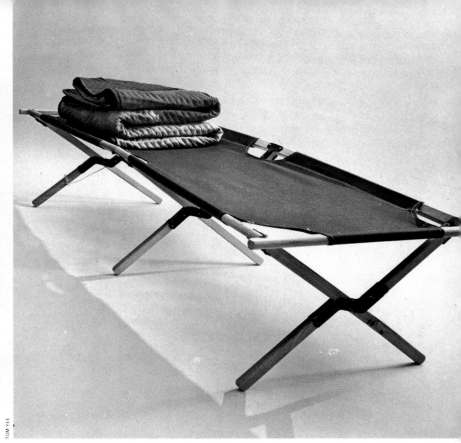

PRESHRUNK *Cotton Department of Mental Health pillowcases by Springs Mills, distributed by Karoll's, Inc. ($4 each); at Manhattan Ad Hoc.*

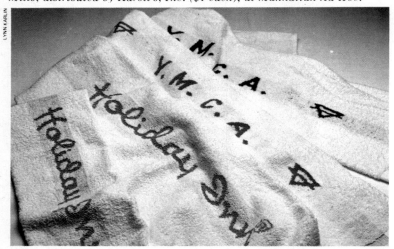

MOTEL AND HOSTEL *Unpretentious monogrammed bath towels that say Holiday Inn and Y.M.C.A. ($5 each); at Manhattan Ad Hoc.*

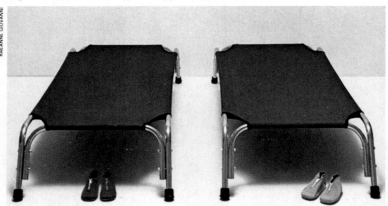

OUT OF SCHOOL *Nursery school stackable resting cots can be used for home nap time too. These navy canvas cots are $26; from Childcraft.*

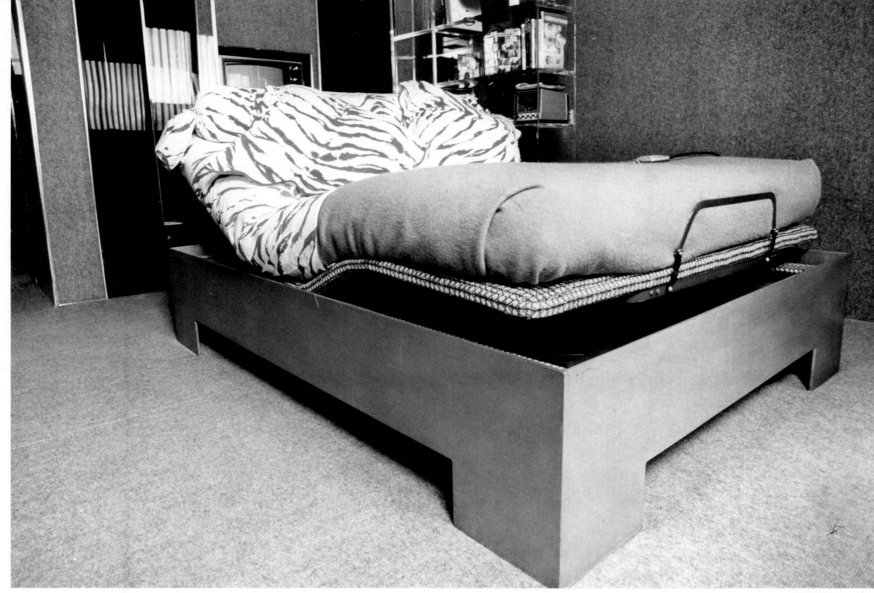

PETER M FINE

BEDS AND LINENS

A WELL BED *To watch the TV set be-hind the head of his bed, above, Robin Roberts raises and then leans against the foot of this electric bed designed by Jay Spectre.*

CLEAN CUT *Simmons's easy-to-clean stainless steel crib, left, sells for $700 plus $53 for the mattress (also available in yellow and white); at L. W. Sleepwell.*

MONDO RUBBER

One of the few fond memories of a hospital stay is the electric bed that goes up and down and can raise the head and bend the knees at a push of a button. Sources listed in the Yellow Pages under Beds, Hospital sell the real things for about $1,100, including mattress and wood head and footboards. If you are willing to forego the elevator feature (which raises the whole bed) and settle for merely raising head and knees, hospital-inspired electric beds (for use with your own headboard) can be had for less. A. Wittenberg in New York City sells a queen-sized Posture-Ease electric bed (with which you use your own mattress) for $880; Simmons makes the Sybarite (an extra-long twin complete with mattress, spring, frame, and casters) that lists for $850 through Simmons dealers—it boasts 1,001 positions; and Frank Hall & Sons sells the Select-A-Rest (with mattress), $915 for twin size and $1,282 for queen size. Other nontraditional bed and linen solutions are institutional linens, nursery school or camp cots, and for purists, stainless steel hospital cribs. Do purists have children?

117

FRENCH GOVERNMENT TOURIST OFFICE

OUTDOOR FURNITURE

Who could imagine London parks without their deck chairs, Paris gardens without their slatted chairs (among the earliest mass-produced chairs), and Italian markets without their huge umbrellas? For years these familiar pieces of commercial outdoor furniture have survived the weather and the vicissitudes of style. Admired for their durability, as well as for their charm, many of these classics have been made continuously for more than fifty years by the same manufacturers. Until recently no one thought of using these classics at home, but why not? Unlike the gaudy, fringed, flowery outdoor furniture available to consumers, these blend in perfectly with the patios of modern houses. Other outdoor ("site") furnishings being borrowed today from commercial sources include advertising umbrellas and playground equipment.

MARKET VALUE *Huge market umbrella that traditionally shielded fruit and vegetables from the noonday sun is used in a private garden setting. Made of canvas and wood, this ample umbrella sells for $410 at D/R.*

118

ELYSE LEWIN/FAMILY CIRCLE

PARK HERE *Classic French folding park furniture (about $150 the set) is available from Williams-Sonoma.*

SAFETY SLIDE *Red, white, and blue playground spiral slide is 7 ft. 7 in. high ($1600); from American Playground Device Co.*

RESORTFUL *Sun & Leisure's molded fiber-glass contour lounge like those used at resorts ($200); at Bailey-Huebner in Bendel's.*

MICHEL TCHEREVKOFF

DRINK UP *Famous brand promotional vinyl advertising umbrellas are suitable as beach umbrellas. Prices start at $41 at Zip-Jack.*

119

DANIEL MILES KRON

ROBERT PERRON

RAEANNE GIOVANNI

JESSICA STRANG

CONVER-SIONS

Most of the items in this book are shown doing the same job residentially that they did industrially, but on these two pages and on the following two are "conversions"—ex-industrial items doing something different from what they were designed to do. Coffee-grinder lamps, manhole-cover tabletops have given conversions a bad name, but there are times when the end transcends the means. Wheel hubs, available from any tire shop, make excellent occasional tables, as do the wooden pallets that are used extensively in the warehousing industry as trays (after being loaded with goods, they are moved by forklift trucks). There are 2,000 pallet manufacturers in the United States. A standard double-faced pallet (wood-slatted top and bottom) is usually 40 by 48 by 5 inches high. New, they cost about $20, but because the old ones are not in demand, dealers will sometimes sell them for as little as $5.

TIRES *Architect Paul Rudolph suggested tractor tires, above left, for furniture; the client upholstered them in elastic.*

WHEELS *"Tables," at left, are American Racing wheels, $50 to $75 from tire shops.*

AUTOMOTIVE *Americans aren't the only ones furnishing with car parts; in the English interior pictured above an auto bumper is used as a wall shelf.*

PETER M. FINE

RAEANNE GIOVANNI

A VERY GOOD GEAR *When photographer Peter M. Fine found an old machine gear on the street in New York's printing district, he turned it into a telephone table in his loft.*

BEAM TABLE *Ward Bennett turned an I beam found on a construction site into a cigarette table.*

121

CONVERSIONS

RAEANNE GIOVANNI

FRANK KOLLEOGY

SUPPORT SYSTEM
Bretford's 24-by-18-by-14-inch-high black base for cassette holders can be used as a coffee table ($49); from Fuller Stationers.

CONCRETE STACK
Piled-up paving stones make an end table in London. (In New York, designer Richard Knapple has stacked plate glass for tables.)

JESSICA STRANG

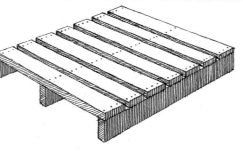

DRAWINGS BY CHAS B SLACKMAN

ON THE SKIDS *Patino/Wolf Associates used industrial pallets as tables, at right, in the apartment of jewelry designer Elsa Peretti.*

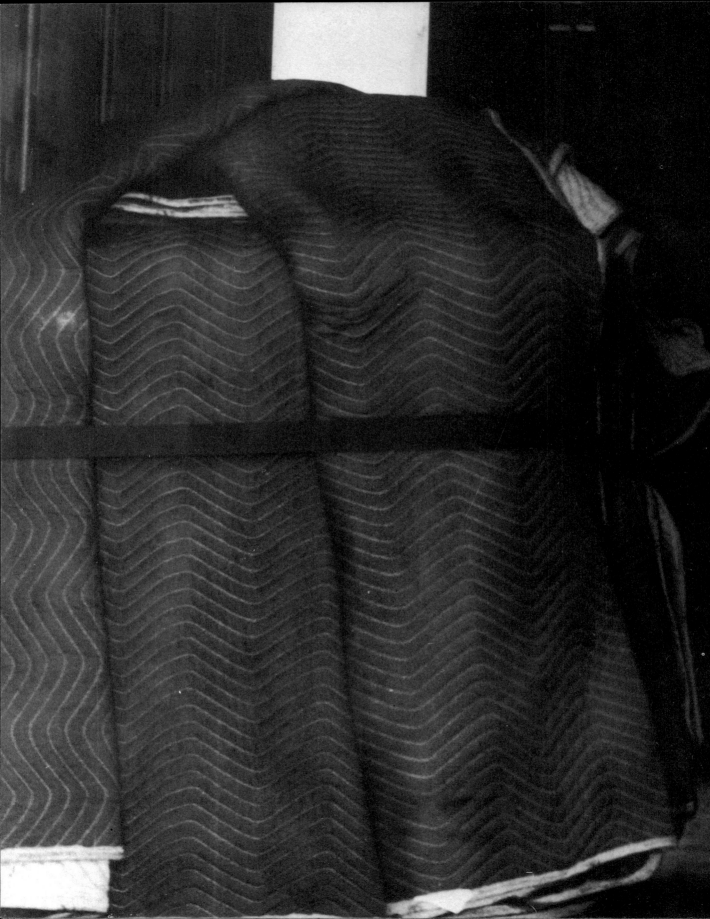

MATERIALS

128 SONOTUBES
In their work life Sonotubes are used as forms for pouring concrete, but for years these fiberboard columns have been put to other ingenious uses.

130 TOPS
There is more to counter- and table-top materials than marble and plastic laminates: ask a chemical lab technician what's impervious to heat, ask an art supply store what's a perfect cutting board, or ask a designer to suggest a handsome, underrated, underutilized material.

132 FABRICS
With the use of artists' canvas for upholstery, sailcloth for curtains, and movers' quilts for wall-to-wall padding, velvet and satin may be endangered species.

136 INDUSTRIAL CARPETING
Industrial carpet sounds like it comes straight out of the factory; actually it comes straight out of the office and off the diving board.

138 WINDOW DRESSING
Once upon a time window shades without draperies over them were seen only in schools and factories. Today a variety of window shades, meant to be used unadorned in the home, are available in materials that were engineered for commercial installations.

140 METALS
From the quilted metal walls of the diner to corrugated aluminum roofing to embossed steel dockplate used in the boiler rooms of battleships, there are a number of industrial metals worthy of your consideration.

144 RUBBER
After years of worshipping the marble floor, the residential market is now kissing the ground-covering material pioneered in an Italian subway.

148 CERAMIC TILE
Quarry tile, which used to be walked on only in factories and firehouses, has been social climbing—and so has that commercial staple, white subway tile.

150 MATS AND SLATS
Whether you want an unusual path or a wall-to-wall raised floor, the mats that keep workers from sliding on restaurant kitchen floors are an untapped design resource.

152 WALLS
Have you ever wondered when you threw out the plastic packing from an appliance if it could serve another purpose? Well, it can.

154 GLASS BLOCK
Glass block started its career in residential service but soon became associated with commercial projects. It's coming back home again.

OVERLEAF *Movers' pads photo, courtesy Rennert Mfg. Co., Inc., inset; Tim Romanello's apartment, photo, Charles Wiesehahn.*

Art and industry were interwoven, literally and figuratively, in the late 1920s, when Anni Albers, who taught weaving at Germany's Bauhaus school, created a new drapery fabric for a labor union school using ordinary cellophane on the front for light reflection and chenille on the back for sound absorption.

Today industrial materials are being used more blatantly—"woven" instead into the "fabric" of the room. Nowhere is the defection from conventional sources more obvious than in our new acceptance of industrial and commercial materials. Where previously the town and country houses of the rich were the models for taste and style, now corporate offices, public buildings, space technology, and real work environments are the trend setters. The traditional classics—carved wood moldings, marble and malachite walls, the fringed and tassled valences, richly veneered tabletops, velvets, and brocades—are now being supplanted by contemporary classics—materials originally developed not for their look or their opulence but for their performance, in total disregard of a fashion. Butcher block was one of the first materials to assert its practicality; covered-wagon canvas is now an accepted slipcover material; nylon spinnaker cloth makes water-repellent shower curtains; artists' canvas is used as upholstery. The inexpensive movers' pads—quilted not for looks but to add extra strength and softness—make wonderful wall and platform padding. Embossed rubber flooring, which led a productive life in train stations, is now a favorite in kitchens, as is the studded floor of the freight elevator. The new taste for these honest industrial products can be seen as a rejection of the hoked-up materials—phony brick floors, ersatz vinyl pretending to be Alhambra ceramics—that pass as home furnishings today.

If we had to choose one material that symbolizes the spirit of high-tech and the industrial aesthetic, it would be steel dock plate. It has evolved in the last 100 years from a sunken-ribbed pattern, developed as a nonskid surface for use in the boiler rooms of coal-burning ships, to a raised diamondette pattern in the 1920s, to the raised nondirectional Super Diamond Floor Plate pattern "designed" in 1932 by Leon Lieberman, product manager of the Alan Wood Steel Co. in Philadelphia and unsung design hero. Illustrated on the cover of this book, this four-way pattern was a success not for decorative reasons but because it allowed the steel to be laid in any direction without a disruption of the pattern. How many times a day do you walk over a cellar door on a city street made of this ubiquitous material? You'll also see it in stadiums, on Navy vessels, on trucks, and loading docks. However, it took an interior-design team, who lifted it out of context and used it on the raised hearth of an Easthampton home (see page 140), to see the beauty and timelessness of this ordinary material that has never won any design awards.

In this chapter we have illustrated a number of common industrial materials that, like dock plate, have been, or could be, used effectively in the home. The world of twentieth-century materials is still ripe for exploration.

RAE-ANNE GIOVANNI

TV COLUMN *Designers Robert Bray and Michael Schaible used a carpeted Sonotube (from Raw Equipment Company) as a free-standing armoire in a New York bedroom. The clients use it to store their TV set and a selection of midnight snacks.*

THE VERSATILE SONOTUBE

Yale architecture students may have been the first to recognize the potential of the Sonotube—a patented fiber form used to pour concrete columns and footings for bridges, buildings, and raised highways. At least ten years ago the students were putting these industrial forms to work at school as kiosks for posters and messages. As far as we could ascertain, about 1970 Sonotubes made their first publicized residential appearance—in *House &*

Garden magazine—as revolving closets in a bedroom designed by architect Paul Rudolph. Since then the popularity of Sonotubes has spread; today you can find them used as beds, pedestals, table bases, closets, and even free standing decorative columns. Sonotubes come in a variety of diameters (which are measured by the inside opening) from 6 inches to 48 inches—in 2-inch increments. The standard length is 18 feet but a Sonotube can easily be

cut down with a skill saw, handsaw, or sharp knife. The tube is a beige color and the trademark is repeated all over it. But even when the tube is painted, the pattern of the fiber, wound in a spiral, is visible. The Sonotube is manufactured by Sonoco Products Company, which has distributors listed in the Yellow Pages under Concrete Construction Forms and Accessories. A 3-by-10-foot Sonotube sells for about $120. Getting it home is another problem.

JOANNE SEADOR

TURNABOUT *Architect Paul Rudolph employed Sonotubes as revolving bedroom closets in this New York apartment.*

ARCHITECTONIC *Although they hold nothing up, this group of Sonotubes, painted white, lend a structural quality to this San Francisco apartment designed by Ron Oates.*

PERFECT PEDESTALS *In the bedroom of London fashion designer Zandra Rhodes, carpet tubes, covered in fabric, hold plants.*

SLEEP TUBES *Jim and Penny Hull, of Culver City, California, designed the Toobline furniture system using fiber tubes, but Sonotubes can be used to make similar beds.*

129

TOPS

Marble stains, wood scratches, lacquer chips, plastic laminate can be scorched by hot pots. So what does industry use for trouble-free tabletops? Johns Manville's Colorlith is an asbestos-cement "stone" used widely in laboratories. Colorlith can be had 1¼ inches thick in 4-by-8-foot sheets in green, dark brown, charcoal gray, and white. For extra stain resistance there is Colorceran—Colorlith with a ceramic-like coating. These laboratory tops and others can be ordered from firms listed in the Yellow Pages under Laboratory Equipment and Supply. A 4-by-4-foot by 1¼-inch Colorlith tabletop in charcoal gray is $189 from Asbeka Industries; brown and white are 20 and 25 percent higher, respectively.

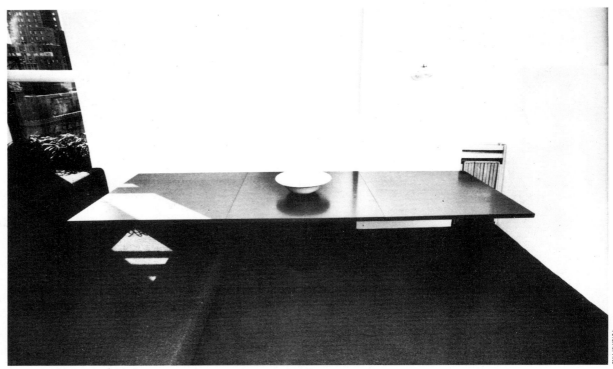

JOHNS-MANVILLE CORP

PETER M. FINE

ACID TEST *Designer Robert Bray used a three-piece Colorlith "stone" top, above, for an 11-foot-long table in his own apartment. Apollo Woodworking cantilevered the top from a steel column bolted to the floor.*

SAFETY GLASS *Designer Joseph Paul D'Urso put wire glass (traditionally used in windows for security and fire retardance) to work as the top of an elegant coffee table shown opposite, top and bottom).*

HARD EDGE *Vinyl or wood edges are offered by most restaurant table makers; these by Johnson Industries.*

TOM YEE

CUTPROOF *"Piccolo," a green and white paper-cutting board, is impervious to scratches. An excellent surface for hobby work or cutting cheese, an 18-by-24-inch piece is $30 at Sam Flax.*

FABRICS

PHOTOGRAPHS BY DAVID RILEY

Stanley Rennert was a traveling man. As a manufacturer of furniture pads and covers in the 1950s, he learned firsthand of the specific needs of the moving industry and was in a position to change the basic production techniques of the movers' material. The result? Rennart's longer-lasting ZIG-ZAG pattern and locked stitching technique, which keeps each stitch independent of the next. A further product improvement was the introduction of colorfast quilt materials to protect furniture from discoloration. The evolutionary history of other industrial fabrics is similar. Whether synthetics or naturals, industrial fabrics were developed to meet the need of every trade. But it is only recently that designers have used them in different contexts. Spinnaker cloth makes a very good shower curtain; laundry bag mesh a pleasing curtain; movers' furniture pads and artists' canvas a different covering for elegant sofas. One of the best sources for industrial fabrics and canvas is John Boyle and Co.

BIG IN BUSINESS *John Boyle's plastic Pro (from $2) is used for tank liners, sulphur-pi covers, and pole-vault pads.*

SEVEN SHEETS TO THE WIND *Aquino's 40-inch-wide Spinnaker Ripstop nylon (about $6 per yard) is sold through sailmakers all over the world.*

ARMY, NAVY, & MARINE *John Boyle and Co., the secret source of many decorators, sells cotton Army duck in all weights and a wide variety of colors (prices start at about $2 per yard).*

SITTING DUCK *Canvas and duck are terms that can be used interchangeably. Designer Lee Bailey used artist's canvas, unsized, as upholstery fabric on a sofa.*

MOVING PICKS *Rennert makes its movers' quilts in a variety of colors, sizes, and fabrics. Turn the page to see how one designer used them.*

DAVID RILEY

FABRICS

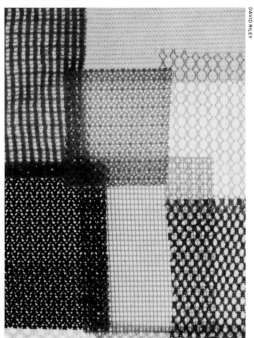

DAVID RILEY

TRADE SECRETS *Nylon meshes from United Textile Corp. are used to make hats, laundry bags, and shoes. This company makes fishnet too.*

DUFFLE BAGGING *The higher the number, the thinner the cotton duck; John Boyle and Co. sells it 120 inches wide (from $4 to $8 per yard).*

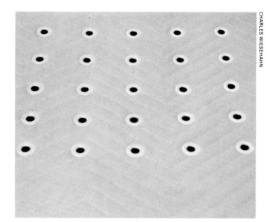

CHARLES WIESEHAHN

PADDED PAD *Designer Tim Romanello used movers' pads from Rennert ($3.50 to $5.50 per square yard) to cover the bed, floor, and cabinets in his one-room apartment, right. Grommets were used for the stereo speaker, above. This fabric must be sanitized before use.*

PETER M. FINE

SWIM CHAMP *Diving board cocoa matting, above, and in detail below, covers the floor and bed platform of Renny Reynolds's bedroom.*

PETER M. FINE

COMMERCE OR INDUSTRY *Designers Douglas Kahn and Stephanie Mallis covered the walls, steps, bookcases, and floor of this open-plan apartment, at left, in khaki-colored commercial carpet.*

"INDUSTRIAL" CARPET

Sisal and cocoa matting, once found only on diving boards and around pools, and "industrial" carpet are becoming more and more popular as wall-to-wall carpeting for residential use. "Industrial" carpet is really a misnomer; rather it should be called "commercial" carpet, as it refers to the tightly woven, level-loop construction carpeting that is commonly used in offices because of its long-wearing properties and ease of maintainance. "Industrial" carpet, because of its low pile, lends itself to platform covering and upholstered wall installations that are trademarks of the industrial-style interior. Nearly every carpet manufacturer has industrial- or commercial-grade carpeting in its line in a number of fibers and fiber combinations.

COURTESY NEW YORK CITY DEPARTMENT OF PARKS AND RECREATION

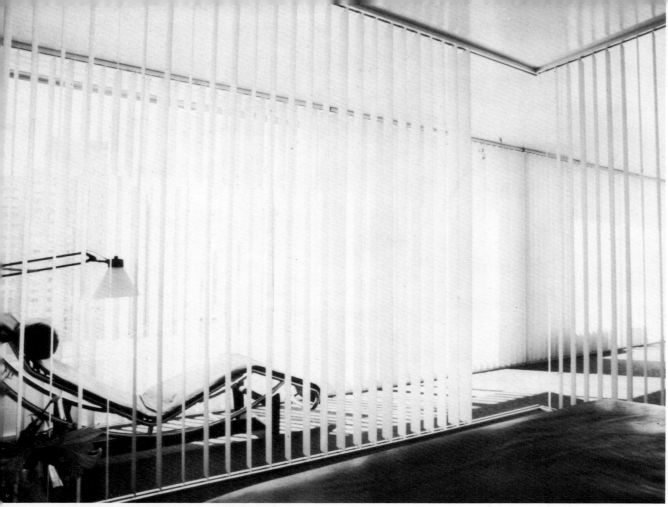

DOUBLE-ENTENDRE *Designer Joseph Paul D'Urso used two layers of vertical blinds in this apartment for New York shoe designer Reed Evins. One set of blinds partitions off the bedroom area; the other set covers the windows.*

SCREENING *Designer Thomas Boccia sewed stiff Roman shades, using*

WINDOW DRESSING

The association of personal modesty with window coverings has been a Victorian legacy. Long after the advent of central heating and picture windows, a home was considered "naked" without its full complement of draperies, curtains, and window shades. But traditional trappings could be a problem on picture windows, not to mention an expense. Tired of sun rot and moisture condensation problems as well as cleaning and

rehanging costs, interior designers were the first to experiment with less cumbersome window treatments pioneered in the "curtain-walled" office buildings that proliferated after the 1951 Lever Brothers Building. Today the bare window look is ubiquitous: going it alone are vertical blinds, pleated shades, venetian blinds, or window shades—all previously acceptable as lone window coverings only in factories, schools, or offices.

Today even the see-through Mylar shades used in store windows to control fading have been appropriated for the home, where they are used to control glare without losing view. With nakedness no longer an issue, advances in window coverings now have less to do with style than with the development of ever-better environmentally engineered fabrics that can control heat gain in summer and loss in winter.

MICHAEL DATOLI

fiber-glass screening from Tetko Wire Cloth Co. Isabel Scott also makes such shades using Owens Corning Fiberglas Co. screening.

PETER M. FINE

SUN SCREEN *On ceiling-to-floor windows Lila Schneider, of Korman-Schneider, uses Holland Shade Co.'s perforated Dijonglas shades to cut heat inflow.*

FADEPROOF *Store windows employ amber cellophane shades to prevent fading or to make food look more appetizing; today mylar shades keep out hot sun at home. This shade by Holland.*

RAE-ANNE GIOVANNI

MECHANISTIC *Joel Berman's Mecho Shade has an easily removable roller for a seasonal change of cloth.*

139

EMBOSSED METALS

DANIEL MILES KRON

Dock plate, tread plate, checker plate, boiler plate (at left and below) are all names for a heavy-duty, 3/16 to ¾ inch thick, embossed steel material that was first developed as nonskid flooring for use on destroyer decks, in engine rooms, and as a loading-dock surface. In 1932, the Alan Wood Steel Company first manufactured its patented four-way diamond pattern which has been in demand ever since. Today, most steel companies make embossed patterns, which are sold through distributors by weight (from $19 to $400 per 100 pounds, plus a cutting fee)

depending on the base material, which ranges from aluminum to carbon steel to stainless steel. Pressed tin ceilings, pictured at right, were introduced during the Civil War as an economical replacement for ornamental plasterwork. Barney-Brainum Shanker Steel is still pressing the metal sheets. A 2-by-8-foot sheet sells for about $10 a sheet. Professional installation ($1.50 a square foot including material) of the hard-to-handle, thin, sharp-edged tin is recommended. Look in the Yellow Pages under Ceilings-Metal for installers.

LEONARD NONES

RED OVERHEAD *This tinplate dropped ceiling was designed and installed by lighting consultant Paul Marantz and architect Alan Buchsbaum.*

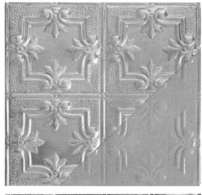

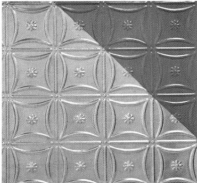
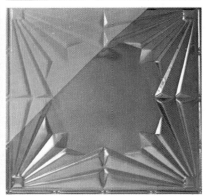

LEONARD NONES

SAMPLING *Barney-Brainum Shanker Steel's pressed tin ceilings come in many patterns. The sheets can be painted or left in the natural silvery finish.*

RAE-ANNE GIOVANNI

FIREPLACE *Bray-Schaible covered a client's hearth, left and above, with Alan Wood's "Super Diamond Floor Plate" from Bushwick Iron and Steel.*

MORE METALS

Think metal: galvanized corrugated steel, stainless steel, cyclone metal fencing. Metals (machined or custom-made, shiny or matte) come in many forms: sheets, rolls, sections; quilted, embossed, drilled, mirrored. They can be used to cover, support, and adorn walls, floors, and ceilings. Restaurant equipment companies make quilted wall panels to order; lumberyards and builders' supply sources carry corrugated steel; or look in the Yellow Pages under Steel Distributors and Fabricators, or Aluminum.

CONDUITS *Swedish architect Andrejs Legzdins used curved galvanized corrugated sections of drainage conduits for the furniture in the converted dairy in which he lives near Stockholm.*

STEEL PEGBOARD *An 18-by-46-inch sheet; $95 at The Professional Kitchen.*

ON THE FENCE *The cyclone fencing used by designer Joseph Paul D'Urso for the Calvin Klein showroom is an original divider. It's easy to hook clothes hangers onto it.*

142

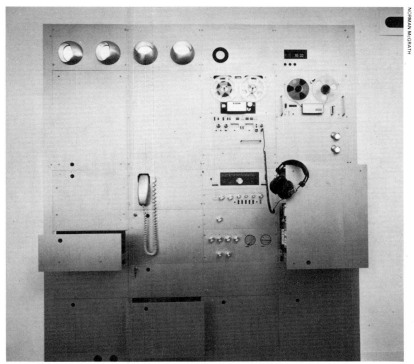

NORMAN McGRATH

IN CONTROL *A custom-made wall system designed by architect Michael Wolfe holding professional sound equipment was faced with aluminum panels.*

CHARLES WIESEHAHN

DINER SPECIAL *The quilted stainless steel wall panels from the Empire Diner are made by restaurant equipment manufacturers.*

NORMAN McGRATH

MIRROR IMAGE *A stainless steel laminate ceiling was chosen by designer John Saladino as a reflective device in this New York apartment.*

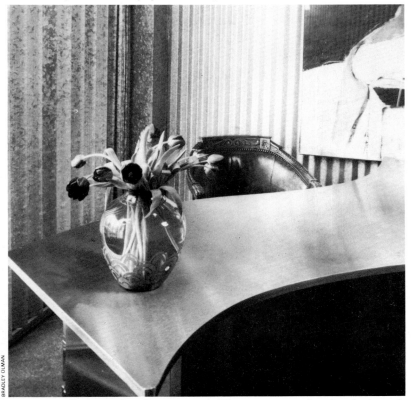

BRADLEY OLMAN

STEELWORK *Designer Jay Spectre used fifteen corrugated galvanized steel sheets, purchased in a lumberyard, to panel his office.*

JASON INDUSTRIAL, INC.

RUBBER

The hard-wearing, water-proof, and insulating properties of rubber flooring make it ideal for home use. The current favorite of designers is embossed-pattern flooring developed in Italy in the 1940s. A group of Italian architects designed a ribbed pattern, convinced the Pirelli Tire Co. to manufacture it, and had it installed in Rome's main railway station, where it has endured. The "studded" pattern of raised circles, designed to minimize grit abrasion was introduced in the 1960s and has been used in the Milan subway and on the Apollo II spacecraft. Pirelli and other brands of industrial nonskid flooring are available in tiles, runners, or wide rolls and come in a variety of patterns. Jason Industrial is the United States source for Pirelli. Other rubber manufacturers are U.S. Mat & Rubber Co., American Floor Products, and Mondo.

MONDO RUBBER

CARLA DE BENEDETTI

SUBWAY STYLE *Nonskid black Pirelli rubber was a good choice for both these stairs, left. It's about $2.50 a square foot uninstalled, from Jason Industrial.*

UP THE WALL *Ribbed-texture rubber flooring was applied to both walls and floor, above, by Milanese architect Eleonore Peduzzi Riva.*

RUBBER

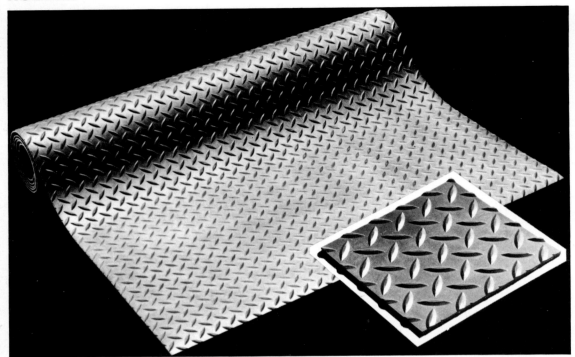

PETER AARON

RUNNER-UP *Slip-resistant rubber runner from American Floor Products Co. has an embossed deck plate design. It's $275 retail for a 25-foot roll, 36-inches wide.*

BILL HELMS FOR THE FORMICA CORP.

STUDDED *Any vinyl tile can be studded with metal. Designer Joseph Paul D'Urso had these red tiles studded by Charles Luria. Roblan Manufacturing Co. also studs tiles for about $4 per square foot.*

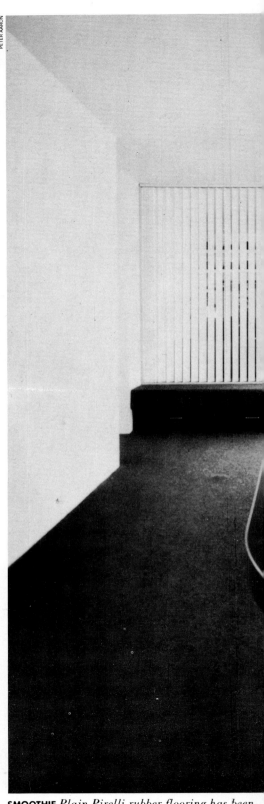

SMOOTHIE *Plain Pirelli rubber flooring has been used for this dining tabletop by designer Joseph*

DAVID RILEY

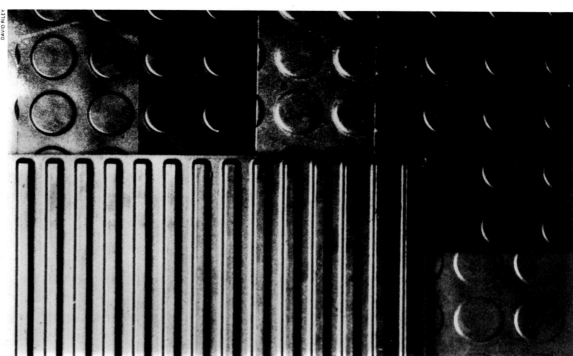

TEXTURAL *Embossed circles (Mondo) and stripes (Pirelli) in a range of colors are available in tiles or runners starting at $2.25 a square foot. Write to the manufacturers for dealer names.*

JAIME ARDILES-ARCE

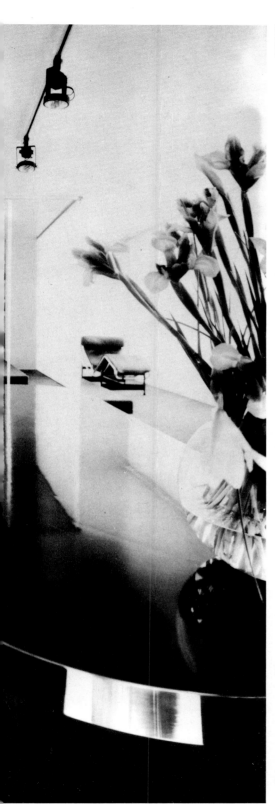

Paul D'Urso in a New York residence. Surprisingly, gleams like a metal top.

WELL PLACED *Designer Juan Montoya chose hard-wearing Pirelli rubber flooring for the surface of this at home work counter. Writing on it can be a problem.*

PETER M FINE

RUGGED *Tan industrial-grade quarry tile, laid on the square, covers the floor of a stately apartment house kitchen renovated by designer Richard Penney.*

JOANNE SEADOR

FRANK KOLLEOGY

REVIVED *Commercial mosaic tiles by American Olean lead a new life; architect Stephen Levine used them to surface the area around a platform bed.*

CARLA DE BENEDETTI

CERAMIC TILE

Ceramic tile is as old as ancient Egypt. But in the recent past, certain patterns, shapes, and finishes of ceramic tile became typecast as either commercial or residential. Colored and decorated tiles were considered residential, and plain shiny white tiles institutional, best suited for subways and fish markets. Small mosaic tiles were used in swimming pools and public lavatories, and quarry tile, the workhorse of the tile family, was for plants, hospitals, malls, and firehouses. But stereotyping began to wane after World War II as architects and designers began exploring the sensual and visual possibilities of commonplace materials. Today these "commercial" tiles are suitable for any room in the house.

WET LOOK *Hygienic white tiles, right, associated with butcher shops and subways, have sensuous appeal in a Milanese bedroom designed by Claudio Dini.*

MATS AND SLATS

Raised duckboards in either vinyl or wood are used to prevent slips on wet floors in restaurants, boats, and around pools. Vinyl duckboards—which come in brilliant colors—are used to cut down on noise in horse stalls and could be used as a sound-absorbing floor covering at home as well. They are a natural for kitchens or baths too. Another industrial mat that is being recognized as useful in the home is the ordinary striated rubber matting found in apartment house lobbies, where it's used on rainy days. It comes in white and black as well as colors, and it can make a perfect do-it-yourself wall-to-wall rubber floor.

TEDRUTH PLASTICS CORP.

DAVID RILEY

ROBERT PERRON

ROPE TRICK *Byron and Susan Bell twisted cargo rope into a rug.*

WOODY *Brabrook's duckboard, left, is made of kiln-dried red oak. Cactus Mat's boardwalk, above, combines hardware slats with shock-absorbing runners.*

ROBERTO BROSAN

SEAWORTHY *Ward Bennett's slatted fence was originally used as boat floors.*

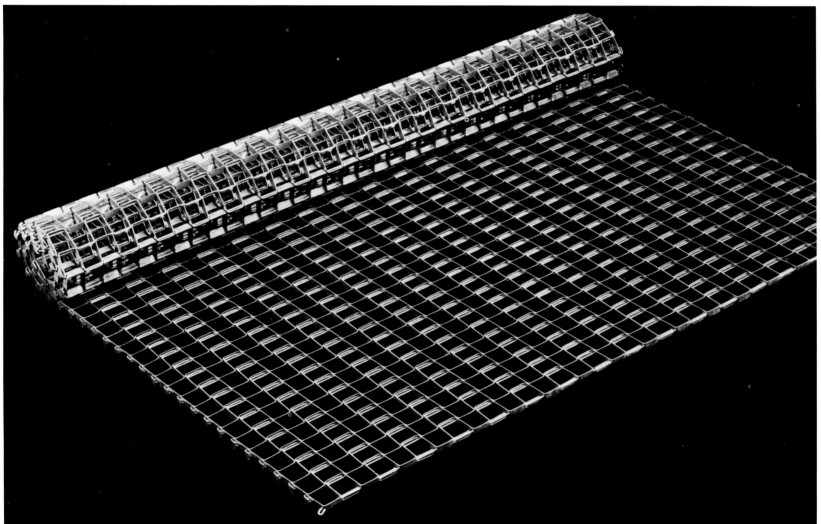

PLASTIC PRESENCE *Tepromark International's vinyl duckboards, left, are flame resistant, and water-, rot-, rust-, and chip-proof ($4 per square foot).*

SCRAPE METAL *Flexible ⅜-inch-thick steel mat from American Floor Products is good for scraping sand, snow, sawdust, and gravel from shoes.*

ABRASIVE *The U.S. Plywood Co. experimented with a specially treated sand-covered material for both the interior and exterior of this house.*

NORMAN McGRATH

WALLS

There is more to wall coverings than plywood veneers, painted Sheetrock, posy-covered wallpaper, and Chinese murals. Industrial research programs are responsible for the development of many new materials, but often it is the architect and designer, constantly searching for new materials, who conceive of residential applications for them. The last two decades have seen a wave of experimentation. There is hardly a material today that is considered unfit for residential walls, be it brown paper bag wallpaper or aluminum foil-backed insulating material—the poor person's silver foil. After Louis Kahn demonstrated in the 50s the beauty of unfinished concrete in his public buildings, raw cinder block, humble peg-board (elevated from the basement workshop), corrugated cardboard, and even the molded plastic material used to package appliances have been seen on walls at home. The time for experimentation isn't over yet. All you need is imagination to transform an industrial material into a decorating tool. But do as the professionals do—use the material in abundance.

UNICUBE CORP.

152

EDUCATIONAL EXPERIENCE *When children visit Yann Weymouth and Peter Coan of Redroof Design they can draw on the architects' school blackboard door.*

CONTAINERIZATION *Styrofoam, usually used as packing material, has been carved into kitchen utensil-shaped niches by Rome architect Lino Schenal.*

PEG O' MY HEART *Architect Ira Oaklander used white-enameled ¼-inch peg-board nailed on 2-by-4-inch framing to build this platformed seating.*

CONCRETE PROPOSAL *Architect Roland Coate chose exposed concrete for the living room walls of his Venice, California, residence.*

153

CIRCLE/SQUARE *Glass blocks are international. Italian architect Giuliana Corsini built an interior partition in a kitchen using a circular patterned glass block.*

GLASS BLOCK

JOANNE SEADOR

As early as 1903 there were architectural experiments with glass lenses—or glass block as it is now called. However, this material did not flourish until the 1930s, when it became synonymous with the work of Le Corbusier and other international-style architects, who used it primarily in factories, schools, and commercial buildings. In fact, Le Corbusier and other leading architects had been strongly influenced by the Maison de Verre, a Paris house (designed in 1928 by engineer/designer Pierre Chareau) that was sheathed (see page 12) in glass block, which, according to architectural historian Kenneth Frampton, the manufacturer, Saint Gobain, would not guarantee to be weatherproof. Fifty years later this glass house, still standing, is an architectural landmark, and glass block is an acceptable material for the home, often used for interior rather than exterior walls. Glass block comes in many sizes and styles. Molded in two identical pieces and seamed together, its construction makes it sound-absorbent and insulating. It is also impact and fire resistant, and depending on the pattern, it can give visual privacy while still letting in light. Write Pittsburgh Corning Corporation, the largest manufacturer of glass block, for a catalog. Used glass block, in current and discontinued styles, can be bought from wrecking companies.

TOM YEE COPYRIGHT ©1973 BY THE CONDE NAST PUBLICATIONS, INC.

GLASS HOUSING *This curved wall of glass block in a New York apartment designed by the architectural firm of Gwathmey & Siegel serves two functions: It screens out noise but still transmits natural daylight to the windowless space.*

CHARLES NESBIT

LIGHT WAVE *Architect Alan Buchsbaum used glass block for a stepped-down undulating wall partitioning his bedroom from the rest of his Soho loft. On waking in the windowless room he can sense the weather from reflections in the glass.*

CHOICES *Five of Pittsburgh Corning's glass-block patterns; sold by Supro Building Products for under $2 per 6-inch-square block.*

LIGHTING

OVERLEAF *Factory photo, courtesy Library of Congress; inset, Peter M. Fine photo.*

ndustrial lighting has always been light years ahead of residential lighting. Mines, railroads, and lighthouses needed good lighting much more urgently than did homes, so new advances were usually adopted first by industry. Even Thomas Edison's own home, according to *The Social History of Lighting* by William T. O'Dea, was not among the first homes to go electric. If it had, it would probably have been lit by Edison lamps, circa 1883— bouquets of glass flowers with electric light bulbs in their centers. These lights were a far cry from the no-nonsense fixtures used at the same time in industry.

The product world still operates on what design historian Herwin Schaefer called the "two-track" system: on one track is the form-follows-function industrial product; on the other track is the form-follows-style residential product. Often the residential product has extra added rosettes.

The two tracks have been on a collision course ever since World War II, when commercial- and industrial-inspired lighting started infiltrating the home. While many people remember those years for the ferment in Italian product design with an accent on colorful molded plastic products, it was also the time when little picture lights gave way to spotlights on electrified ceiling tracks (right out of museums and art galleries), when the old-fashioned globe over the medicine cabinet gave way to backstage-type bare bulb fixtures, when the coffee table was underlit with neon right out of the advertising world, and drafting-type lamps turned up on night tables. But the contemporary industrial product became almost indistinguishable from the real industrial product in the 1960s when, as Emilio Ambasz points out in the foreword to this book, the Castiglione brothers designed the Toio lamp—a lamp made of automobile headlights. The logical next step was to go back to the source. Why wear designer jeans when you can wear Levis? "Industrial fixtures are terrific," said lighting designer Paul Marantz, "because they are well-made and exceedingly honest. Nobody sat down to make a saleable item with any of these fixtures. They were designed for a purpose: if a fixture needed a screw on the left side, it had a screw on the left side, no matter what the screw would do to the fixture's appearance. Industrial fixtures are not self-conscious design. There is no fashion about them."

But there is a fashion for them. And there is a tremendous variety to be had. There are nearly thirty pages of industrial lighting manufacturers listed in the Thomas Register, a comprehensive catalog of American manufacturers and dealers, under such esoteric headings as Emergency Lighting; Temporary Lighting; Portable Lighting; Airport, Navigation, and Aisle Lights; Beacon, Cargo, and Christmas Tree Lights; Dental, Dust-Tight, Flagpole, and Foglights; Footlights; Floodlights; Trouble Lights; Taillights; Underwater Lights; Votive Lights; and would you believe, Deodorizing Lights. On the following pages we have endeavored to show the diversity of fixtures available from commercial and industrial sources that have potential for home use. But we use the word available advisedly. Not all the lights shown are available in standard consumer outlets. Hardware stores and wholesale electrical supply houses—where electricians buy—are the best sources. But not all those outlets want to sell to consumers who need special attention, so do your homework before you go shopping. It is important to understand, for instance, that low-voltage fixtures, such as the ones used in automobiles, planes, and on boats, need special transformers to make them usable at home.

However, as sure as dressing-room lights were made for the home, factory lights and airplane lights will eventually turn up in retail stores. But watch out, some manufacturer is bound to try to make them more appealing with rosettes!

ITALIAN WORKERS *Architects Clara and Umberto Orsoni installed four Italian factory lamps with European mountings in this kitchen.*

CARLA DE BENEDETTI

THE FACTORY LIGHT

LIBRARY OF CONGRESS

If there is one universal lighting fixture it is the RLM, the generic name for porcelain-on-steel incandescent light reflectors. Although it is hard to pinpoint exactly when it was first designed or manufactured, we know that by the 1930s the RLM was a well-established form of lighting in factories and warehouses. We also know that the fixture gets its name from the Registered Luminaire Manufacturers Institute, a standards group (now known as the RLM Standards Institute Group, Inc.) to which lighting manufacturers belong and which controls the conformance of fixtures to RLM specifications and national electrical codes. RLM's have always been, and still are, inexpensive and ubiquitous. They have been getting out of the factory for some time—trading up successively from restaurants to showrooms to architects' offices. Their first homecoming was through the back door into the kitchen, but today they are acceptable in every room in the house. Although the number of manufacturers who make these fixtures has dwindled, the names to look for are Abolite, Appleton, Benjamin Electric, and Spero. Originally sold in parts through electrical supply shops, the fixtures have been resourcefully assembled by some distributors—for instance, New York's Harry Gitlin Lighting—so that total units can be purchased. Recently, RLM's have also been turning up in hardware stores and lighting shops. For sources, check the Yellow Pages under Electrical Supply. These fixtures start at about $18 each, unassembled.

MICHAEL DATOLI

NORMAN McGRATH

RAEANNE GIOVANNI

ON THE TRACK *Architect Carolyn Levy of L.S.K Designs used track mounted RLM's from The Lighting Center for her own kitchen.*

GREEN LIGHT *Hung from a chain, an RLM lamp illuminates the plant-filled reading and dining corner in artist Jack Ceglic's Soho loft.*

BLACK BEAUTY *The RLM reflector, tabletop, table base, and slate floor are all black in designer Ward Bennett's summerhouse.*

ELLIOT FINE

RAEANNE GIOVANNI

SUMMER STOCK *Three hanging domes light a beach house kitchen designed by architect Carl Hribar in Fire Island, N.Y.*

WHITE ON WHITE *Architect Kenneth Walker chose a white porcelain-on-steel reflector to match the white cabinets and hardware in his country kitchen.*

THE FACTORY LIGHT

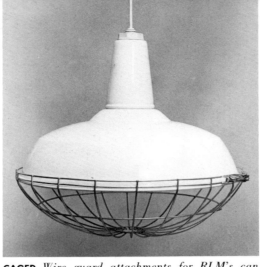

CAGED *Wire guard attachments for RLM's can protect the bulb—they look good too; 18-inch guard is $18 at The Lighting Center.*

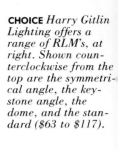

CHOICE *Harry Gitlin Lighting offers a range of RLM's, at right. Shown counterclockwise from the top are the symmetrical angle, the keystone angle, the dome, and the standard ($63 to $117).*

WHAT'S IN STORE *The Italian factory lamp is similar, but not identical, to its American counterparts. Femi in Milan supplies it to the European Fiorucci shops.*

THE SOURCE *Abolite now makes its RLM's in white, green, yellow, blue, red, or black; retails from $35 to $45, depending on size, through dealers.*

ANGLED *BumpZoid Architects installed symmetrical RLM's in this kitchen. Sources: Appleton, Benjamin Electric, Hubbell Lighting, and Crouse-Hinds.*

NUMBERED *Angled RLM's spotlight the numbers on the entrance to architect Barton Myers's narrow, 25-foot-wide residence in Toronto.*

162

HOLOPHANE
AND VAPORTIGHT

In the nineteenth century glass was recognized as a permanent material which would not deteriorate on contact with contaminents like heat, fumes, dirt, and moisture. England's Holophane Company developed a way to manufacture efficient and safe glass reflectors for foundries, machine shops, gymnasiums, and exposition halls; these lights were often installed with protective outer aluminum shades or underside grilles. Nowadays, the word "Holophane" is generally used for all prismatic glass-shade fixtures, while "Vaportight" describes a fixture category in which the bulb is sealed off from vapors in an airtight protective glass cover. New York lighting consultant Paul Marantz was one of the first to champion the residential use of Holophanes and Vaportights, finding them particularly suitable for bathrooms and kitchens where steam and humidity are a problem. But Holophane and Vaportight fixtures can be ordered through some electricians' supply stores or you can write to the manufacturers listed in the back of this book for names of dealers in your area.

TRIPLE PLAY *Architect Alan Buchsbaum (working with lighting consultant Paul Marantz) used industrial fixtures in three residential installations: At far left, closed-bottom Holophane fixtures in a bathroom; above left, a group of Holophane lights over a kitchen counter; and above right, a Vaportight wall bracket over a sink.*

165

ALTERNATIVE LIGHTS

DAVID RILEY

DAVID RILEY

PETER M FINE

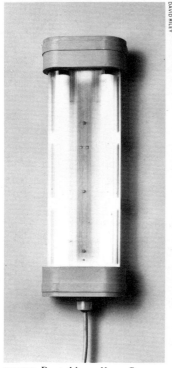

TWINS *Portable yellow fluorescent fixture from the Daniel Woodhead Co. (about $115).*

SAFETY FIRST *Daniel Woodhead hand lamp features a hook, a yellow rubber handle with an outlet, a one-piece insulating material socket, and a stainless steel cord clamp ($15); from Morsa.*

CAGED *Appleton Vaportight taxi call-light has been wall mounted by designer Richard Penney in this New York Park Avenue bathroom.*

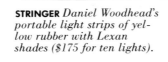

STRINGER *Daniel Woodhead's portable light strips of yellow rubber with Lexan shades ($175 for ten lights).*

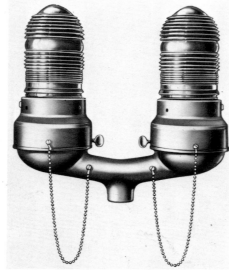

PHOTOGRAPHIC *Harwood's aluminum reflector has a swivel clamp ($6), right.*

WARNING *Red lights, left, mark towers and air-navigation obstructions; from the Crouse-Hinds Co.*

ON GUARDS *Daniel Woodhead's heavy-duty steel wire guards can dress up bare bulbs (about $2.50 to $4.50).*

HARD HAT *Woodhead's temporary light strips, right, are used on construction sites ($200 for ten lights).*

BIG LIGHTS

Deep-bowl fixtures (often referred to as Hi-Bays, Lo-Bays) fitted with 300-, 400-, or 500-watt lamps were being manufactured as early as 1917. Made with ventilating caps, these fixtures were subsequently used outdoors, often as street lighting, or indoors in airplane hangars and assembly plants, where they were traditionally positioned as high as possible down the center aisle, thus "Hi-Bay."

Designers have co-opted these lamps because of their appearance, often asking manufacturers to fit them with smaller sockets to accommodate lower wattage bulbs. Deep-bowl fixtures and Hi-Bays are well suited to lighting high indoor spaces; they can also be used over tables in low-ceilinged rooms. Major manufacturers: Abolite, Hubbell, and Spero. See High-Tech Directory for addresses.

CENTER STAGE *A large white enameled deep-bowl factory lamp was the choice of Swedish architect Andrejs Legzdins in this dining area.*

THOROUGHFARE *Italian architects Griffini and Montagni deployed a row of bright-red deep-bowl streetlights, right, in a Milanese hallway.*

JEREMIAH O. BRAGSTAD

EARLY SIDEWALK *In the United States, before sodium vapor streetlights were installed, "Radio Wave" lights like this Abolite were used.*

STREET FARE *Architect Susan Bragstad used "Radio Wave" lights ($45), left, in James Stockton's kitchen; from Abolite.*

ROBERT PERRON

CHARLES NESBIT

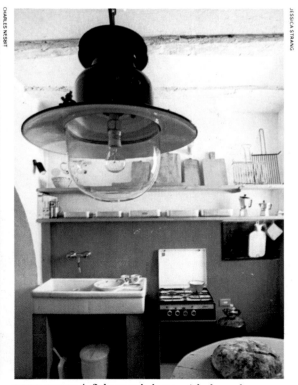

JESSICA STRANG

STREET SCENE *Architect Turner Brooks combined a shallow dome light with a conduit pipe.*

GARAGE LIGHT *Alan Buchsbaum's glass-lined Abolite deep bowl, above, is dimmer-controlled.*

GOOD CATCH *A fisherman's lamp with deep glass bowl is the focal point in this English kitchen.*

SOURCES OF ILLUSION

The photographer, filmmaker, set designer, and display artist are all masters of illusion, and one of their most important tools is light. The lights used by photographers, besides casting light on a subject, have to be lightweight, portable, adjustable, and adaptable to many problems, attributes which make these lights ideal for residential as well as professional use. The photographer's folding umbrella, the most exquisitely functional reflector, is fast becoming the darling of architects. Other professional pieces of lighting equipment that could be adapted for the home are three-color theatrical border lights, disco strobes, blinking marquee lights, dimmers, and department store showcase bulbs. Check the Yellow Pages under Stage Lighting Equipment, Lighting Systems and Equipment, and Photographic Equipment and Supplies.

ON LOCATION *William Conklin's floor lamp: a tripod and photo umbrella ($20 for both), and a "can" light.*

BACKSTAGE *Designer Juan Montoya surrounded a mirror with bare bulbs in porcelain sockets.*

HARDWARE SPECIALS *Ordinary $1 and up reflectors were ceiling-mounted here on gooseneck sockets for general illumination.*

INTERMITTENCE *Architect Alan Buchsbaum punctuated a wall with $1 incandescent showcase bulbs.*

BOUNCE *Clamp-on spot plus photo umbrella ($21 at Lowel-Light) sheds soft light, right. Design: John Van Hamersveld.*

170

NORMAN McGRATH

FRENCH GOVERNMENT TOURIST OFFICE

NEON LIGHT

The neon lights finding their way into homes today were born in physics laboratories at the end of the nineteenth century when it was discovered that an electric current passed through a tube filled with colorless neon gas produced a brilliant reddish orange glow. Other gases produced other colors, but the term "neon" became generic. French physicist Georges Claude unveiled the first commercial neon sign in Paris in 1910. From the mid-1920s to the late 1940s, when other types of signs began to compete, neon reigned over everything from nightclub marquees to shoe shine parlor windows. However, as neon's light dimmed commercially, its star brightened aesthetically. By the 1960s—with pop artists creating neon "sculpture"—commercial neon signs began to be appreciated as authentic industrial folk art. You can order neon, custom-made, from $6 to $40 per running foot, from sources listed in the Yellow Pages under Signs or Lighting.

OVERHEAD LIGHTING *In a dining room by architects Mayers and Schiff, neon light is used as graphic art.*

RAINBOW ROOM *Designer Colin Birch and lighting designer Ralph Bisdale ran high-voltage, four-color neon across a bathroom ceiling.*

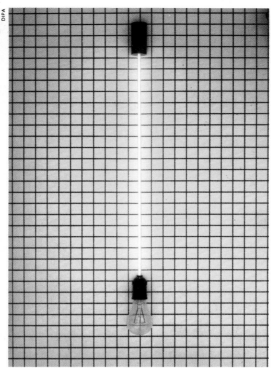

LIGHT LINE *The neon cord lights up, the bulb doesn't, on this neon pun by Zen for Dipa, an Italian manufacturer.*

BUCOLIC *A neon cow graces a renovated barn designed by architect William Grover of Moore Grover Harper; the cow would cost $750 today.*

SILVER LINING *A London designer hung a cloud of neon in a stairwell. Wherever the neon goes, there has to be a bulky transformer nearby.*

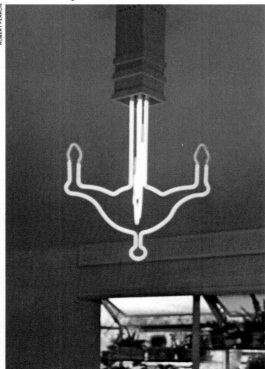

CANDLE LIGHT *Architect Mark Simon of Moore Grover Harper designed this chandelier made by Jo-Ran Neon of North Haven, Connecticut.*

HOOPLA *Ben Benedict and Carl Pucci, the Connecticut architects known as BumpZoid, used a neon basketball hoop as a front-door light.*

173

IN STOCK *Photographer Armen Kachaturian made his living-room spotlights out of hardware store staples—ordinary goosenecks and stainless-steel shades.*

TRACK AND SPOT LIGHTS

Although the electric filament lamp, introduced in 1879 by Thomas Edison, did not come into common household use until the 1920s, it was adopted almost immediately for theatre lighting. It took less than 100 years to make the theatrical spotlight—or a reasonable facsimile—a standard household lighting device. The one innovation which hastened the domestication of the spot was the electrified ceiling track, a late 1920s innovation. Track light-ing started its career in fac-tories, then moved to store windows, in-store displays, exhibitions, offices, art gal-leries, and museums, out of which it moved naturally into the homes of modern art col-lectors wanting to emulate the gallery environment. Although people considered a row of frankly commercial, exposed spotlights an anachronism in living rooms, attitudes changed when the cost of re-cessed lighting rose in direct relationship to the wages of plasterers, carpenters, and electricians. Track lighting, after all, is reusable; it can be connected to an existing ceil-ing outlet, and the lights on it can be rearranged by the homeowner without tools. Other spotlight paraphernalia adaptable for home use are dimmers, colored gels, fram-ing spotlights, and barn door (adjustable shutter) lights. Shop for them in the Yellow Pages under Lighting Fixtures-Retail and Stage Lighting Equipment.

NORMAN MCGRATH/FIORUCCI

RIGHT TRACK *Designer Joseph Paul D'Urso chose classics: Lightolier ceiling track ($12 per foot) and spotlights (from $45 each).*

GRAB BAR *Michael Schaible used Lighting Services' spots, sliding clamps, and coiled cords.*

FOOTLIGHT *$15 "can" lights were used as uplights by architect Rita Bormioli (with Joseph Lembo). Source: Harry Gitlin.*

SEE SPOTS *Put on a show with Ralph Bisdale's spotlights; from $58 to $75 at Manhattan Ad Hoc.*

STAGEY *"Barn doors" get direct light from Lighting Services' spot, above, at Ward Bennett's.*

TRUCK SPOT *Phoenix's yellow Pogolite, right, a pole light used in loading trucks, costs about $170.*

175

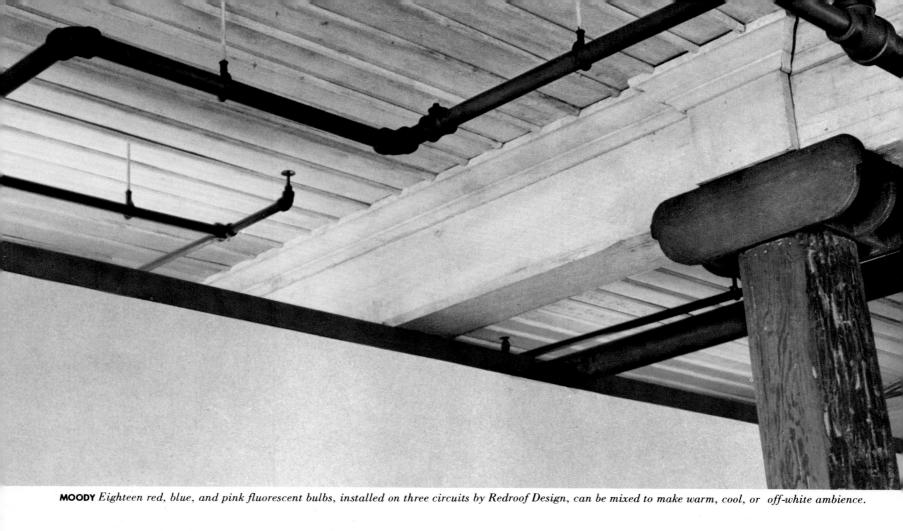

MOODY *Eighteen red, blue, and pink fluorescent bulbs, installed on three circuits by Redroof Design, can be mixed to make warm, cool, or off-white ambience.*

MOOD LIGHTING

STUDIO 54 COURTESY RON DOUD

The ability of light to influence emotion is as old as fire, shooting stars, volcanoes, lightning, and fireworks. Multiple lights and blinking lights have always been festive. And although scientific tests have proved that red light can raise the pulse and blue light lower it, one doesn't need a scientific study to know that a southern exposure is cheerier than a northern one. The only thing new about mood lighting, besides the wealth of man-made sources of it, is the fact that people are willing to

invest money to have such lighting in their homes. Today, even though wasting ever-more-costly electricity is frowned upon, the possibilities of changing one's environment with light are nonetheless being explored. "Theatrical mood light is necessary," said fabric designer Jack Lenor Larsen, "because as our living spaces get smaller we need to differentiate the uses of the same space." Instead of imitating the rock-crystal chandeliers of Versailles, today's designers

mimic the lights of rock concerts, airport runways, marquees, bridges, oil refineries, and the discotheque. Disco lighting effects can be created at home with portable control boards, sound-light pulsers, laser beams, colored gelatins, slide projections, and spotlights—all of which can be bought at a theatrical lighting company. Other commercial sources of mood lights are Christmas tree lights; signal lights; fiber optics; or really low energy votive candles, from religious supply shops.

176

LANDING GEAR *Hubbell obstruction lights with blue bulbs edge the floor of Alan Buchsbaum's bedroom simulating an airport runway.*

DISCO-TECH *In his white living room designer Mario Lo Cicero wrapped layers of colored gels from Times Square Stage Lighting around fluorescent tubes.*

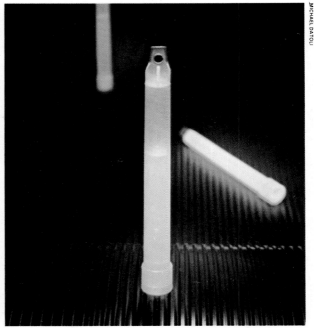

AGLOW *Two chemicals inside American Cyanamid Corp.'s portable Lite-Stick (three for $5) give off a glow.*

SUNNEX, INC.

TASK LIGHT

The seventeenth-century lacemakers' condenser light, a candle surrounded by four glass globes filled with water, was one of the major advances in work light after the candle. Copperplate engravers of the day used an adjustable-arm, wall-mounted oil lamp with an oilpaper diffuser. Today's work lights are direct descendants of these early lights. Workers still need diffused shadowless light and adjustable light sources for glare control, attributes that are equally important in reading lights for the home. So, while there is still a market for traditional lamps that look like candles, there is a growing market for industrial task lights. The Luxo Company claims to be the largest manufacturer in the world of adjustable-arm lights. The Luxo light dates back at least to 1937, when Jac Jacobsen, a Norwegian manufacturer, saw a spring-balanced, adjustable-arm work light in England, bought the patent, and renamed the light Luxo. In 1951, after success in Scandinavia, the company expanded to the United States and today sells over 400,000 lamps per year, mostly to industrial users. The Luxo (which comes with a selection of mounting devices for floor, wall, or tabletop) is available to consumers through art supply stores, stationers, and lighting shops. The lamp, which can be had in different sizes, colors, and with sockets for fluorescent as well as incandescent bulbs, sells for from $22 to over $100, depending on the model. Flexible gooseneck pharmacy lamps, used by doctors and manicurists and lately by top decorators for reading lights, can also work at home. They are available in medical supply stores. Low-voltage marine lights or the 747 reading lights can be used at home if they are equipped by an electrician with a built-in or remote transformer to convert the fixture to household current. For other sources check the High-Tech Directory.

MACHINE SHOP *Low voltage Sunnex halogen lamp (from $72); the magnifier attachment is optional.*

MICHAEL DUNNE

STUDIO *Piano + Rogers, architects, opted for a Photax reflector lamp; available in six sizes.*

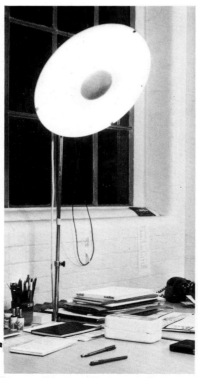
RAEANNE GIOVANNI

CHARETTE *Architects Yann Weymouth and Peter Coan specified a chrome Luxo drafting lamp as a bedside light.*

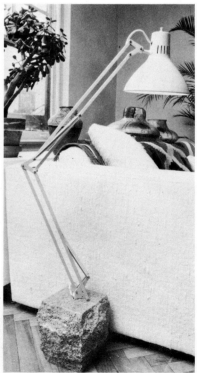
PETER M. FINE

BASIC *Instead of using the standard Luxo base, designer Ivan Chermayeff mounted his Luxo in granite.*

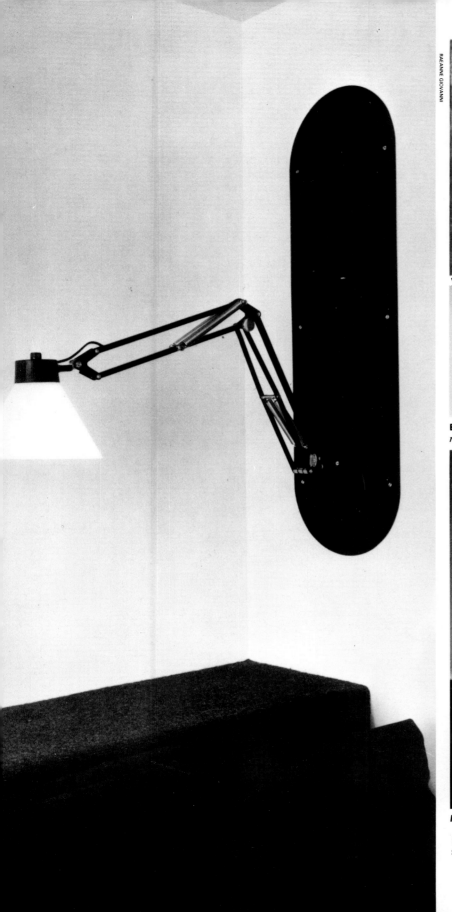

RAEANNE GIOVANNI

MICHAEL WOLFE

AIRBORNE *Architect Michael Wolfe installed Wemac 20-watt airplane reading lights, left, over a bed.*

NAUTICAL *Perko swivel shield marine light, right, is 2⅝ inches wide, and costs $7.*

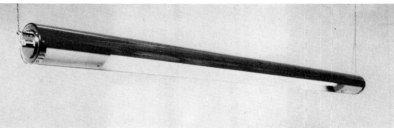

ROBERTO BROSAN

EX-OFFICIO *Swedish SuperTube has a 39-inch-long sturdy but lightweight aluminum casing that holds a fluorescent ($110); at Scandinavian Design.*

CARLA DE BENEDETTI

MEDICAL *Pharmacy lamps were placed over a wall by architect Fulvio Raboni.*

SOUND-LIGHT *Bray-Schaible Design hung a special Luxo wall lamp, left, with white glass shade by Harry Gitlin Lighting on a custom speaker grille.*

179

THE WORKS

OVERLEAF *Con Ed guardrail photo, courtesy Consolidated Edison Co. of New York, Inc.; inset, Ward Bennett bathroom, photo, Raeanne Giovanni.*

There is a new inside-out look about some homes today—a flaunting of pipes, vents, conduits, electrical wires, and forced-air ducts—increasing our awareness of how different the contemporary house is from those that existed before electricity, indoor plumbing, central heating, and air conditioning. Architect Barton Myers's Toronto home, pictured on the next page, is a perfect example of the new frankness about the "works" of the house. With its massive heating ducts passing through the dining room with boiler-room nonchalance, the Myers house is bound to become a touchstone for integrating the service functions of a house with its ceremonial aspects.

Even in the less obvious domain of electrical cords there is a new frankness. Instead of hiding behind sofas, cords are now surfacing in industrial-style projects—newly coiled and presentable—like contemporary underwear that is so attractive it is being worn as outerwear. There is also talk these days about computer floors. A counterpart to the dropped ceiling, the computer floor is a modular, raised floor panel system that, by leaving an air space under the new floor surface, allows cords to come and go, surfacing at any point they're needed. A computer floor, which can be covered with carpet tiles, is becoming a standard in offices where telephone wires, computer terminals, and electrical outlets have to be constantly relocated. Today this system is considered an office solution, but when computers start coming home in full force, the floors won't be far behind.

Meanwhile the flow of equipment and ideas from commercial users to the residential kitchen and bathroom is as pervasive as we have seen it to be in furniture, storage, lighting, and materials. Commercial influences in the kitchen and bath are by no means new. The compact residential bathroom adjoining the bedroom was originally inspired by a Boston hotel where, in the early 1870s, sinks with running water first became adjuncts to bedrooms.

And years before standardized kitchen cabinets were available for the home, efficiency experts were looking at the interrelatedness of hotel kitchens as a model for home kitchens. But today we are not borrowing the *idea* of the commercial kitchen and bath; we are borrowing the *fixtures* per se.

The tremendous new interest in gourmet cooking is bringing commercial kitchen equipment into the home: massive stoves, see-in refrigerators, orange juice squeezers, and coffee urns. And in the bathroom there is a new sangfroid. In demand among taste setters are stainless steel hospital scrub sinks with knee-action faucet controls or wrist-action handles. Nothing commercial is sacred, from the office water cooler to the public lavatory sink-cum-medicine chest-and-soap-dispenser to the shower tower for group showers.

From the Navy we want to borrow the built-in ironing board with a door latch that is so strong that even a torpedo hit will not open it accidentally. From the scaffolding dealer some designers have appropriated shoring posts to hold up hammocks. But one scaffolding company in particular is offended by this idea. The company fears that home use of its products will make the company look . . . less professional. "Our things are for industry," we were scolded by a salesman, affronted at the "trivializing" of his product.

No, it is not always easy to buy industrial products for the home from companies that prefer first of all to sell 1,000 of something rather than just one piece. We are not advising you misrepresent yourself, but in certain dealings it is better to "infer" that you want a hospital sink for a doctor's office you are building than to say you are putting it in your powder room. Being an engineer, designer, or an architect are the best credentials, but for those who are not, familiarity with product terminology is essential.

EXPOSED PIPES

They were the first things to be covered up, and they tended to stay that way at least until they burst and needed changing. But now architects and designers are adopting a new approach to pipes and letting them all hang out. In lofts, renovations, or even new buildings the pipes needed for hot and cold water, heat, and ventilation are becoming the focal point of the design. Once rediscovered they are painted in bright colors, both for identification and for visual excitement. Sometimes pipes lead a double life—as sculpture as well as heat conductors. Better to have these uncovered ducts reach up and sweep around than to have large areas where covering them up would mean ruining the space. Some people paint them, others leave them in their natural state. Pennsylvania architects Annie and Peter Bohlin of Bohlin and Powell had a local foundry make them a new semicircular radiator that not only heats their living room but provides them with a conversation piece.

UNCONVENTIONAL APPROACH *Architect Barton Myers left the mechanical servicing systems uncovered and unfinished when he designed the house he lives in on a reclaimed site in downtown Toronto.*

RUNAROUND *Ventilation ductwork was ceiling-hung and painted red by architects Edward S. Knowles and John Immitt when they renovated the police academy stable as a residence for New York artist Lowell Nesbitt.*

CONDUCTIVE *Jeffrey Hannigan channeled electrical power through exposed conduits for Fisher & Marantz.*

OPEN HEARTH *Architect William Bruder likes materials left natural—ergo his exposed ductwork.*

PIPE DREAM *Stephanie Mallis and Douglas Kahn shelved around a hot-water pipe.*

SCULPTURAL *When New York architect Christine Bevington had this wood-paneled living room renovated, she replaced the old radiators with a system of imaginative pipes that both heat and decorate the space.*

HOT IDEA *Architects Bohlin and Powell bent radiation pipe into arched radiators.*

RAEANNE GIOVANNI

SUBWAY FARE *The subway grating covering the warm-air ducts in Ward Bennett's summer home contrasts with the wood decking out the window.*

RETURN REQUESTED *Curlicues are out. Ceiling diffusers like these commercial ones by Tuttle & Bailey are designers' choices.*

MOVING AIR

Designers today are looking up at the air ducts in public buildings and down at subway gratings. "I love subway gratings," says designer Robert Bray, "because they're beautiful and they never warp." The material is so strong that designer Ward Bennett was able to turn a five-story air shaft into usable outdoor space (without depriving the downstairs neighbors of light or air) by laying steel beams with subway grating over them. Subway grating sources include Irving Grating, Borden, and Register and Grill Manufacturing Co. Other industrial ventilation hardware includes commercial grills, perforated meshes, and utilitarian-looking ceiling fans used in factories to recirculate the machine heat that rises to the ceiling.

UNITED STATES STEEL CORP

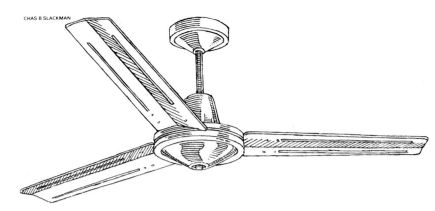

CHAS B SLACKMAN

RUNS HOT AND COLD *To cut down on heating costs some factories recirculate heated air with fans; Modern Supply's 48-inch D.E.M.C. is $179.*

RAEANNE GIOVANNI

PUNCHED OUT *Under this window architect Yann Weymouth used one of Berkley Perforating Co.'s patterns as a radiator cover.*

RAEANNE GIOVANNI

SWITCH *Ward Bennett used a light grill as an air vent.*

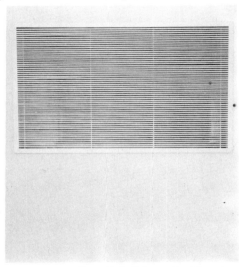

RAEANNE GIOVANNI

PUBLIC VECTOR *Bray-Schaible used a Titus industrial vent in a home.*

PETER M FINE

STRONG AND AIRY *Inside Ward Bennett's flat the grating covers heating ducts; outside it covers a five-story air shaft.*

RAEANNE GIOVANNI

SPEAKERS TOO *In Ward Bennett's country home the subway grating on the edge of the raised platform conceals speakers and heating ducts.*

PETER M. FINE

DANIEL MILES KRON

OCCUPIED *Designer Jay Spectre tried to buy an airline lavatory for client Robin Roberts; when he failed he had the American Metal Restaurant Equipment Co. make a copy of one. Getting TWA soap is more difficult.*

PETER M. FINE

CHEMISTRY *David Fabricators sell stainproof lab sinks ($100 to $125) similar to one used by John Saladino.*

JEFF PERKELL

DANISH MODERN *Made for universities, epoxy-coated Vola fixtures are imported by Architectural Complements.*

THE BATHROOM

Although bathroom renovations are at an all-time high, few people are aware of the wealth of options available from laboratory, hospital, and institutional catalogs. There are freestanding hospital tubs (the contemporary counterpart of the old-fashioned oval tub) and faucets that can be turned on with an elbow, or a foot. From chemical laboratory supply sources there is the stainproof resin sink that looks as if it were crafted by a potter; and from the institutional supplier there is a full range of products from tampon and liquid soap dispensers to urinals. One marvelous institutional item is an all-in-one sink unit complete with medicine cabinet, paper towel holder, soap dispenser, and light. More esoteric are the shampoo sinks from beauty supply houses; heart-shaped tubs, the staple of the honeymoon hotel; and fiber glass baptismal pools that come with dramatic flights of steps. For sources, see our directory. Or ask your plumber to get some industrial catalogs for your perusal.

STRIPPED *Tana Hoban used Speakman brass medical faucets, dechromed, in her bathroom.*

FREESTANDING *Designer Ward Bennett had a roomy hospital tub installed in his summer home.*

THROW AWAY *Halbrand's disposable hospital toothbrushes ($1.50 per dozen); Manhattan Ad Hoc.*

ENCLOSURE *Square white ceramic tiles surround this Kohler tub used in hospitals on raised bases in a New York bathroom designed by Bray-Schaible.*

HANDLE WITH CARE *Yann Weymouth and Peter Coan of Redroof Design favor hospital faucets.*

189

THE BATHROOM

DOUBLE DUTY *The Hospital Ware lavatory ($950), above, has a swing-away cabinet that conceals the toilet.*

SOAPY *A foot-operated liquid soap dispenser from the Bradley Corp.*

MEN'S *This wall-hung urinal from Briggs would be a useful addition to any home bath.*

TWO IN ONE *Bradley double toilet-roll dispenser with ashtray in shelf is good insurance against running out.*

SHAMPOO *This hairdresser's sink from Marble Products is available through Takara-Belmont (about $200).*

HIGH AND DRY *Architect Christine Bevington specified a lavatory hand dryer as a hair dryer.*

SHOWER STALL *Designer Richard Penney used this Charles Parker Co. washroom soap holder ($15).*

TORKIL GUDNASON

RICHARD PENNEY

ALL TOGETHER NOW *Multiple shower head from the Bradley Corp. is perfect for large families.*

LADIES' *This stainless steel tampon dispenser could be wall-hung in any home bathroom ($150); from Bradley Corp.*

NAPKIN DISPOSAL

PUSH

DOCTOR'S ORDERS *A scrub sink with instrument trays has a knee-controlled faucet ($950); from Elkay.*

SUPER BOWLS *Bradley Corp.'s built-in lavatory units include the one below, with its extra-large bowl and overhead light ($354), and the foot-controlled model, left, with its hidden spout and towel and cup dispenser ($372).*

SUPPORT HARDWARE

DAVID RILEY

Some people still think that fleurs de lys and lions' head hooks are the only solution for hanging up possessions. But there is much to learn from the professionals, because no one knows how to hang it all up better than they do. The butcher shop's meat racks and hooks are the latest pieces of support hardware that are being adapted to hold heavy, oversized roasting pans and spaghetti pots in the home. Sources include Bazaar De La Cuisine, The Professional Kitchen, Marlo Manufacturing Co., and New London Equipment (which will make hanging racks to order). Hospital grab bars hung on the ceiling instead of the wall can also support a *batterie de cuisine*; ceiling-hung metal pipes can provide a flexible system for curtaining off a room; trusty Con Edison guardrails can double as convenient freestanding towel racks that easily fold away when not in use. And don't forget the heated hotel towel rack, one piece of support hardware no bathroom should be without. Source? Hammacher-Schlemmer.

ANDREW HOLMES

HOSPITALITY *Heated pipe towel rack in the bathroom that architects Richard and Susan Rogers designed warms and holds an efficient number of towels.*

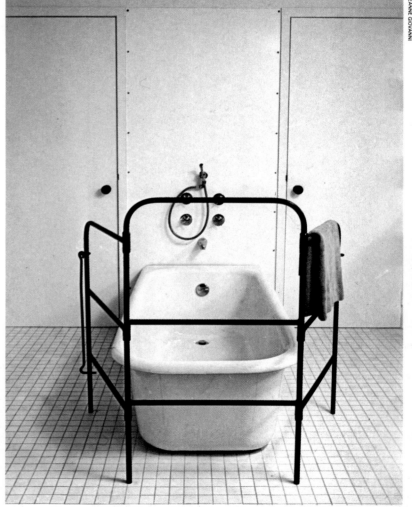

RAEANNE GIOVANNI

CON JOB *Designer Ward Bennett's bath towel hangs on a black spray-painted Con Edison guardrail manufactured by Schaffer Metal Products (about $50).*

192

LYNN KARLIN

GRIDWORK *Sid Diamond's wall-rack system at the Manhattan Ad Hoc House-wares store supports a panoply of kitchen equipment.*

RAEANNE GIOVANNI

GRABBY *Architect Leslie Armstrong of Armstrong/Childs had hospital grab bars fastened to the ceiling and equipped with oversized butcher hooks.*

PETER M. FINE

BASIC PIPE *A bar of steel tubing running parallel to the window is a neat solution for hanging equipment in this New York kitchen.*

DAN WYNN

FOR PROS *Able Metalcraft made this straight-edged ceiling-hung pot and pan rack that can hold even the largest cooking utensils. Design, Colin Birch.*

LYNN KARLIN

CURTAINS *Ron Doud's system of industrial metal pipes provides a flexible solution for dressing-room space in the Harriet Love Shop in New York.*

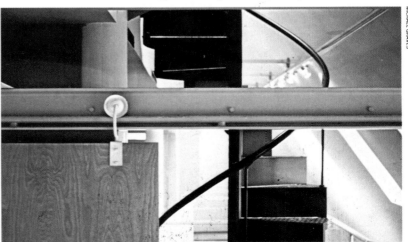

MICHAEL GRAVES

OPEN-DOOR POLICY *Architect Michael Graves used a 4½-inch lawnmower wheel and a section of steel tubing to make this sliding-door track.*

SUPPORT HARDWARE

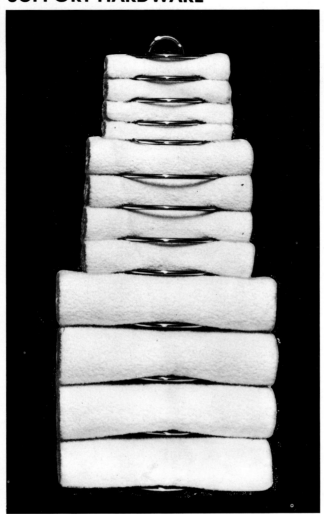

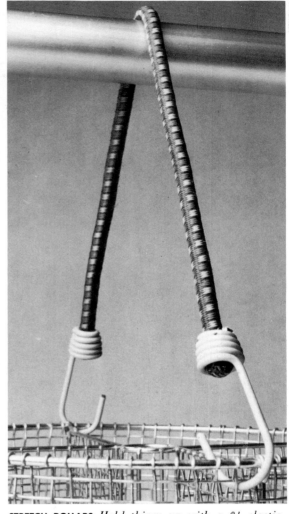

BE MY GUEST *Plaza's chrome-plated towel rack ($7.35), designed by a motel owner, discourages towel waste and space.*

STRETCH DOLLARS *Hold things up with a $1 elastic strap hook from a bicycle shop.*

HANG-UPS *Stainless steel mop holder, hooks, and shelf unit, right, by Bradley ($90.20); Esposito Sales.*

SHELF LIFE *Esposito Sales also sells the Bradley fold-down toilet booth shelf ($21.95), below.*

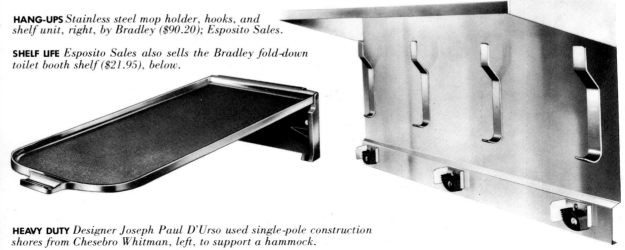

HEAVY DUTY *Designer Joseph Paul D'Urso used single-pole construction shores from Chesebro Whitman, left, to support a hammock.*

KA-LOR CUBICLE & SUPPLY CO.

PETER AARON

DRAPERY HARDWARE

The swagged curtains and drapes of opera houses and nostalgia-prone hotels are not one of the many industrial trappings being appropriated for residential use by designers. If curtains are called for, designers are borrowing the utilitarian cubicle curtains of the hospital and nursing home, or the curtains that partition off gymnasium space. Mister Cubicle and Ka-Lor Cubicle Co. are two New York area dealers in cubicle hardware. In other cities check the Yellow Pages under Hospital Equipment and Supplies. Draperies in office buildings have to be easy to remove for cleaning. One device to facilitate removal is the snap on/off heading and track available from major drapery hardware manufacturers such as Grabar and Kirsch. These sources offer another piece of hardware developed for use outside the home: the push-button, power-operated drapery opening and closing mechanism that, like the light dimmer, originated in the theatre.

MEDICAL TREATMENT *Canvas bed curtains supported by Imperial Fastener hospital cubicle ceiling track are used for sound and light control in a bedroom designed by Joseph Paul D'Urso. Curtains are two-toned.*

CONVERTIBLE *David Barrett ties back his curtains, above, with grommets, left, like those on old convertible car tops.*

HANDY RAIL *Patino Wolf used bannisters from Julius Blum, top right, as curtain rods.*

Rx *Philip Ferrato hung nylon sailcloth shower curtains, right, from Mr. Cubicle's hospital ceiling track ($3 per foot); curtain by Hild Sails.*

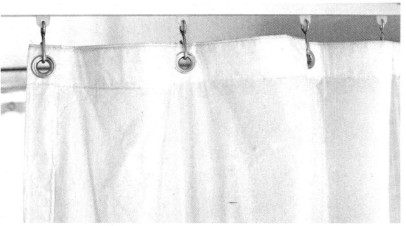

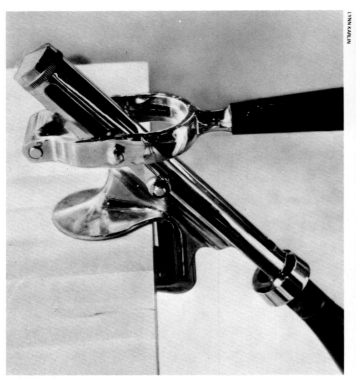

CORKERS *Sommelier's corkscrew, available at The Professional Kitchen for about $63, would work well at home.*

CROWD PLEASER *Stainless steel coffee urn that can be carried full ($222); from The Professional Kitchen.*

CAMPFIRE *The 24-ounce Optimus 77A camp stove comes with two pots and a fry pan ($18); from Eastern Mountain Sports.*

SMALL APPLIANCES

Steam cookers, blenders, fryers, choppers, roasters, peelers, orange squeezers, hot chocolate makers, beverage dispensers, crepe makers, tenderizers—there's a professional appliance for every household kitchen task. And although they're not inexpensive, there's a lot to be said for investing in these heavy-duty appliances. It's only recently that commercial appliances have been considered appropriate for home use. They are functional alternatives to the flower-appliquéd, pastel-colored appliances prevalent in housewares departments. However, items such as the large-bowled, heavy-duty mixers that can whip up two dozen eggs at once are not yet stocked in most hardware, kitchenware, or department stores. Although many of these commercial appliances are not inexpensive to run or that easy to have installed, they will repay you in superbly efficient service whether you're cooking for two or twenty. The combined dish dispenser/plate warmer, shown opposite, is a good investment for party givers—and the "laboratory" automatic-stirring hotplate could make perfect hollandaise, even in a dormitory.

DEEP FRIED *Fried food lovers can get a professional deep fat fryer made by Frymaster from $402.*

CHARLES NESBIT

LYNN KARLIN

PULL THE LEVER *Architect Alan Buchsbaum has a Pavoni espresso machine.*

HOT PLATES *Electric dispenser from Shelley Mfg. Co. ($331) warms a stack of plates.*

CUT UP *Restaurant chopping and slicing machine by Robot-Coupe ($430); from The Professional Kitchen.*

REVVED UP *Waring's one gallon, stainless steel commercial blender ($57) is a heavy-duty appliance.*

LYNN KARLIN

STIRRED UP *Corning's laboratory hotplate with built-in stirrer ($150 by mail order); from Arthur H. Thomas.*

MACHINE SHOP *Commercial restaurant heavy-duty mixers, whippers, blenders, food processors, slicers, and choppers are available with a wide variety of attachments from The Professional Kitchen.*

199

CHEF'S SPECIAL *Architect Donald Mallow specified a South Bend range (about $2,000 list) for the New York kitchen of artists Milton and Shirley Glaser.*

KITCHEN APPLIANCES

DANIEL MILES KRON

For years professional stoves and refrigerators were a well-kept secret. Seemingly unavailable to nonprofessionals, they were hidden away in the back of steak houses and Chinese restaurants or behind the counters of coffee shops. Recently, with the upsurge in interest in cooking and the dearth of domestic help, more amateur cooks are turning to professional restaurant equipment for sturdy, hard-wearing, and reliable service. The restaurant stove—as well as the glass-front refrigerator—are becoming the new status symbols in the modern kitchen. Capable of maintaining high, even heat, restaurant stoves are available in a range of configurations with oversized ovens, griddles, salamander grills, and six-burner setups as standard options. And the refrigerator/freezers that showed off a selection of pies in the coffee shop now accommodate anything in the home from the Thanksgiving turkey to a full case of champagne. Prices start at about $1,500 for new professional ranges.

HIGHLY QUALIFIED *Writer Barbara Goldsmith and movie director Frank Perry chose a six-burner Garland restaurant stove for their kitchen.*

COLD STORAGE *Art dealer Louis K. Meisel and his wife, artist Susan Pear Meisel, inherited this sliding-door refrigerator with their loft.*

ORIENTAL INFLUENCE *Leslie Armstrong of Armstrong/Childs Architects selected this Anets modular range for the kitchen she planned for harpsichordist Albert Fuller, an expert Chinese cook. Two sets of burners are separated by a large griddle area that's convenient for simmering large stockpots.*

201

KITCHEN APPLIANCES

LYNN KARLIN

JULES BACKUS

STACKED UP *Double-door stainless steel refrigerator units from Raetone retail for about $1,285 each at The Professional Kitchen.*

BLOODMOBILE *Secondhand hospital blood bank has been recycled into a home refrigerator unit by the Ant Farm, the San Francisco-based design group.*

RAE-ANNE GIOVANNI

GRILLWORK *Bray-Schaible Design had this South Bend gas range with an overhead salamander grill fitted into this clinically clean New York kitchen.*

RAE-ANNE GIOVANNI

CAMPSITE *Portable solar camping stove ($150 from Dean & DeLuca) is used to heat soup in the sunny apartment of New York designer Robert Bray.*

JAIME ANDILES-ARCE

SOLID FRONT *Three under-the-counter stainless steel cold storage units were installed in this kitchen by designer Joseph Paul D'Urso.*

NURSES' AIDE *Hospital nourishment center from Market Forge incorporating refrigerator, storage, and cooking facilities would work well at home.*

203

OFFICIOUS *Shoulder-height corridor handles placed on each of the doors in this closet-lined dressing room punctuate the space with color.*

SERGE KORNILOFF

RAEANNE GIOVANNI

ARCHITECTONIC *Overscaled white pulls from Ironmonger strike a commercial note in architect Kenneth Walker's kitchen on Long Island.*

PULLS

Hardware is the jewelry of the home, but too often it consists only of the poorly designed ornate facsimiles of past cultural glories available in local hardware stores. Meanwhile, outside the home, the market proliferates with sleek, handsome opening and closing devices developed for functional needs. Bold, highly visible door pulls are necessary on the glass doors of public buildings; on boats hardware must be flush to save space and prevent bruised hips in close quarters; in hospitals the bold grab bars are strong arms on which to lean. Lately architects and designers have been bringing home the hardware they've encountered on commercial and industrial jobs. Resourceful homeowners can do the same by searching out architectural hardware dealers, and marine and medical supply sources.

PHIL KOENIG

SHIP AHOY *Shiny chrome nautical ring pull, right, is $4.50 from Manhattan Marine & Electric Company.*

DANIEL MILES KRON

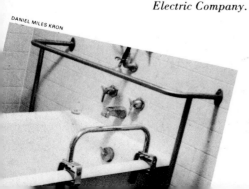

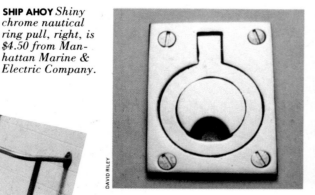

DAVID RILEY

NO SCREWS *Kenneth Cooke improvised this pull, above left, from hardware store suction cups.*

SAUNA *Wooden pull from Metos Sauna, above, is impervious to changes in temperature.*

SMOOTH GOING *Forms and Surfaces' nylon cabinet pulls, left, are popular with furniture makers.*

RAIL WAY *Ward Bennett fitted no-sag redwood doors on wheels, right, with boxcar latches.*

HELPING HANDLE *Hospital grab bars from the Charles Parker Co. were specified by architect Christine Bevington for these kitchen drawers.*

OPEN-DOOR POLICY *A pair of bright red nylon door pulls (similar ones are available from the Ironmonger, $50 each) were used for this London shop.*

ROLL AWAY *Designer Martin Lipsitt used this eight-rung wood shop ladder on rollers to reach the high storage cabinets in this Brooklyn kitchen.*

STEELWORKER *Designer Joseph Paul D'Urso chose this three-step steel safety warehouse ladder to allow his client access to his hanging pots.*

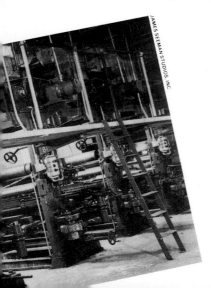

LADDERS

There's nothing harder to find than a good-looking functional step stool or ladder. Those available to the consumer market are often flimsy, unsteady, too low—in other words, not safe. Industrial sources can supply a ladder for every use. There are shop ladders, library ladders, metal folding ladders, ships' ladders, rolling ladders, pulpit ladders, all useful for safely reaching the top shelf. If you want to reach the *roof*, material equipment handling dealers can supply elevating work platforms. Check the Yellow Pages under Ladders.

BIG WHEELS *Fidelity's ladder has self-retracting ball casters (about $134).*

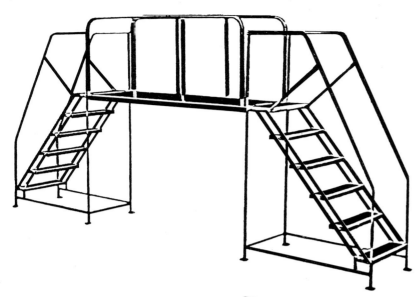

DOUBLE TIME *Work platform with two staircases, nonskid steps, and crossover is available on special order from Spiral Steel Products Corporation.*

COMBINATION CART *Putnam Rolling Ladder's oak library cart comes with folding steps; the 38" x 31" x 15" size is $125.*

ALL ABOARD *Aluminum yacht-boarding ladder is $550 at Pompanette.*

REST STOP *Pulpit ladder ($162) from Putnam Rolling Ladder Co. has safety brakes.*

STEP ON IT *Rubbermaid office step stool ($25.95) has safety treads.*

KICKY *Movable step stool ($18.95) won't slip, wobble, or roll.*

BOOKISH *Eighty-four-inch-high oak library ladder is $98 from Putnam Rolling Ladder Co. Track is $2 a foot uninstalled.*

ROBERTO BROSAN

FIDELITY PRODUCTS

ROBERTO BROSAN

207

INNER BEAUTY *Loose connections are visible with Daniel Woodhead Co.'s industrial plugs, above. The number 85447 plug is about $3 from Morsa in New York or write Woodhead for other dealers.*

UNIVERSAL COIL *Piano + Rogers used coiled extension cords, right, in their London office. In this country, coiled or retractile cords as they are called, are made by the Daburn Company.*

DIM TRIM *Joseph Paul D'Urso's rheostat cove, above, was made in chrome by Wainland.*

LOW VOLTAGE *Ward Bennett favors Electro Systems' Touch-Plate light-up switches, above.*

ELECTRICAL HARDWARE

Wallpaper-camouflaged electric-switch plates are not part of the industrial scheme. Just as plumbing pipes, heating ducts, and ventilation grills are exposed and celebrated in the industrial style, electrical cords, plugs, switches, and receptacles are highlighted, not hidden. There is a wonderful array of electrical equipment with which to industrialize the home. Exposed wires will no longer be an eyesore when they are replaced with the "retractile"-type ones used on telephones or those available in a wide array of colors from Daburn Electronics & Cable Corp. A most unusual piece of industrial electrical hardware is the see-through electrical plug from Daniel Woodhead, not made that way for novelty, but because it's a practical way to see if there is trouble at connection points.

WALK ON IT *You can drive over Daniel Woodhead's cord protector; $12 to $40.*

208

LEONARDO FERRANTE

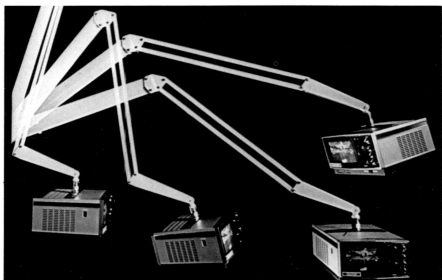

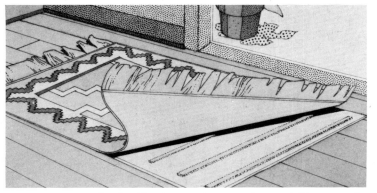

CONNECTIONS *Don't hide cords, flaunt them with retractile cords like the ones, above, used in an English interior.*

PATIENT'S SET *Bunting's wall-mounted color TV on a spring arm, left, lists for about $700; a black-and-white set is about $400.*

CRIME PREVENTION *Inspired by the warning mats in stores, Nutone makes an electronic floor-mat detector, above, for the home.*

209

BROOM CLOSET

Sometimes the most unglamorous jobs spawn the most efficient equipment. One of the most compactly conceived pieces of equipment is the maid's cart that travels from room to room in hotels and makes the rounds, after hours, in offices. Everything needed to do the job is at hand. Yes, homemakers can learn a thing or two about energy saving from janitors: slop buckets on wheels, large fire-safe and odor-resistant garbage receptacles, floor sinks that can accommodate hanging mops, and retractable ironing boards are just a few of the efficient items that can be found at sources listed in the Yellow Pages under Janitors' Supplies. Beam Supply, Inc., in New York City is a typical example of a janitorial supply store that would be willing to sell direct to a consumer. Although this store sells mostly to institutions, it has its share of householders coming in to buy the better-quality mops and brooms and the specially formulated polishes that have more wax than their consumer product counterparts.

CLEAN-UP PROGRAM *An assortment of janitorial supplies at Manhattan Ad Hoc includes mops, work gloves, washboards, and a maid's cart.*

PRESSING IDEA *Iron-A-Way's ship's locker is equipped with a 46-inch ironing board, timer, and appliance outlet ($197).*

STEELWORKERS *A selection of galvanized steel tubs—some on wheels, some with handles—for washing the dog or mopping the floor is always in stock at Manhattan Ad Hoc.*

STREET SEEN *English designer Brian Asquith devised this steel and polyethylene trash container.*

ROUNDUP *Ward Bennett sprayed this United Receptacle waste can with black paint.*

SNOOTY *Doorless snoot from United Receptacle fits the top of a 55-gallon drum.*

BAG IT *Metropolitan Wire Corp.'s trash cart was specified by Joseph Paul D'Urso.*

FIBER *I.C.F. carries this Zanotta trash can, inspired by a vulcanized industrial one.*

BIG ONE *These garbage cans have a 48-gallon capacity; from United Receptacle.*

TOP CHOICES *United Receptacle sells these adjustable, self-closing, enamel-finished heavy-gauge steel tops that can convert 15-, 30-, or 55-gallon drums into waste containers.*

OPEN WEAVE *Manhattan Ad Hoc carries Howard Metalcraft's mesh can ($60).*

HOLE IN ONE *Fire-safe trash can from United Receptacle comes in five colors.*

JANITORIAL *No more lifting full buckets with Elkay's low-down service sink.*

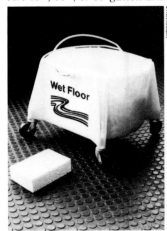

KICK IT *Cheery yellow rolling bucket ($25); from The Professional Kitchen.*

ON WHEELS *Galvanized steel four-wheeled bucket ($31); from Manhattan Ad Hoc.*

POSTED *Post-mounted English litter bin has a woven removable basket.*

LITTER LINE-UP *Manhattan Ad Hoc shows and sells the oversized plastic trash containers found in fast-food emporiums.*

FINISHING TOUCHES

216 WALL GRAPHICS
The taste for large-scale images has been driven home by the billboard. Now photo blowups are pushing picture arrangements off the wall.

218 FOOD PREPARATION
Professional cooking equipment is available in every city if you know where to buy it. Its forms are dictated by function, and it functions very well indeed.

220 TABLETOP
The green-edged china from the local greasy spoon suddenly looks good enough to eat off of. Other restaurant tabletop items making appearances at home are sugar shakers, napkin holders, disposable salt shakers.

224 LABORATORY GLASS
Flasks, beakers, fleakers, test tubes, and bell jars—the everyday utility and beauty of chemical glass is undisputed. Why then is it not sold at every department store? In this chapter we present six pages of laboratory glass in its infinite variety.

230 MIRRORS
Security mirrors are not just to catch a thief. When you see the other possible uses of these common commercial devices, you may want to steal the ideas.

232 PLANTERS
It is hard to surpass the common clay pot as the quintessential planter, but there are a number of industrial containers that take exceedingly well to plants—for instance, a pig trough.

234 WEIGHTS AND MEASURES
The doctor's scale has never won any design awards, and probably never will, but then the pretty bath shop floor scale never won any accuracy awards. On these pages we present doctors' and grocers' scales, commercial clocks, and a small electronic scoreboard for you to use imaginatively.

236 ANTIQUES
People who wouldn't think of giving houseroom to a truck wheel-hub coffee table cherish their old wagon wheels. Herewith a sampling of some retired pieces of commercial and industrial equipment doing something decorative with their old age.

238 INDUSTRIAL-INSPIRED
Imitation is the sincerest form of flattery, and there is no shortage of industrial flattery. An inspired bookcase from Italy has steel joists like those of a factory ceiling, and there are lamps available that look like auto headlights.

OVERLEAF *Laboratory photo, courtesy New York Public Library Picture Collection; inset, tabletop arrangement by Joseph Paul D'Urso, photo, Michael Dunne.*

like an add-a-pearl necklace, the bride's china, crystal, and silver have traditionally been considered good investments with resale value. These possessions, which are the sacramental objects of the entertainment ritual, have also been regarded as status investments, and as such, were supposed to be the most expensive and elaborate a bride could afford. This attitude evolved from earliest times when a trousseau was actually part of the dowry—a matching grant, so to speak, from the bride's family to compensate for money paid by the groom to the father of the bride. In certain cultures it was even customary for the prospective bridegroom to inspect a girl's trousseau to make sure it was valuable enough. Although the bartering of brides is a thing of the past, the importance of the china pattern and other trousseau items lingers vestigially along with the veil, and something blue. Homemakers going counterculture and selecting, for instance, restaurant china for its wholesomeness, durability, and classic design are not merely exercising freedom of choice but are thumbing their noses at the antiquated notion that hand-painted sets of porcelain or crystal goblets are social necessities. In this chapter we've tried to point out a variety of nontraditional finishing touches for the home that are available from commercial and industrial sources.

For those who want to sample the industrial environment before making a large investment, a tabletop item or a piece of chemical glass provides an inexpensive initiation. Laboratory glass has been moving in and out of your awareness for years. Much admired by the 1920s avant-garde designers, it was included in the Machine Art exhibit at the Museum of Modern Art in 1934. Although today it is still a favorite of many designers, it continues to be virtually unavailable (except from a few florists) in standard consumer outlets. To buy it you have to go to laboratory equipment supply houses. But it's well worth the trip because these outlets offer one of the least expensive and most beautiful assortments of glass being made today. Every large city has a restaurant supply house, and these emporiums offer a wealth of items that would be useful at home. Some restaurant suppliers will only sell china by the three dozen or more, or sell to "retail" customers on slow days; but others will sell small quantities, and some dealers even have on hand bins of used china or seconds that are often enhanced—or spoiled, depending on your taste—by restaurant monograms. If you have trouble getting a foot in the door, say you are opening a small motel or coffee shop or buying for your club.

Besides these tabletop items, this chapter includes information about security mirrors that can reflect more than shoplifters, and wall graphics that are alternatives to wallpaper. Needless to say, off-the-beaten-track industrial sources do not gift wrap, do not have bridal registries, do not accept exchanges and give refunds, and do not always welcome the small customer. If courtesy and service are important, look for items of commercial origin in your favorite department store where little by little these formerly low-status items are beginning to turn up. But all the addresses and all the leads we supply can't beat your own alert sleuthing. The handsome disposable salt and pepper shakers shown on page 221 were first sighted on a New York University cafeteria table. It took six phone calls to find the manufacturer and then the distributor. To avoid buying 72 pair we arranged for them to be sold at a retail store.

NORMAN McGRATH

BIG PICTURE *Architect Charles Gwathmey of Gwathmey & Siegel had a huge photographic enlargement made of an original 1905 photograph. The fourteen-section mural was made by Merit Studios.*

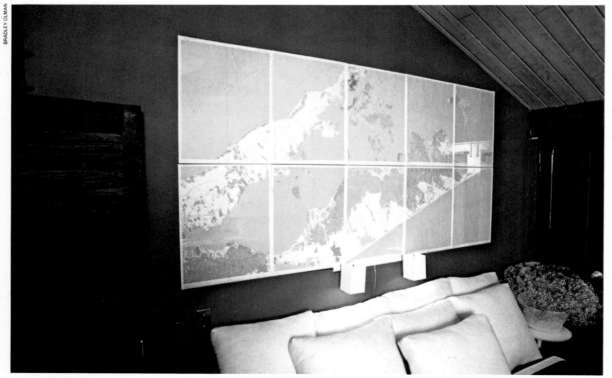

BRADLEY OLMAN

WORLD IS FLAT *Designer Lee Bailey framed a group of ten United States Geological Survey maps (about $1.75 each at Hammond) and hung them as a group. With more wall space you could cover a lot of territory.*

3M CO.

WALL GRAPHICS

The automobile put the billboard on the map, and the billboard in turn gave us a taste for large-scale images. Original billboard sheets can sometimes be purchased directly from billboard companies such as Foster and Kleiser. Another commercial solution to the blank-wall problem is the photo mural, which was originally used as an eye-catcher at conventions, trade shows, and fairs. Using an enlargement process, black-and-white photo blowups can be made from any photo for about $5 a square foot and up. A new photo-enlargement process owned by the 3M Company creates Architectural Paintings, which can cost from $11 to $25 per square foot. These full-color reproductions, made from any photo, negative, or artwork, are painted electronically by computer. Movie and theatre posters, campaign broadsides, and maps can also be pressed into service.

COMPUTER GRAPHICS *The giant rose in the kitchen at right was the brainchild of architect Alan Buchsbaum. It was photographed by Charles Nesbit and enlarged and painted electronically by the 3M process.*

CHARLES NESBIT

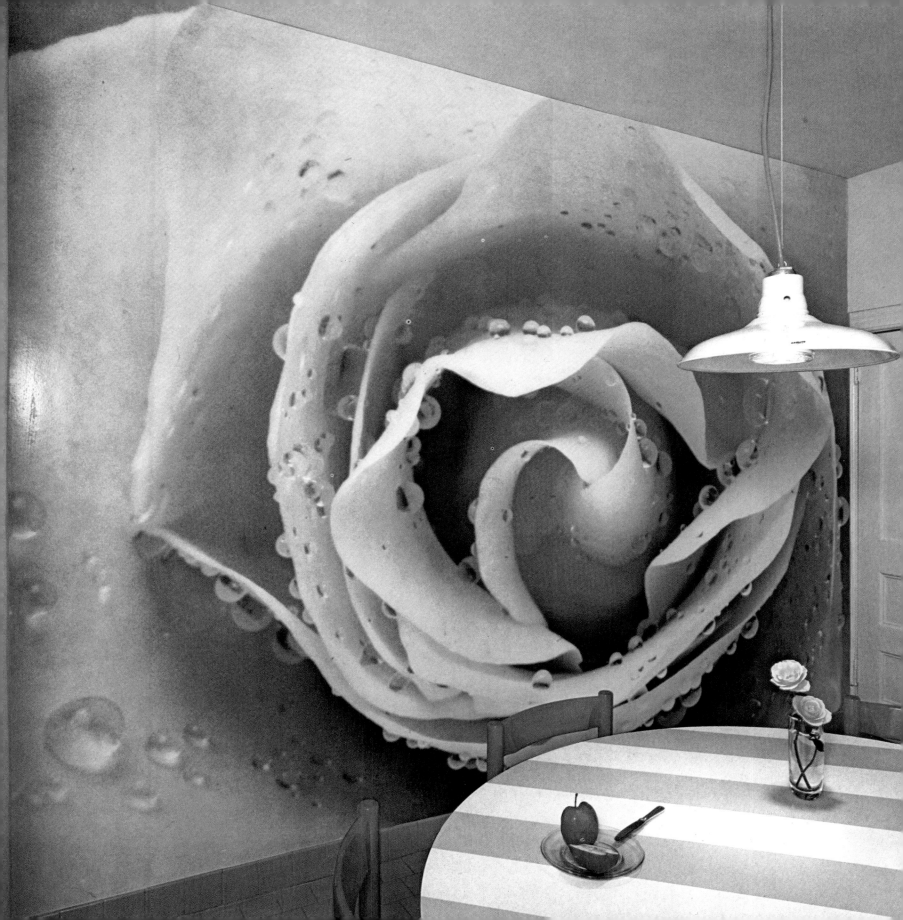

DANIEL MILES KRON

PREPARATION

Professional equipment may not make you into a James Beard, but it will certainly help get you started. Chefs, restauranteurs, and just plain good cooks have always invested in this equipment, which is well made, extremely durable, and impervious to capricious changes in style. Oversized, professional equipment is often expensive but can last forever. Look for it in restaurant supply stores, kitchen shops, and, increasingly, in the housewares departments of major department stores.

OVEN READY *Handled braziers ($84 to $113); Professional Kitchen.*

PHOTOGRAPHS BY LYNN KARLIN

DRESSING UP *Airtight stainless steel hospital supply dressing jars double as kitchen canisters ($9 to $30); from The Professional Kitchen.*

FOOD STORE *Polyethylene Rubbermaid food storage containers go from deep freeze to steam heat ($5 to $15); from Manhattan Ad Hoc.*

BIG DIPPER *Graduated stainless steel four-quart urn dipper ($18); from Manhattan Ad Hoc Housewares.*

STOCK UP *Sixteen-quart stockpot ($92); from The Professional Kitchen.*

SUPER STRAINER *Restaurant-sized stainless steel colander on a base ($40); from The Professional Kitchen.*

CHOOSE YOUR WEAPONS *The Professional Kitchen sells a large selection of kitchen knives and cleavers for chefs or amateur cooks.*

HANG-UPS *A display of ladles, funnels, and strainers is indicative of what's in store at The Professional Kitchen.*

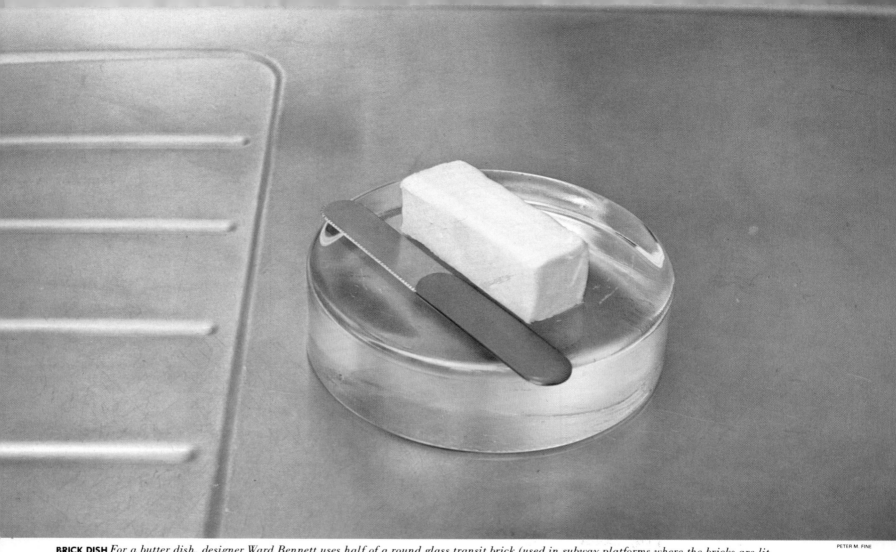

PETER M. FINE

BRICK DISH *For a butter dish, designer Ward Bennett uses half of a round glass transit brick (used in subway platforms where the bricks are lit from underneath when the trains arrive). Similar "dishes" are available from Pittsburgh Corning glass-block dealers for about $7 apiece.*

PETER M. FINE

COOLING OFF *Designers Harry Schule and Ned Marshall use a red firefighter's bucket as a wine cooler in their home.*

LYNN KARLIN

CATERED *This tin-lined copper bain-marie has bronze handles and holds three 2-quart pots ($300); from The Professional Kitchen.*

COLUMN A *They're standard as serving dishes in every Chinese restaurant. Dish and cover are available for $11.25 at Manhattan Ad Hoc Housewares.*

COLUMN B *Blue Delph is a Chinese restaurant pattern available from Cook's Supply Corp. The teacups are about $25 for three dozen pieces.*

TEA FOR ONE *Individual teapot and creamers are typical restaurant ware; teapot about $6, creamers about $1.50; from The Professional Kitchen.*

DINER *Federal Restaurant Supply mugs are $18 a dozen.*

GREEN BAND *Jackson hotel china ($49 for three dozen plates) is from Cook's.*

S & P *Morton's institutional shakers are $1.00 the pair, filled.*

COURTESY NEW YORK PUBLIC LIBRARY PICTURE COLLECTION

TABLETOP

The obligatory two sets of trousseau dishes never included Chinese restaurant ware or Horn-and-Hardart-type mugs. But the tables are turning. Today restaurants wanting to make an impression buy Spode, and radical homemakers are discovering the homely good looks of commercial tabletop items. Certainly the taste for restaurant china, etc., has been helped along by a tremendous increase in eating out, gourmet travel tours, and catered at-home parties. The first restaurant item to come home was the giant pepper mill, then the heavy-duty chafing dish, and next the who-cares-if-it-breaks-in-the-dishwasher, all-purpose wineglass, and fat-edged china. However, soon the trip to the restaurant supply house to buy by the two dozen may no longer be necessary. Specialty stores and department stores are starting to offer these commercial products—at higher prices. While there are few yet undiscovered restaurant tabletop items, we did stumble on one virgin institutional item: Morton's disposable, filled white plastic salt shakers and gray plastic pepper shakers. We've arranged for Manhattan Ad Hoc Housewares to sell them.

221

TABLETOP

SAUCY *Sauce server comes with long-handled ladle ($15 the set); one of the restaurant serving pieces available from Manhattan Ad Hoc Housewares.*

SMOKING SECTION *White ceramic ashtray has a slot to hold the restaurant's imprinted matchbook ($6.50); from Manhattan Ad Hoc Housewares.*

TABLE SERVICE *Restaurant salt and pepper shakers have glass bodies and metal screw-on tops ($.95 each); from Manhattan Ad Hoc Housewares.*

DINER SPECIALS *Paper napkin holder ($7.75), syrup server ($4.75), and stainless steel tray ($14) are all cafeteriaware carried by Manhattan Ad Hoc.*

EASY DOES IT *Dishwasher-proof trays help reduce spillage, breakage, and noise ($35 to $75 a dozen); from The Professional Kitchen.*

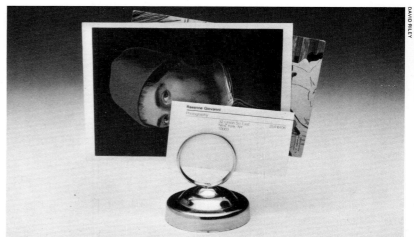

YOUR TABLE IS READY *Menu, table number, or reserved sign holder doubles as a note holder ($1.95); from Manhattan Ad Hoc Housewares.*

DECANTER *Twelve-cup stainless steel pourer ($14); Professional Kitchen.*

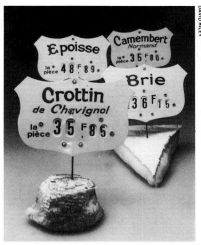

COMBIEN *French cheese shop markers are from Paris's Papeterie Moderne.*

ICE SHOW *Plastic ice mold ($20); from The Professional Kitchen.*

CRÈMES *A trio of milk jugs ($2.50 to $22); from Manhattan Ad Hoc.*

PIZZAZZ *Bari Restaurant and Pizza Equipment sells a $6 pizza paddle.*

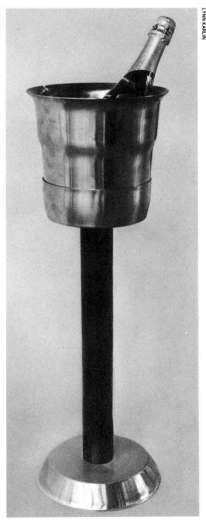

HOT STUFF *Ceramic mustard jar with spreader ($5.75); Manhattan Ad Hoc.*

POURERS *Sugar shaker ($1.25) and creamer ($1.50); Manhattan Ad Hoc.*

IN FLIGHT *Plastic-handled stainless steel cutlery is Air France issue.*

COOL *Restaurant champagne cooler is $200; from The Professional Kitchen.*

TYPE CAST *Vinyl "Dekplate" foam-backed typewriter pads from U.S. Mat & Rubber Co. make high-tech placemats; they're about $3.50 apiece.*

LABORATORY GLASS

Borosilicate (borax plus silica) glass, the first glass capable of withstanding sudden jolts of heat and cold, was developed by the Corning Glass Works in 1912 for use in railway signal lanterns. In 1915 Corning's borosilicate Pyrex-brand cookingware and laboratory glass were introduced. Vycor, a 96 percent silica glass, so heat resistant that a piece of it could be heated to 900° F and then plunged into ice water without breaking, was introduced in 1939. This material is used in sunlamps, manned spacecraft viewports, and in certain pieces of laboratory glass. Reasonably priced, heat-resistant laboratory glass in a myriad of sizes and shapes, proscribed by function, not fashion, is made primarily by Corning (Pyrex and Vycor), Kimble (Exax and Kimax), and Nalge (Nalgene), and is sold by dealers listed in the Yellow Pages under Laboratory Equipment.

RAEANNE GIOVANNI

RAEANNE GIOVANNI

TALL ORDER *Architect Rita Bormioli and designer Joseph Lembo used specimen cylinders, right, for juice and medical tubing straws.*

PATRICK JACOB

ARMEN KACHATURIAN

EXPERIMENTAL *Designer Robin Drake of Eisenman & Enoch puts flowers in test tubes.*

PLAT DU JOUR *Crystallizing dish, left, makes a gourmet soufflé or baking dish.*

BATTERY JARS DE CUISINE *The most expensive item of laboratory glass in this photograph is the crystallizing dish used as a salad bowl ($14.49); from Arthur H. Thomas Co. The other pieces shown cost from 86 cents for the milk beaker to $8.25 for the dressing jar holding the pasta.*

225

PHOTOGRAPHS BY RAEANNE GIOVANNI

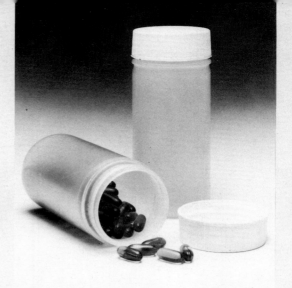

STERILIZED *Polypropylene mason jars have sealable caps ($13.62 for six); from Arthur H. Thomas Co.*

THE BELL JAR *Laboratory bell jar, 18-inches high, can protect an art object ($150); from Arthur H. Thomas Co.*

PORCELAIN *Laboratory evaporating dishes ($2.62 each) can hold pushpins, or even melted butter.*

STORAGE OPTIONS *Glass jars with screw-on tops, from the Arthur H. Thomas Co., hold from 1 to 16 ounces (cost from $2.75 to $11.75 a dozen).*

CHARGER *John Saladino stores logs in an SGA Scientific battery jar ($210).*

OVERSCALED *Ward Bennett uses a flat-bottomed laboratory flask to hold a large frond; he orders his lab glass through a physician friend.*

THE RED AND THE BLACK *Red glass flasks (125 to 500 milliliters) are about $4.60 apiece; black Teflon, $7 to $13 each; from Arthur H. Thomas.*

227

RAEANNE GIOVANNI

LAB GLASS *The $37 18-by-6-inch jar at the extreme left is the most expensive item of chemical glass on this page. The other flasks and cylinders sell from $4.30 to $18 at Arthur H. Thomas Co., a mail-order house.*

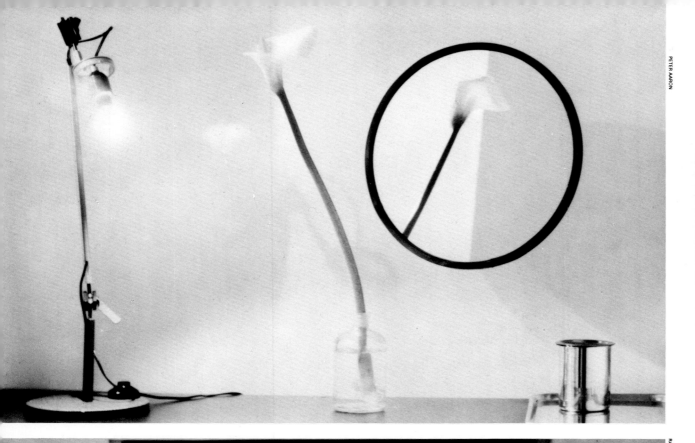

PETER AARON

RAEANNE GIOVANNI

SOCIAL SECURITY *The round dressing-table mirror in the apartment at left, designed by Joseph Paul D'Urso, is a detection mirror.*

HINDSIGHT *Architect Turner Brooks uses a rearview mirror, above, in a bathroom for shaving.*

ART OF DETECTION *A convex security mirror, right, on the ceiling reflects another on top of a column in a bedroom designed by Bray-Schaible.*

ON DISPLAY *The mirror mosaics of the display industry are used to panel a bathroom at right; available from Chic Display Co.*

DOOR AND CEILING *In a New York apartment by Bray-Schaible Design, an overhead mirror in the living room, left, was installed as if it were a detection mirror. In the bedroom an Eliason supermarket door (about $130) used as a closet door, above, has mirrored "window."*

RAEANNE GIOVANNI

DANIEL MILES KRON

MIRRORS

The round mirror in the front hall is the symbol of hospitality. The round security mirror in a department store is the symbol of hostility to the shoplifter, but lately it's being lifted by designers who are using it decoratively in the home. (Where else can you get a ready-made round mirror? In an auto supply store.) In addition to preventing theft, industrial mirrors are used to prevent accidents, e.g., to see around the corners of hospital corridors and warehouse aisles. Industrial mirrors can be had flat or convex, square or round, in glass or in nonbreakable plexiglass. A typical flat outdoor-type rubber-framed safety mirror, 20 by 30 inches, with rounded corners, sells for about $116 at Allsteel Scale Co. Industrial mirrors are listed in the Yellow Pages under Automotive Parts and Supplies (where you can buy rearview mirrors), or look for detection mirror sources listed under Mirrors.

SERGE KORNILOFF

231

GOOD MIXER *Large cement trough on wheels that can be turned to face the light holds a mini-jungle in Ward Bennett's Long Island house.*

VINTAGE *On Kenneth and Mary Walker's terrace geraniums grow out of halved wood barrels once used for wine and whiskey distilling.*

OFF-STREET PARKING *Rosenwach's California redwood planters with encircling benches furnish many public areas. Planters are shipped assembled.*

F H LAWSON CO (A TAPPAN CO)

HELLO DOLLY *Galvanized steel dolly with 3-inch rubber swivel wheels makes a good base for a large plant ($35); from A. Liss.*

LYNN KARLIN

232

CHARLES WIESEHAHN

DANIEL MILES KRON

PLANTERS

Recently, large plants became *de rigueur* in the office landscape. It was just a matter of time until these mini-jungles invaded the home. As the plants got larger, it became increasingly difficult to find containers to hold them. Looking beyond small clay pots, designers and architects started investigating other sources for reasonably priced yet efficient planters. Wheels were a necessity so that plants could be moved to face the light and from room to room, to vary the exposure with the season. The logical places to look were in commercial site furnishing catalogs. Other solutions were improvised. Agway, Sears, and other farm equipment sources all carry a selection of galvanized metal animal feed tubs, which make perfect planters. Whiskey distilleries often sell their used barrels, and these make very good outdoor planters; or follow Ward Bennett's example and simply plant your tree in a metal cement mixing trough, already equipped with wheels.

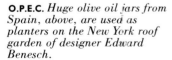

O.P.E.C. *Huge olive oil jars from Spain, above, are used as planters on the New York roof garden of designer Edward Benesch.*

FEEDER *In the office of Jules Fisher and Paul Marantz a galvanized animal feeding tub, left, holds the plants.*

À LA MODE *Ward Bennett used large layer cake baking pans as plant saucers, right.*

PETER M. FINE

233

SCALES AND CLOCKS

COURTESY OF SEARS ROEBUCK AND CO

There is more to weighing and measuring than the typical puny bathroom scale. Industry offers scales with which to weigh your loaded auto, or an elephant, or weigh-count almost anything electronically. For a long time the doctor's scale has been the *de rigueur* piece of commercial equipment for serious weight watchers. But now, for those who are as rich as they are thin, there is a fully electronic industrial "deck" scale that can be recessed into the floor, flush (perhaps in front of the refrigerator); it comes with 25 feet of cord leading to a remote digital display unit that could be recessed into the wall. Manufactured by Weigh-Tronix, this 24-by-24-inch-square scale sells for $3,470. In the industrial clock department, marine clocks and school clocks are a viable alternative to the "decorator" clocks offered in most retail stores. And if you want to time your resident football or basketball team consider a small electronic scoreboard timer.

DANIEL MILES KRON

SCOOPED *Produce scale ($12) is in Sears Farm Catalogue.*

INSTITUTIONAL *Howard Miller clock can be ceiling mounted, $155.*

LYNN KARLIN

TO MARKET, TO MARKET *Market scale, based on the combination lever and spring principle, is made of cast iron with a baked enamel platter ($114); from The Professional Kitchen.*

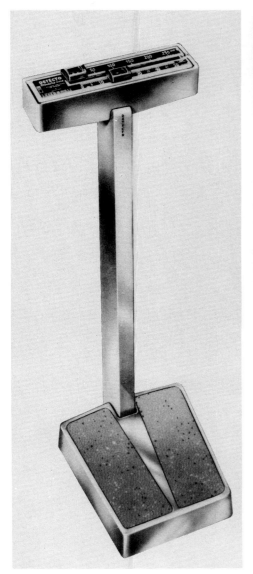

FRANKLIN INSTRUMENT CO

TWO-FACED *Electric or battery operated, this $245 Howard Miller clock can be cantilevered.*

OFFICE HOURS *Franklin 12-inch-wide clock ($10.33); from C&H.*

CLINICAL *Detecto's doctor's scale weighs to every 4 ounces ($120); from Allsteel Scale.*

WHAT'S THE SCORE? *The electric Fair-Play Scoreboard has red numerals ($798); from Mellor Gym Supply.*

RAEANNE GIOVANNI

WEATHER FORECASTS *Architect Kenneth Walker had a ship's barometer, humidity meter, and wind velocity instrument built into the wall of his waterfront Long Island summerhouse.*

EIGHT HUNDRED POUNDER *Detecto's digital shop scale on wheels ($1,060); from Allsteel Scale.*

LIBRARY OF CONGRESS

ANTIQUES

Old pharmacists' chests, gas street lights, apothecary jars, architectural remnants, early office equipment, little red schoolhouse desks, streamlined jukeboxes are all being rediscovered, refinished, replated, repolished, and recirculated. Even in the antiques market, retired "workers" can have social security.

JERRY TUBBY-ELIZABETH WHITING & ASSOCIATES

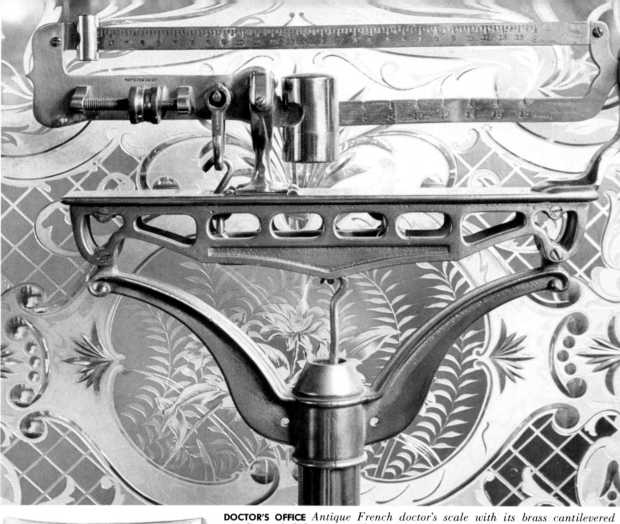

DOCTOR'S OFFICE *Antique French doctor's scale with its brass cantilevered weights and elaborate metalwork is a collector's item.*

MICHEL TCHEREVKOFF

DANIEL MILES KRON

CAPITAL *Reproduction repoussée zinc capitals, above, sell for $75 to $200; Kenneth Lynch & Sons.*

HOSPITABLE *The Village Stripper occasionally has old hotel medicine cabinets, left.*

SCHOLARLY *The storage wall, right, in designer Bob Gill's home is early schoolroom.*

JESSICA STRANG

RESTAURANT REVIVAL *The old restaurant range used in a New York apartment has acquired the cachet of a classic car.*

DANCE REVIVAL *Colorful push-button jukebox that used to play records in a rock and roll bar now adds pizazz to this London home.*

LAWFUL *This London interior has been renovated keeping the wood-paneled partitions that used to divide the office spaces of a law firm.*

RAILROADED *Movie director Frank Perry and writer Barbara Goldsmith have a turn-of-the-century railway station light in their kitchen.*

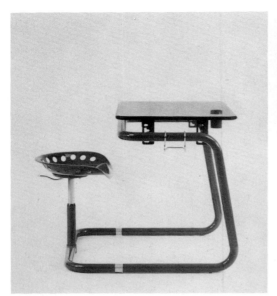

INTERNATIONAL CONTRACT FURNISHINGS, INC.

WORKPLACE *Child's desk with tractor seat by Marc Berthier is sold at Habitat, France.*

METALWORK *Stack chair and table by Englishman Rodney Kinsman for OMK is epoxy over steel; ICF lists the table for $109, the chair for $59; Conran's retails the chair for $48.*

PETER M. FINE

ALDO BALLO

ALDO BALLO

HEADLIGHT *Italian architect Achille Castiglione designed this light for Flos ($150); from AI.*

TOUCHÉ *Milanese architect Gae Aulenti designed this fencing-inspired lamp for Artemide.*

OPEN JOIST *Italian designer Giotto Stoppino's shelf unit for Acerbis ($790); from Abitare (doors, $32).*

INDUSTRIAL-INSPIRED

To the bank of traditional decorative images—flora and fauna, scrolls and cherubs, astrological signs and plain geometry—has recently been added a new category: industrial iconography. Today, for example, we find jewelers offering bracelets that fasten with real gold screws and fashion designers who are reinterpreting hospital scrub suits and other work clothes as street clothes. It's only natural that lighting, furniture, and fabric designers would look to industry as a source for new ideas. On these pages we present just a few home products that the industrial landscape has inspired.

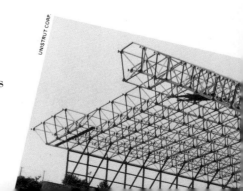
UNISTRUT CORP

238

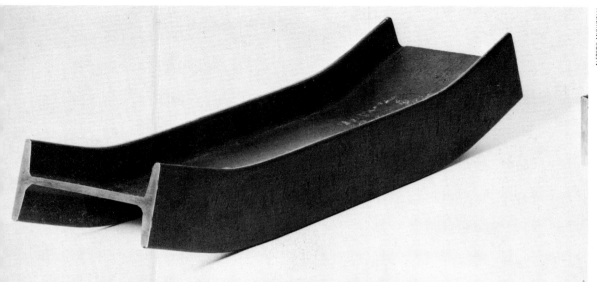

I BEAM *Milanese architect Enzo Mari has been adapting industrial parts since the early 1960s. Here an iron I beam has been bent and shaped into a serving piece; manufactured by Danese, Milan.*

ON THE GRID *Knock-down wire bin is by Guido De Marco for Castelli ($72); from Ambienti.*

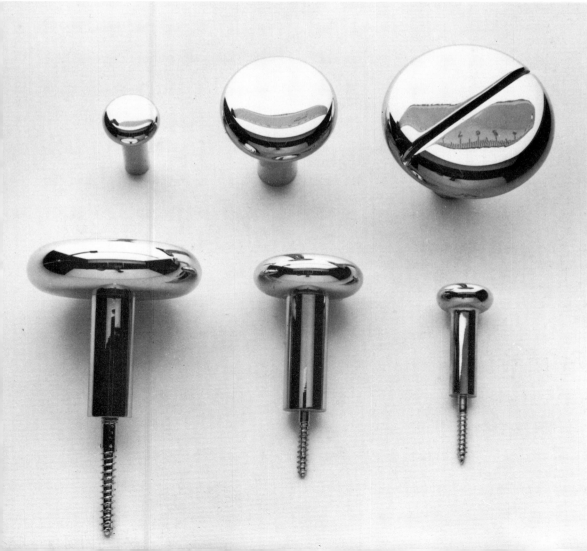

SOFT STEAL *Quilted chintzes by Etalage, above, were inspired by deck plate and graph paper.*

UNSCREWED *Munich-based designer Ingo Maurer did these polished chrome pulls, left.*

239

LYNN KARLIN

THE HIGH-TECH DIRECTORY

Pictured above are some useful guide books that are veritably the Baedekers of industrial exploration: The Thomas Register and Sweet's Catalogue File (both of which, as we explained in the introduction to the book, are available at libraries), the Yellow Pages, and some manufacturers' catalogs. On the following pages we have listed according to chapter sequence the addresses of the various sources named throughout the book, as well as others not previously mentioned. The symbol (M) stands for manufacturer; (W) for wholesaler or dealer (some of whom will sell only through architects or designers); (R) for retailer; and (M.O.) for mail order. However, you should probably start your inquiry with the manufacturer. While many manufacturers do not sell directly to consumers, without being coaxed, they will supply catalogs and product information and refer you to a dealer in your area. And remember, consider any prices listed in this book merely as a guide and subject to change.

STRUCTURAL

Windows

Amelco
Box 32
Glen Cove, NY 11542 (M)
Double-glazed venetian blind windows

Amrol Corp.
2001 Troy Ave.
New Castle, IN 47362 (M)
Rolling shutters

William Bloom and Son, Inc.
25 Almeida Ave.
East Providence, RI 02914 (M)
Microstructures

The Bogert and Carlough Co.
508 Straight St.
Paterson, NJ 07509 (M)

Carda Window Corp.
Box 877
Chester, PA 19013 (M)

Defender Ind., Inc.
255 Main St.
New Rochelle, NY 10801 (M.O.)

Disco Aluminum Products, Inc.
P.O. Box 1019
Selma, AL 36701 (M)

Forms & Surfaces
Box 5215
Santa Barbara, CA 93108 (W)

Hillaldam Coburn Ltd.
Red Lion Rd.
Surbiton, Surrey, England (M)
Rolling garage doors

Manhattan Marine & Electric Co., Inc.
116-118-120 Chambers St.
New York, NY 10007 (R)

Marmet Corp.
410 Bellis St.
Wausau, WI 54401 (M)

Overhead Door Corp.
P.O. Box 97
Elmsford, NY 10523 (M)

Perko, Inc.
16490 N.W. 13 Ave.
P.O. Box 64000-D
Miami, FL 33164 (M)

Roblin Architectural Products
Div. of United Steel & Wire
Battle Creek, MI 49016
   Azusa, CA 91702 (M)

Rure Assoc., Inc.
P.O. Box 112
Middlesex, NJ 08846 (W)

Sears Farm and Ranch Catalog
Sears Roebuck and Co.
Sears Tower
Chicago, IL 60684 (R)

Therma-Roll Corp.
512 Orchard St.
Golden, CO 80401 (M)

   4600 Post Oak Pl. Dr.
   Suite 209
   Houston, TX 77027

Trio Ind., Inc.
33 Platt Rd.
Shelton, CT 06484 (M)
Custom-made windows in quantity

J. C. Whitney & Co.
1917-19 Archer Ave.
P.O. Box 8410
Chicago, IL 60680 (R)

Young Windows
P.O. Box 387
Conshohocken, PA 19428 (M)

Greenhouses

Campbell Mfg. Co., Inc.
1262 Viceroy Dr.
Dallas, TX 75247 (M)

Dome East Corp.
325T Duffy Ave.
Hicksville, NY 11801 (M)
Geodesic systems

Duracote Corp.
358 N. Diamond St.
Ravenna, OH 44266 (M)
Light reflective shades for greenhouses

El Patio Products Corp.
P.O. Box 125
Houston, TX 77002 (M)

English Greenhouse Products Corp.
Davis & Copewood Sts.
Camden, NJ 08103 (M)

General Products Mfg. Co.
P.O. Box 32-T
Morristown, NJ 07960 (M)

Hydroculture, Inc.
10014 W. Glendale Ave.
Glendale, AZ 83507 (M)

Lasco Ind., Inc.
3255 E. Miraloma
Anaheim, CA 92806 (M)
Translucent fiber-glass sheet only

Lord & Burnham
Irvington-On-Hudson, NY 10533 (M)

National Greenhouse Co.
P.O. Box 100
Pana, IL 62557 (M)

Roper
IBG
P.O. Box 100
Wheeling, IL 60090 (M)
Ickes-Braun sunhouses

   IBG of Canada
   P.O. Box 2000
   90 Bartlett Rd.
   Beamsville, Ontario

Sears Farm and Ranch Catalog
Sears Roebuck and Co.
Sears Tower
Chicago, IL 60684 (R)

Warren/Sherer
W. Industrial Rd.
Marshall, MI 49068 (M)

Doors

Amrol Corp.
2001 Troy Ave.
New Castle, IN 47362 (M)

William Bloom and Son, Inc.
25 Almeida Ave.
East Providence, RI 02914 (M)
Microstructures

Bldg. Products Mfg. Co.
Div. of HUTCH Mfg.
3690 Dunn Rd.
Detroit, MI 48211 (M)

Cantor Bros.
57 Park Ave.
Bay Shore, NY 11706 (M)

Dynaflair Corp.
555 Broad Hollow Rd.
Suite 104
Melville, NY 11746 (M)

   108 Nordic Ave.
   Pointe Claire, Quebec H9R 3Y 2 Canada

   Suite 214
   159 Bay St.
   Toronto, Ontario M5J 1J7 Canada

Eliason Corp.
Easy Swing Door Div.
P.O. Box 2128
Kalamazoo, MI 49003 (M)
Aluminum doors

Forms & Surfaces
Box 5215
Santa Barbara, CA 93108 (M)

Hillaldam Coburn Ltd.
Red Lion Rd.
Surbiton, Surrey, England (M)

Overhead Door Corp.
P.O. Box 97
Elmsford, NY 10523 (M)
   24 Van Zant St.
   East Norwalk, CT 06855 (M)

Paniflex Corp.
430 E. 165 St.
New York, NY 10456 (M)

E. C. Payter Ltd.
Coneygre Industrial Estate
Tipton, Staffordshire, England (M)

Robot Ind.
7041 Orchard
Dearborn, MI 48126 (M)
Automatic doors

Sears Farm and Ranch Catalog
Sears Roebuck and Co.
Sears Tower
Chicago, IL 60684 (R)

Stanley Door Operating Equipment
Div. of The Stanley Works
Farmington, CT 06032 (R)
Automatic door-opening hardware

Jim Walter Doors
3825 Henderson Blvd.
Tampa, FL 33609 (M)

THE HIGH-TECH DIRECTORY

Total Rooms

Acoustic Standards
1227 W. Trenton Ave.
Orange, CA 92667 (M)

Air-Tech Ind., Inc.
9 Brighton Rd.
Clifton, NJ 07012 (M)

Robert K. Berner Assoc.
388 Lakeview Ave.
Clifton, NJ 07011 (W)

William Bloom and Son, Inc.
25 Almeida Ave.
East Providence, RI 02914
  (M)

Carefree of Colorado
2760 Industrial La.
Broomfield, CO 80020 (M)
Screen enclosures

Center for Exhibit Systems
645 N. Michigan Ave.
Chicago, IL 60611 (M)
Paperboard display systems

CID Assoc., Inc.
P.O. Box 10
Dept. 6
Allison Park, PA 15101 (W)

Ellis Sauna
Showroom:
18 W. 56 St.
New York, NY 10019 (M)

  Factory Sales & Showroom:
  P.O. Box 204
  Mack Rd.
  Middlefield, CT 06455

Lintern Corp.
8667 Station St.
Mentor, OH 44060 (M)
Crane cabs and control rooms

MacLevy Products Corp.
92-21 Corona Ave.
Elmhurst, NY 11373 (M)
Sauna rooms

MEG Merchandising Equip.
  Group
100 Bidwell Rd.
South Windsor, CT 06074 (M)

Meteor-Siegen
Apparatebau Paul Schmeck
  GmbH
Frankfurter StraBe 27
Postfach 10 08 01 (M)
Dark rooms

Metos Sauna
13000 Bellevue Redmond Rd.
Bellevue, WA 98005 (M)

Herman Miller, Inc.
Zeeland, MI 49464 (M)

  600 Madison Ave.
  New York, NY 10022

Herman Miller of Canada Ltd.
19th Floor
155 University Ave.
Toronto, Ontario M5H 3B7
  Canada

Herman Miller Ltd.
London Information Centre
2 Goodge St.
London W1P 1FE England

Sears Farm and Ranch Cata-
  log
Sears Roebuck and Co.
Sears Tower
Chicago, IL 60684 (R)

Tri-State Ind., Ltd.
1436 Williamsbridge Rd.
Bronx, NY 10461 (M)
Funeral tents

Ungermann Enterprises, Inc.
P.O. Box 847
Simi Valley, CA 93063 (M)

Van Dyke-La Arc Co., Inc.
Woonsocket, SD 57385 (M)

Visual Displays, Inc.
1 Huntington Quadrangle
Melville, NY 11746 (W)

Wenger Corp.
1077-S Wenger Bldg.
Owatonna, MN 55060 (M)
Acoustical music rooms

Screens/Partitions

Adirondack Direct
276 Park Ave. S.
New York, NY 10010 (M.O.)

Anthonsen & Kimmel
440 Park Ave. S.
New York, NY 10016 (W)

Ascot Steel Equip. Co., Inc.
45-35 39 St.
Long Island City, NY 11104 (M)

The Brewster Corp.
Old Saybrook, CT 06475 (M)

Butler Mfg. Co.
BMA Tower
Penn Valley Pk., Kansas C
Kansas City, MO 64141 (M)

Center for Exhibit Systems
645 N. Michigan Ave.
Chicago, IL 60611 (M)

Claridge Products and Equip.,
  Inc.
P.O. Box 910
Harrison, AR 72601 (M)

Forms & Surfaces
Box 5215
Santa Barbara, CA 93108 (M)

Global Steel Products Corp.
95 Marcus Blvd.
Deer Park, NY 11729 (M)

Hertz Furniture Systems Co.
220 Fifth Ave.
New York, NY 10001 (W)

Liskey Aluminum, Inc.
P.O. Box 8746
Baltimore, MD 21240 (M)

Logan Co.
200 Cabel St.
Louisville, KY 40206 (M)
Mesh partitions

Manutan
32 Bis, boulevard de Picpus
75012 Paris, France (W)

MEG Merchandising Equip.
  Group
100 Bidwell Rd.
South Windsor, CT 06074 (M)

J. A. Preston Corp.
71 Fifth Ave.
New York, NY 10003 (M.O.)

Rosemount Office Systems,
  Inc.
Airlake Industrial Pk.
Lakeville, MN 55044 (M)

Sanymetal Products Co., Inc.
1701 Urbana Rd.
Cleveland, OH 44112 (M)
*Shower stalls and toilet
  enclosures*

Spiral Steel Products Corp.
32-15 58 St.
Woodside, NY 11377 (W)

Jim Walter Doors
3825 Henderson Blvd.
Tampa, FL 33609 (M)

Exterior Components

Fiberdome, Inc.
P.O. Box 11
Lake Mills, WI 53551 (M)
Dome-shaped roofs

Manutan
32 Bis, boulevard de Picpus
75012 Paris, France (W)
Offers an open-air shed

Miracle & Jamison
Miracle Recreation Equip. Co.
P.O. Box 275
Grinnell, IA 50112 (W)
Geodesic domes

Unadilla Silo Co., Inc.
Unadilla, NY 13849 (M)
Silo domes

Structural Systems

Donn Access Floors, Inc.
P.O. Box 1000
Forest Hill, MD 21050 (M)

Inland Steel
30 W. Monroe St.
Chicago, IL 60603 (M)
*Metals, component building
  systems*

Liskey Aluminum, Inc.
P.O. Box 8746
Baltimore, MD 21240 (M)

Staircases

Abel Metal Co.
1095 Fewster Dr.
Mississauga, Ontario
L4W 1A2 Canada (W)

Access Equip. Ltd.
Maylands Ave.
Hemel Hempstead,
  Hertfordshire
England (M)

American Ornamental Metal
  Co. of Austin, Inc.
Route 3
Box 136-B
Volente Rd.
Leander, TX 78641 (M)

C & H Distr., Inc.
401 S. 5 St.
Milwaukee, WI 53204 (M.O.)

EQUIPTO

Crescent of Cambridge Ltd.
New St.
Cambridge, England **(M)**

Duvinage Corp.
Box 828
Hagerstown, MD 21740 **(M)**
Spiral stairs

Duvinage Sales Offices
  (Partial List):

  Bldg. Utilities & Specialties
    Co.
  P.O. Box 10206
  Knoxville, TN 37919

  R. J. DeWees & Son, Inc.
  P.O. Box 35085
  Dallas, TX 75235

  R. J. DeWees & Son, Inc.
  3100 Audley
  Houston, TX 77006

  Golterman & Sabo
  5731 Manchester Ave.
  St. Louis, MO 63110

  Melville Grant Assoc.
  P.O. Box 175
  Needham, MA 02192

  Frank C. Saunders Co.
  P.O. Box 12097
  Oakland, CA 94694

  Spiral Stairs, Inc. & Charles
    Gilbert Co.
  P.O. Box 96
  Leonia, NJ 17605

Equipto
225 S. Highland Ave.
Aurora, IL 60507 **(M)**

L'Escalier Industriel
67, rue Pierre-Curie
93230 Romainville, Paris,
  France **(M)**

A. Liss & Co.
38-60 13 St.
New York, NY 11101 **(W/R)**

Logan Co.
Div. of ATO
200 Cabel St.
Louisville, KY 40206 **(M)**
Spiral stairs

MacLevy Products Corp.
92-21 Corona Ave.
Elmhurst, NY 11373 **(M)**

Manutan
32 bis, boulevard de Picpus
75012 Paris, France **(W)**

Recreation Equip. Corp.
724 W. 8 St.
Anderson, IN 46011 **(M)**

Spiresca Escaliers-France
65-67 boulevard Romain
  Rolland
92120 Montrouge, Paris,
  France **(M)**

Rene Turpin
41110 Chateauvieux
Paris, France **(M)**

Randle Waltho Ltd.
30a Doyle Rd.
London SE25 England **(M)**

Mezzanines/Railings

Akins Mfg. Corp.
100 Ave. of the Americas
New York, NY 10013 **(M)**

Aluminum Tube Railings, Inc.
430 Madera St.
P.O. Box 118
San Gabriel, CA 91778 **(M)**

Alvardo Mfg. Co., Inc.
10626 E. Rush St.
South El Monte, CA 91733
  (M)
*Railings, pulls, hardware,
  turnstiles*

Ascot Steel Equip. Co.
45-35 39 St.
Long Island City, NY 11104
  (M)

Julius Blum & Co., Inc.
P.O. Box 292
Carlstadt, NJ 07072
"Connectorail" system

Bradley Corp.
P.O. Box 309
Menomonee Falls, WI 53051 **(M)**
Railings for washrooms, grab bars

EQUIPTO

Walter A. Braun Co., Inc.
Home Office:
23 Mackay Ave.
P.O. Box 287
Paramus, NJ 07652

  New York Office:
  303 W. 42 St.
  New York, NY 10036 **(W)**
Folding auditorium stages

Deluxe Systems, Inc.
10 S. Commercial Ave.
Carlstadt, NJ 07072 **(W)**

Dexion
Div. of Interlake, Inc.
135 St. & Perry Ave.
Chicago, IL 60627 **(M)**

  Regional Sales Offices:

  1200 Oakleigh Dr.
  East Point, GA 30344

  369 Passaic Ave.
  Fairfield, NJ 07006

  26711 Woodward
  Suite LL2
  Huntington Woods, MI
    48070

  761 Port Chicago Hwy.
  Pittsburgh, CA 94565

Equipto
225 S. Highland Ave.
Aurora, IL 60507 **(M)**
Prefab railings

Esposito Sales
46 King St.
Port Jefferson Sta.
New York, NY 11776 **(W)**
*Distributes Bradley washroom
  hand rails*

Fibergrate
13604 Midway Rd.
Dallas, TX 75234 **(M)**
Reinforced plastic grating

Fort Steuben Metal Products
  Co.
P.O. Box 268
Weirton, WV 26062 **(M)**

  1532 S. California Ave.
  Monrovia, CA 91016
Mezzanines

Bernard Franklin Co.
4424 Paul St.
Philadelphia, PA 19124 **(M)**
Mezzanines

Globe-Metal Products Div.
U.S. Gypsum
101 S. Wacker Dr.
Chicago, IL 60606 **(M)**

The Ironmonger
446 N. Wells St.
Chicago, IL 60610 **(W)**

Kee Klamp Div.
Gascoigne Ind. Products,
  Ltd.
P.O. Box 207
Buffalo, NY 14225 **(M)**

Lawrence Metal Products,
  Inc.
P.O. Box 400-M
Bay Shore, NY 11706

A. Liss & Co.
35-03 Bradley Ave.
Long Island City, NY 11101 **(W)**

Kenneth Lynch and Sons
177 Factory Rd.
Wilton, CT 06897
Railings

Manhattan Marine & Electric
  Co., Inc.
116-118-120 Chambers St.
New York, NY 10007 **(R)**

Manutan
32 bis, boulevard de Picpus
75012 Paris, France **(W)**

Miami-Carey
203 Garver Rd.
Monroe, OH 45050 **(M)**
Washroom grab bars

Mitchell Mfg. Co.
2778 S. 34 St.
Milwaukee, WI 53215 **(M)**

Perko, Inc.
16490 N.W. 13 Ave.
P.O. Box 64000-D
Miami, FL 33164 **(R)**
Marine railings

Pompanette, Inc.
1515 S.E. 16 St.
Fort Lauderdale, FL 33316

　326 First St.
　Annapolis, MD 21403 **(R)**
Marine railings

Reynolds Metals Co.
Architectural and Bldg.
　Products Div.
P.O. Box 27003
Richmond, VA 23261 **(M)**
*"Reyno Rail III" structural
　railing system*

Sheridan-Martin Assoc.
P.O. Box 186
Somerville, NJ 08876 **(W)**
*Distributes Fibergrate
　mezzanines*

SSI Fix Equipment Ltd.
Kingsclere Rd.,
Basingstoke, Hampshire
　RG21 2UJ
Great Britain **(M)**

Thomas, Inc.
8135 Forsyth Blvd.
St. Louis, MO 63105 **(M)**

SYSTEMS

Scaffolding and Pipes

Ace High Ladder Co., Inc.
611 Jackson Ave.
Bronx, NY 10455 **(W)**

Baker-Roos
Div. of Hugh J. Baker & Co.
P.O. Box 892
Dept. 2018S
602 W. McCarty St.
Indianapolis, IN 46206 **(M)**

Bil-Jax, Inc.
Archbold, OH 43502 **(M)**

C & H Distr., Inc.
401 S. 5 St.
Milwaukee, WI 53204 **(W)**

City Ladder Co.
Div. of Pepper Ladder Co.
152 Getty Ave.
Paterson, NJ 07503 **(M)**

Gilco Scaffolding Co.
517 Jarvis Ave.
Des Plaines, IL 60018 **(M)**

Hollaender Co.
3841 Spring Grove Ave.
Cincinnati, OH 45223 **(M)**
Nu-Rail clamps

Kee Klamp Div.
Gascoigne Ind. Products, Ltd.
P.O. Box 207
Buffalo, NY 14225 **(M/W)**

Perry Mfg., Inc.,
2531 Burton Ave.
Indianapolis, IN 46208 **(M)**

Putnam Rolling Ladder Co.,
　Inc.
32 Howard St.
New York, NY 10013 **(M)**

Raven Enterprises
2424C Bates Ave.
Concord, CA 94520 **(M)**

Rota-Lock
(see Up-Right Scaffolds)

Safway Steel Products
6228 W. State St.
Milwaukee, WI 53201 **(M)**

　26-02 1 St.
　Long Island City, NY 11102

Swing Staging, Inc.
775 Tiffany St. & Lafayette
　Ave.
Bronx, NY 10474 **(M)**

Swiss Fabricating, Inc.
Plant # 2 Myrtle St.
Rocky Mount, NC 27801 **(M)**

　1953 Camp Horne Rd.
　Pittsburgh, PA 15237

Up-Right Scaffolds
1013 Pardee St.
Berkeley, CA 94710 **(M)**

Up-Right Scaffolds
108 Industrial Dr.
Whitby, Ontario L1N 5Z8
　Canada **(M)**

　2410 Bank of Georgia Bldg.
　Atlanta, GA 30304

　519 E. Trade St.
　Charlotte, NC 28202

6677 N.W. Hwy.
Chicago, IL 60631

226 E. 8 St.
Cincinnati, OH 45201

1030 Terminal Tower
Cleveland, OH 44113

616 Carter Tower
Carter Tower Bldg.
Dallas, TX 75261

1515 Cleveland Pl.
Suite 200
Denver, CO 80201

1761 First National Bldg.
Detroit, MI 48226

3317 Montrose Blvd.
Houston, TX 77001

1916 Baltimore Bldg.
Kansas City, KS 66110

5415 York Blvd.
Los Angeles, CA 90042

420 Dermon Bldg.
Memphis, TN 38103

2040 W. Wisconsin Ave.
Milwaukee, WI 53233

44 S. 7 St.
Minneapolis, MN 55402

423 Carondeleto St.
New Orleans, LA 70130

999 Woodcock Rd.
Orlando, FL 32803

1400 Chestnut St.
Philadelphia, PA 19105

530 6 Ave.
Pittsburgh, PA 15219

705 Olive St.
St. Louis, MO 63101

1710 N. Main
San Antonio, TX 78212

2420 University Ave.
San Diego, CA 92104

First National Bank Bldg.
Seattle, WA 98154

99 Highland Ave.
Sommerville, MA 02143

3650 James St.
Syracuse, NY 13206

100 Huyler St.
Teterboro, NJ 07608

422 Washington Bldg.
Washington, DC 20005

Vanguard Mfg. Co., Inc.
100 Temple Rd.
New Ipswich, NH 03071 **(M)**

Werner Co., Inc.
77 Osgood Rd.
Greenville, PA 16125 **(M)**

　10800 W. Belmont
　Franklin Park, IL 60131 **(M)**

Metro

Art et Industrie
132 Thompson St.
New York, NY 10013 **(R)**

Bloomingdale's
1000 Third Ave.
New York, NY 10022 **(R)**

Cook's Supply Corp.
151 Varick St.
New York, NY 10013 **(W)**

Sid Diamond
964 Third Ave.
New York, NY 10022 **(W)**

Japan Erecta Shelf Co.
Shin-Shibuya Bldg.
7th Floor
1-16-10 Dogenzaka
Shibuya-Ku Tokyo 150 **(W)**

Ed Jenks
Star Rte., Box 450-A
49-799 Kam Hwy.
Kaawa, HI 96730 **(W)**

Macy's
Herald Square
New York, NY 10001 **(R)**

Manhattan Ad Hoc House-
　wares
842 Lexington Ave.
New York, NY 10021 **(R)**

Metropolitan Wire Corp.
Wilkes-Barre, PA 18705 **(M)**

　16, avenue des Courses
　1050 Brussels, Belgium

Slotted Angle

Adapto Steel Products
625 E. 10 Ave.
Hialeah, FL 33010 **(M)**

Ascot Steel Equip. Co., Inc.
45-35 39 St.
Long Island City, NY 11104 **(M)**

FOBA

Bruynzeel Sarl
Residence Elysee II
route de la Jonchere
Boite Postale 25
78170 La Celle-Saint-Cloud,
  France **(M)**

Deluxe Systems, Inc.
10 S. Commercial Ave.
Carlstadt, NJ 07072 **(W)**

Dexion, Inc.
369 Passaic Ave.
Fairfield, NJ 07006 **(M)**

Equip. Co. of America
1075 Hialeah Dr.
Hialeah, FL 33010 **(M)**

Equipto
225 S. Highland Ave.
Aurora, IL 60507 **(M)**

Bernard Franklin Co.
4424 Paul St.
Philadelphia, PA 19124 **(M)**

Ind. Handling Co., Inc.
137 Meacham Ave.
Elmont, NY 11003 **(W)**

Kitchen Bazaar
11 rue D'Alencon
(Corner avenue du Maine)
75015, Paris, France **(R)**

A. Liss & Co.
35-03 Bradley Ave.
Long Island City, NY 11101 **(W)**

Lyon Metal Products, Inc.
1933 Montgomery St.
Aurora, IL 60507 **(M/W)**

Material Handling Equip. Co.
111 Union Ave.
Bala-Cynwyd, PA 19004 **(W)**

Pacific Shelving
1901 W. El Segundo Blvd.
Compton, CA 90222 **(M)**

SSI Fix Equipment Ltd.
Kingsclere Rd.,
Basingstoke, Hampshire
  RG21 2UJ
Great Britain **(M)**

Tennsco
P.O. Box 606
Dickson, NJ 37055 **(M)**

Display Systems

Abstracta Structures, Inc.
101 Park Ave.
New York, NY 10017 **(M)**

Adjustable Steel Products
103-5 Greene St.
New York, NY 10012 **(M)**

Alden Systems Co., Inc.
Rte. 9 & 495 Turnpike Rd.
Westboro, MA 01581

  117 N. Main St.
  Brockton, MA 02401 **(M)**

Alka Structures, Inc.
457 W. 45 St.
New York, NY 10036 **(M/W)**

Apton
Div. of Interlake, Inc.
135 St. & Perry Ave.
Chicago, IL 60627 **(M)**

Click Systems, Inc.
115 Michael Dr.
Syosset, NY 11791 **(M)**

Sid Diamond Display Corp.
379 Fifth Ave.
New York, NY 10016 **(W/M)**
Converta

FOBA
AG 8907
Wettswill, Switzerland **(M)**

General Learning Corp.
250 James St.
Morristown, NJ 07960 **(M)**

Hayett Display Co.
207 W. 25 St.
New York, NY 10001 **(M)**

Kee Klamp Div.
Gascoigne Ind. Products, Ltd.
P.O. Box 207
Buffalo, NY 14225 **(M/W)**

Lozier Storage Systems of
  Omaha
4401 N. 21 St.
Omaha, NB 68110 **(M)**

FOBA

Herman Miller, Inc.
Zeeland, MI 49464 **(M)**

Opto, Inc.
162 Northfield Rd.
Northfield, IL 60093 **(M)**

Photo-Care, Ltd.
170 Fifth Ave.
New York, NY 10011 **(R)**
*Sells FOBA & other
  photography systems*

Unicube Corp.
Subsidiary of Gordon Tube
  Products Co., Inc.
1290 Oak Point Ave.
Bronx, NY 10474 **(M)**

Unistrut Corp.
Wayne, MI 48184 **(M)**

STORAGE

Lockers/Wardrobes

Abaco Steel Products, Inc.
1560 Locust Ave.
Bohemia, NY 11716 **(M)**

Able Steel Equip. Co., Inc.
50-02 23 St.
Long Island City, NY 11101 **(M)**

Adirondack Direct
276 Park Ave. S
New York, NY 10010 **(M/W)**

All Enterprises
Box 729
Petoskey, MI 49770 **(M)**
Multisided closet units

Blickman Health Ind., Inc.
20-21 Wagaraw Rd.
Fair Lawn, NJ 07410 **(M)**

Bucksco Mobile Service Equip.
Quakertown, PA 18951 **(M)**
Wardrobes on wheels

C & H Dist., Inc.
401 S. 5 St.
Milwaukee, WI 53204 **(M.O.)**

Dahnz Ind. (U.S.A.), Inc.
2 Park Ave.
New York, NY 10016 **(M)**

  1051 Clinton St.
  Buffalo, NY 14206
Modular plastic locker system

Claridge Products and
  Equipment, Inc.
P.O. Box 910
Harrison, AR 72601 **(M)**

Dallek, Inc.
534 Broadway
New York, NY 10012 **(M)**

  287 Madison Ave.
  New York, NY 10016 **(W/R)**

Deluxe Systems, Inc.
10 S. Commercial Ave.
Carlstadt, NJ 07072 **(W)**
Sells new and used products

Equipto
225 S. Highland Ave.
Aurora, IL 60507 **(M)**

Evans Metal Products, Inc.
435 Park Ave. S.
New York, NY 10016 **(M)**

Fidelity Products Co.
705 Pennsylvania Ave. S.
Minneapolis, MN 55426 **(M.O.)**

Frank Eastern Co.
625 Broadway
New York, NY 10012 **(M/W)**

Bernard Franklin Co.
4424 Paul St.
Philadelphia, PA 19124 **(M)**

F. E. Hale Mfg. Co.
P.O. Box 187
Herkimer, NY 13350 **(M)**

Hallowell, Div. of Standard
  Pressed Steel Co.
Hatfield, PA 19440 **(M)**

Hausmann Ind. Inc.
130 Union St.
Northvale, NJ 07647 **(M)**

Herman Miller, Inc.
Zeeland, MI 49464 **(M)**

Hertz Furniture Systems Co.
220 Fifth Ave.
New York, NY 10001 (**W**)

Homak Mfg. Co., Inc.
4433 S. Springfield Ave.
Chicago, IL 60632 (**M**)

Horizon Steel Products, Inc.
223 Water St.
Brooklyn, NY 11201 (**M**)

Itkin Bros., Inc.
290 Madison Ave.
New York, NY 10017 (**R/W**)

A. Liss & Co.
35-03 Bradley Ave.
Long Island City, NY 11101
(**W/M.O.**)

Lozier Store Fixtures, Inc.
4401 N. 21 St.
Omaha, NB 68110 (**M**)

Lyon Metal Products, Inc.
1933 Montgomery St.
Aurora, IL 60507 (**M**)

MacLevy Products Corp.
92-21 Corona Ave.
Elmhurst, NY 11373 (**M/W**)

Manutan
32 bis, boulevard de Picpus
Paris, France 75012 (**W**)

Medart
9701 Higgins Rd., Suite 216
Rosemount, IL 60018 (**M**)

Metalstand Co.
11200 Roosevelt Blvd.
Philadelphia, PA 19115 (**M**)

Paniflex Corp.
430 E. 165 St.
New York, NY 10456 (**M**)

Penco Products, Inc.
Oaks, PA 19456 (**M**)

R & G Affiliates
205 Lexington Ave.
New York, NY 10016 (**W**)

Shure Mfg. Corp.
1601 S. Hanley Rd.
St. Louis, MO 63144 (**M**)

Spiral Steel Products Corp.
32-15 58 St.
Woodside, NY 11377 (**W**)
Carries Medart lockers

Systeme Fix
2 rue du Canal
Basse Ham
Yutz, France 57110 (**M**)

Watson Mfg. Co., Inc.
335 Harrison
Jamestown, NY 14701 (**M**)

Winston Technologies
6780 Eighth St.
Buena Park, CA 90621 (**M**)
Manufacturers of the Simplector Space Odyssey tape cassette file

Cabinets and Drawers

AAA Restaurant Equip.
284 Bowery
New York, NY 10012 (**W**)

Able Steel Equip. Co., Inc.
50-02 23 St.
Long Island City, NY 11101 (**M**)

Adirondack Direct
276 Park Ave. S.
New York, NY 10010 (**M/W**)

Akro-Mils
Div. of Myers Ind.
Akron, OH 44309 (**M**)

Alfredo
Centrol Ind. Europea
22078 Turate, Italy (**M**)

American Metal Restaurant
Equip. Co.
43-04 19 Ave.
Long Island City, NY 11105 (**M**)

Amsco
American Sterilizer Co.
2424 W. 23 St.
Erie, PA 16512 (**M**)

Architectural Supplements,
Inc.
150 E. 58 St.
New York, NY 10022 (**W**)

Art Metal Construction Co.
2121 Walnut St.
Philadelphia, PA 19103 (**M**)

Ascot Steel Equip. Co., Inc.
45-35 39 St.
Long Island City, NY 11104
(**W**)

Auto World
701 N. Keyser Ave.
Scranton, PA 18505 (**R**)

Bretford Mfg., Inc.
9715 Soreng Ave.
Schiller Park, IL 60176 (**M**)

COURTESY SEARS ROEBUCK AND CO.

Cases, Inc.
1745 W. 134 St.
Gardena, CA 90249 (**M**)

C & H Distr., Inc.
401 S. 5 St.
Milwaukee, WI 53204 (**W**)

Charette Drafting Supply
Corp.
212 E. 54 St.
New York, NY 10021 (**R**)

1 Winthrop Sq.
Boston, MA 02110

44 Brattle St.
Cambridge, MA 02138

31 Olympia Ave.
Woburn, MA 01801

Coyne & Paddock
100 Ave. of the Americas
New York, NY 10013 (**M**)

Dallek, Inc.
534 Broadway
New York, NY 10012

287 Madison Ave.
New York, NY 10016 (**W/R**)

Deluxe Systems, Inc.
10 S. Commercial Ave.
Carlstadt, NJ 07072 (**W**)

D/R
Design Research
53 E. 57 St.
New York, NY 10022 (**R**)

Dolin Ind., Inc.
475 President St.
Brooklyn, NY 11215 (**M**)

Edsal Mfg. Co., Inc.
4400 S. Packers Ave.
Chicago, IL 60609 (**M**)

Equipto
225 S. Highland Ave.
Aurora, IL 60507 (**M**)

Evans Metal Products, Inc.
432 Park Ave. S.
New York, NY 10016 (**M**)

Fidelity Products Co.
705 Pennsylvania Ave. S.
Minneapolis, MN 55426 (**W**)

Sam Flax, Inc.
55 E. 55 St.
New York, NY 10022 (**R**)

Fort Steuben Metal Products
Co.
P.O. Box 268
Weirton, WV 26062

1532 S. California Ave.
Monrovia, CA 91016 (**M**)

Frank Eastern Co.
625 Broadway
New York, NY 10012 (**M/W**)

Bernard Franklin Co.
4424 Paul St.
Philadelphia, PA 19124 (**M**)

Fuller
45 E. 57 St.
New York, NY 10022 (**R**)

Hallowell
Div. of Standard Pressed
Steel Co.
Harfield, PA 19440 (**M**)

J. L. Hammett Co.
100 Hammett Pl.
Braintree, MA 02184 (**W/R**)

Helit
Friedrich Hefendehl
5883 Kierspe 1
Postfach 1146 Germany (**M**)

Hertz Furniture Systems Co.
220 Fifth Ave.
New York, NY 10001 (**W**)

Homak
4433 S. Springfield Ave.
Chicago, IL 60632 (**M**)
Shop tables

Horizon Steel Products, Inc.
223 Water St.
Brooklyn, NY 11201 (**M**)

Hunt Mfg. Co.
1405 Locust St.
Philadelphia, PA 19102 (**M**)

Inter-Graph, Ltd.
979 Third Ave.
New York, NY 10022 (**W**)

Jatel Steel Products, Inc.
262-280 Starr St.
Brooklyn, NY 11237 (**M**)

A. Liss & Co.
35-03 Bradley Ave.
Long Island City, NY 11101
(W/M.O.)

Lyon Metal Products
1933 Montgomery St.
Aurora, IL 60507 (M)

Mail Order Plastics
56 Lispenard St.
New York, NY 10013 (R)

Manutan
32 Bis, boulevard de Picpus
75012 Paris, France (W)

Marlo Mfg. Co., Inc.
140 Fifth Ave.
Hawthorne, NJ 07506 (M)

Mattick Business Forms
333 W. Hintz Rd.
Box P
Wheeling, IL 60090 (M)

Mayline Co., Inc.
619 N. Commerce St.
Sheboygan, WI 53081 (M)

Meilink Steel Safe Co.
P.O. Box 2847
Toledo, OH 43606 (M)

Ohio Medical Products
3030 Airco Dr.
P.O. Box 7550
Dept. 353
Madison, WI 53707 (M)

Charles Parker
290 Pratt St.
Meriden, Ct 06450 (M)

Plan Hold
17621 Von Karman Ave.
Irvine, CA 92714 (M)

Pollard Bros. Mfg. Co., Inc.
5504-08 N.W. Hwy.
Chicago, IL 60630 (M)

Safco Products Co.
H.P. Div.
7425 Laurel Ave. S.
Golden Valley, MN 55426 (M)

Shure Mfg. Corp.
1601 S. Hanley Rd.
St. Louis, MO 63144 (M)

Spiral Steel Products Corp.
32-15 58 St.
Woodside, NY 11377 (W)

SSI Fix Equipment Ltd.
Kingsclere Rd.,

Basingstoke, Hampshire
RG21 2UJ
Great Britain (M)

Visi-Shelf File, Inc.
105 Chambers St.
New York, NY 10007 (M)

Waldner's
222 Old Country Rd.
Mineola, NY 11501 (R)

920 Conklin St.
Farmingdale, NY 11735 (R)

N. Wasserstrom and Sons, Inc.
2300 Lockbourne Rd.
Columbus, OH 43207 (M)

Waterloo Ind., Inc.
300 Ansborough Ave.
Waterloo, IA 50704 (M)

Westinghouse Architectural
Systems
Westinghouse Corp.
4310 36 St. S.E.
Grand Rapids, MI 49508 (M)

Yorkville Ind., Inc.
55 Motor Ave.
Farmingdale, NY 11735 (M)

Zero-West
777 Front St.
P.O. Box 509
Burbank, CA 91503 (M)
Electronic fixture cabinets

Zero-East
288 Main St.
Monson, MA 01057

Zero-South
14501 49 St. N.
P.O. Box 6275
Clearwater, FL 33520

Open Shelving

AA Steel Shelving
169 Mercer
New York, NY 10012 (R, W, M)

Abaco Steel Products, Inc.
1560 Locust Ave.
Bohemia, NY 11716 (M)

Able Steel Equip. Co., Inc.
50-02 23 St.
Long Island City, NY 11101 (M)

Adirondack Direct
276 Park Ave. S.
New York, NY 10010 (M.O.)

LYON METAL PRODUCTS, INC.

Adjustable Steel Products Co.
103-5 Greene St.
New York, NY 10012 (M)

Alfredo
Central Ind. Europea
22078 Turate, Italy (M)
Steel and wire shelving

AMCO
901 N. Kilpatrick St.
Chicago, IL 60651 (M)
Wire shelving unit

Architectural Supplements
Inc.
150 E. 58 St.
New York, NY 10022 (W)

Art et Industrie
132 Thompson St.
New York, NY 10013 (R)

Art Metal Construction Co.
2121 Walnut St.
Philadelphia, PA 19103 (M)

Ascot Steel Equip. Co., Inc.
45-35 39 St.
Long Island City, NY 11104 (M)

Barattini
Via Clavature, 9
Bologna, Italy (M)

Bay Products Div.
American Metal Works, Inc.
8701 Torresdale Ave.
Philadelphia, PA 19136 (M)

Walter A. Braun Co., Inc.
303 W. 42 St.
New York, NY 10036 (W)

L. Brun
19, rue des Halles
Paris, 1, France (W)

Bruynzeel Sarl
Residence Elysee II
Route de la Jonchere
78170 La Celle-Saint-Cloud,
France (M)
Lundia wood shelving

Bucksco
Quakertown, PA 18951 (M)

Caddylak Systems, Inc.
201 Montrose Rd.
Westbury, NY 11590 (M)

C & H Distr., Inc.
401 S. 5 St.
Milwaukee, WI 53204 (M.O.)

Claridge Products and Equip. Inc.
P.O. Box 910
Harrison AR 72601 (M)

Click Systems
Div. of Hammond Ind., Inc.
155 Michael Dr.
Syosset, NY 11791 (M)

The Columbus Show Case Co.
850 Fifth Ave.
Columbus, OH 43212 (M)

The Concord Depot
84 Thoreau St.
Concord, MA 01742 (R)

Cook's Supply Corp.
151 Varick St.
New York, NY 10013 (W)
Wire shelving

Cubicon Corp.
3825 Laclede Ave.
St. Louis, MO 63108 (M)

Dallek, Inc.
534 Broadway
New York, NY 10012

287 Madison Ave.
New York, NY 10016 (W/R)

Deluxe Systems, Inc.
10 S. Commercial Ave.
Carlstadt, NJ 07072 (W)

D/R
Design Research
53 E. 57 St.
New York, NY 10022 (R)

Dexion
135 St. & Perry Ave.
Chicago, IL 60627 (M)

Sid Diamond
150 E. 58 St.
New York, NY 10022 **(W)**
Metro shelving

Display Equip. Mfg. Co.
711 S. Orchard St.
Seattle, WA 98108 **(M)**

Dolin Ind., Inc.
475 President St.
Brooklyn, NY 11215 **(M)**

The Door Store
3140 M St. N.W.
Washington, DC 20007 **(R)**

Edsal Mfg. Co., Inc.
4400 S. Packers Ave.
Chicago, IL 60609 **(M)**

Equip. Co. of America
1075 Hialeah Dr.
Hialeah, FL 33010 **(M)**

Equipto
225 S. Highland Ave.
Aurora, IL 60507 **(M)**
Steel shelving

Evans Metal Products, Inc.
432 Park Ave. S.
New York, NY 10016 **(M)**

Fidelity Products Co.
705 Pennsylvania Ave. S.
Minneapolis, MN 55426 **(M.O.)**

Sam Flax
55 E. 55 St.
New York, NY 10022 **(R)**

Fort Steuben Metal Products
Co.
P.O. Box 268
Weirton, WV 26062

1532 S. California Ave.
Monrovia, CA 91016 **(M)**
Steel shelving

Frank Eastern Co.
625 Broadway
New York, NY 10012 **(M)**

Bernard Franklin Co.
4424 Paul St.
Philadelphia, PA 19124 **(M)**
Steel shelving

Fuller Stationers
45 E. 57 St.
New York, NY 10022 **(R)**

Grayarc
882 Third Ave.
Brooklyn, NY 11232 **(R)**

Don Gresswell Ltd.
Bridge House
Grange Park
London N21 1RB
England **(M)**

Hafele KG
7270 Nagold
West Germany **(M)**

F. E. Hale Mfg. Co.
P.O. Box 187
Herkimer, NY 13350 **(M)**
Glass-door bookcases

Hallowell
Div. of Standard Pressed Steel Co.
Hatfield, PA 19440 **(M)**
Steel shelving

Hamilton Ind.
Div. of American Hosp.
Supply Corp.
1316 18 St.
Two Rivers, WI 54241 **(M)**
Wire shelving

Hertz Furniture Systems Co.
220 Fifth Ave.
New York, NY 10001 **(W)**

Hirsh Co.
8051 Central Park Ave.
Skokie, IL 60076 **(M)**

Hobart Mfg. Co.
Troy, OH 45373 **(M)**

Hodge Mfg. Co., Inc.
55 Fisk Ave.
Springfield, MA 01101 **(M)**

William Hodges & Co.
Div. of Falcon Products
3031 Red Lion Rd.
Philadelphia, PA 19114 **(M)**
Postmaster wire shelving

Horizon Steel Products, Inc.
223 Water St.
Brooklyn, NY 11201 **(M)**

Howard Displays, Inc.
500 Tenth Ave.
New York, NY 10018 **(M)**

Hunt Mfg. Co.
1405 Locust St.
Philadelphia, PA 19102 **(M)**

Industrie Secco
C.P. 101
31100 Treviso, Italy **(M)**

Interlake, Inc.
135 St. and Perry Ave.
Chicago, IL 60627 **(M)**

EQUIPTO

InterRoyal Corp.
Library Div.
One Park Ave.
New York, NY 10016 **(M)**

Lear Siegler, Inc.
Borroughs Div.
3002 N. Burdick St.
Kalamazoo, MI 49007 **(M)**

A. Liss & Co.
35-03 Bradley Ave.
Long Island City, NY 11101
(W/M.O.)

Lozier Store Fixtures
4401 N. 21 St.
Omaha, NB 68110 **(M)**

Lundia, Myers Ind., Inc.
600 Capitol Way
Jacksonville, IL 62650 **(M)**
Wood shelving

Lyon Metal Products
1933 Montgomery St.
Aurora, IL 60507 **(M)**
Steel shelving

Manhattan Ad Hoc House-
wares
842 Lexington Ave.
New York, NY 10021 **(R)**

Manhattan Wire Goods Co.,
Inc.
34-24 Hunters Point Ave.
Long Island City, NY 10011
(M)

Manutan
32 Bis, boulevard de Picpus
75012 Paris, France **(W)**

Market Forge
35 Garvey St.
Everett, MA 02149
Wire shelving

Marlo Mfg. Co., Inc.
140 Fifth Ave.
Hawthorne, NJ 07506 **(M)**

MEG Merchandising Equip.
Group, Inc.
100 Bidwell Rd.
S. Windsor, CT 06074 **(M)**

Metropolitan Wire Corp.
Wilkes-Barre, PA 18705 **(M)**
16, Avenue des Courses
1050 Brussels, Belgium

National Blank Book Co., Inc.
Marketing Dept. OP
Holyoke, MA 01040 **(M)**

Neiman Steel Equip. Co., Inc.
Philadelphia, PA 19134 **(M)**

Pacific Shelving
1901 W. El Segundo Blvd.
Compton, CA 90222 **(M)**

Penco Prod. Inc.
Oaks, PA 19456 **(M)**

Plan Hold
17621 Von Karman Ave.
Irving, CA 92714 **(M)**

Pollard Bros. Mfg. Co., Inc.
5504-08 N.W. Hwy.
Chicago, IL 60630 **(M)**

The Professional Kitchen
18 Cooper Sq.
New York, NY 10003 **(R)**

Republic Steel Corp.
Ind. Products Corp.
1038 Belden Ave. N.E.
Canton, OH 44705 **(M)**

R&W Specialty Mfg. Corp.
504 Metropolitan Ave.
Brooklyn, NY 11211 **(M)**

Sears Farm and Ranch Cata-
log
Sears Roebuck and Co.
Sears Tower
Chicago, IL 60684 **(R)**

Shure Mfg. Corp.
1601 S. Hanley Rd.
St. Louis, MO 63144 **(M)**

Spiral Steel Products Corp.
32-15 58 St.
Woodside, NY 11377 **(W)**

Spur Systems Intl. Ltd.
Watford, Hertfordshire,
England **(M)**

Supreme Steel Equip. Corp.
170 53 St.
Brooklyn, NY 11232 **(M)**

SSI Fix Equipment Ltd.
Kingsclere Rd.
Basingstoke, Hampshire
RG21 2UJ
Great Britain **(M)**

Trim Corp. of America
657 Broadway
New York, NY 10012 **(M)**

Visi-Shelf File, Inc.
105 Chambers St.
New York, NY 10007 **(M)**

Waldner's
222 Old Country Rd.
Mineola, NY 11501 **(R)**

920 Conklin St.
Farmingdale, NY 11735 **(R)**

N. Wasserstrom and Sons, Inc.
2300 Lockbourne Rd.
Columbus, OH 43207 **(M)**

Workbench
470 Park Ave. S.
New York, NY 10016 **(R)**
Lundia shelving

Revolving Storage

Akro-Mils
Div. of Myers Ind.
Akron, OH 44309 **(M)**

All Enterprises
Box 729
Petoskey, MI 49770 **(M)**

C & H Distr., Inc.
401 S. Fifth St.
Milwaukee, WI 53204 **(M.O.)**

Deijon, Inc.
184 Central Ave.
Old Tappan, NJ 07675 **(W/R)**
Revolving book and magazine racks

Delco Assoc., Inc.
522 E. Putnam Ave.
P.O. Box 423
Greenwich, CT 06830 **(M)**

LCO ASSOCIATES, INC.

FRICK-GALLAGHER MFG. CO.

Equipto
225 S. Highland Ave.
Aurora, IL 60507 **(M)**

Frick-Gallagher Mfg. Co.
Wellston, OH 45692 **(M)**

A. Liss & Co.
35-03 Bradley Ave.
Long Island City, NY 11101
(W/M.O.)

Lyon Metal Products
1933 Montgomery St.
Aurora, IL 60507 **(M)**

Manhattan Ad Hoc House-
wares
842 Lexington Ave.
New York, NY 10021 **(R)**

Sperry Univac
1290 Ave. of the Americas
New York, NY 10036 **(M)**

Supreme Equip. &
Systems Corp.
170 53 St.
Brooklyn, NY 11232 **(M)**

Conveyors

Acco-Chain Conveyor Div.
12755 E. Nine Mile Rd.
Warren, MI 48089 **(M)**

Acco-Integrated Handling
Systems Div.

Balles Rd.
Frederick, MD 21701 **(M)**

Aero-Go, Inc.
5800 Corson Ave. S.
Seattle, WA 98108 **(M)**

Allis-Chalmers Ind. Truck Div.
21800 S. Cicero Ave.
Matteson, IL 60443 **(M)**

Alvey/Control Flow
Div. of Alvey, Inc.
9301 Olive Blvd.
St. Louis, MO 63132 **(M)**

American Mfg. Co., Inc.
P.O. Box 1237
Tacoma, WA 98401 **(M)**

AMSCO
American Sterilizer Co.
2424 W. 23 St.
Erie, PA 16512 **(M)**

Aseeco Corp.
8857 Olympic Blvd.
Beverly Hills, CA 90211 **(M)**

Automatic Ind. Machines, Inc.
115 Dell Glen Ave.
Lodi, NJ 07644 **(M)**

Autoquip Corp.
1058 W. Industrial Ave.
Guthrie, OK 73044 **(M)**

A. J. Bayer Co.
Subsidiary of Interlake, Inc.
P.O. Box 276
Shepherdsville, KY 40165 **(M)**

Bilt-Rite Conveyors, Inc.
141 Lanza Ave.
Garfield, NJ 07026 **(M)**

Bunting Magnetics Co.
2100 Estes Ave.
Elk Grove Village, IL 60007
(M)

Engineered Products
Box 6767
Greenville, SC 29606 **(M)**

Ermanco, Inc.
6870 Grand Haven Rd.
P.O. Box 180
Spring Lake, MI 49456 **(M)**

Flexicon, Inc.
1275 Bloomfield Ave.
Fairfield, NJ 07006 **(M)**

Giant Lift Equip. Mfg. Co., Inc.
1871 Revere Beach Pkwy.
Everett, MA 02149 **(M)**

Interlake, Inc.
135 St. & Perry Ave.
Chicago, IL 60627 **(M)**

Interroll Corp.
60 Hoffman Ave.
Hauppauge, NY 11787 **(M)**

Kornylak Corp.
400 Heaton St.
Hamilton, OH 45011 **(M)**

Litton Unit Handling Systems
Storage Systems Dept.
7100 Industrial Rd.
Florence, KY 41042 **(M)**

Logan Co.
Div. of A-T-O
200 Cabel St.
Louisville, KY 40206 **(M)**

McDowell-Wellman
Engineering Co.
113 St. Clair Ave. N.E.
Cleveland, OH 44114 **(M)**

Mallard Mfg. Corp.
101 Mallard Rd.
Sterling, IL 61081 **(M)**

Manutan
32 Bis; boulevard de Picpus
75012 Paris, France **(W)**

Mayfran, Inc.
Div. of Fischer Ind.
P.O. Box 43038
Cleveland, OH 44143 **(M)**

Midland Ross Corp.
Material Handling Div.
10605 Chester Rd.
Cincinnati, OH 45215 **(M)**

MRC Corp., Scanner Systems
Div.
Subsidiary of Scope, Inc.
11212 McCormick Rd.
Hunt Valley, MD 21031 **(M)**

MTD Products, Inc.
Material Handling Equip. Div.
5389 W. 130 St.
Cleveland, OH 44111 **(M)**

Munck Systems, Inc.
315 East St.
Hampton, VA 23670 **(M)**

Nedco Conveyor Co.
Div. C & T Tarlton, Inc.
132 W. Main St.
Rahway, NJ 07065 **(M)**

Nestaway
Div. of Bliss & Laughlin Ind., Inc.

9501 Granger Rd.
Cleveland, OH 44125 **(M)**

New London Engineering Co.
1700 Division St.
New London, WI 54961 **(M)**

Pacific Shelving
1901 W. El Segundo Blvd.
Compton, CA 90222 **(M)**

Power-Pack Conveyor Co.
836 E. 140 St.
Cleveland, OH 44110 **(M)**

Railex Corp.
89-02 Atlantic Ave.
New York, NY 11416 **(M)**

Rapid Installations Co.
4003 Oaklawn Dr.
Louisville, KY 40219 **(M)**

Rapistan, Inc.
507 Plymouth Ave. N.E.
Grand Rapids, MI 49505 **(M)**

David Round & Sons, Inc.
32405 Aurora Rd.
Cleveland, OH 44139 **(M)**

Saratoga Conveyor Corp.
3913 Central Ave.
Hapeville, GA 30354 **(M)**

Scope, Inc.
1860 Michael Faraday Dr.
Reston, VA 22090 **(M)**

Si Handling Systems, Inc.
P.O. Box 70
Easton, PA 18042 **(M)**

Standard Conveyor Co.
2266 N. Second St.
North St. Paul, MN 55109 **(M)**

Stor-Dynamics Corp.
99 Main Ave.
Elmwood Park, NJ 07407 **(M)**

TELELIFT Niederlassung
Postfach 9101
Ehrenstrabe 4
4000 Düsseldorf 1 Germany **(M)**

TELELIFT Technisches Buro
Postfach 311460
1000 Berlin 31 Germany **(M)**

Vac-U-Max
37 Rutgers St.
Belleville, NJ 07109 **(M)**

Jervis B. Webb Co.
Norfolk Conveyor Div.
155 King St.
Cohasset, MA 02025 **(M)**

White Machine Co., Inc.
50 Boright Ave.
Kenilworth, NJ 07033 **(M)**

Wire Storage

Admac Intl.
903 River Acres Dr.
Tecumseh, MI 49286 **(W)**
Elfa system

Art et Industrie
132 Thompson St.
New York, NY 10013 **(R)**
Elfa system

Closet Maid Corp.
P.O. Box 304
720 W. 17 St.
Ocala, FL 32670 **(M)**

Grayline Housewares, Inc.
1616 Berkley St.
Elgin, IL 60120 **(M)**

Hafele K G
P.O. Box 160
7270 Nagold/West Germany
(M)

Housewares, Inc.
1025 Second Ave.
New York, NY 10022 **(R)**

Manhattan Ad Hoc House-
wares
842 Lexington Ave.
New York, NY 10021 **(R)**

Schulte Corp.
11450 Grooms Rd.
Cincinnati, OH 45242 **(M)**
Wire storage systems

Seabon
54 E. 54 St.
New York, NY 10022 **(R)**
Elfa system

Pick Racks

Adapto Steel Products
625 E. 10 Ave.
Hialeah, FL 33010 **(M)**

Akro-Mils
Div. of Myers Ind.
Akron, OH 44309 **(M)**

Butler Ind.
637 Central Ave.
Newark, NJ 07107 **(M)**

Dexion, Inc.
369 Passaic Ave.
Fairfield,NJ 07006 **(M)**

C & H Distr., Inc.
401 S. 5 St.
Milwaukee, WI 53204 **(M.O.)**

Equipto
225 S. Highland Ave.
Aurora, IL 60507 **(M)**

Fenco Design Mfrs.
Cinnaminson, NJ 08077 **(M)**

Fort Steuben Metal Products
Co.
P.O. Box 268
Weirton, WV 26062 **(M)**

Bernard Franklin Co.
4424 Paul St.
Philadelphia, PA 19124 **(M)**

Frick Gallagher Mfg. Co.
201 S. Michigan Ave.
Wellston, OH 45692 **(M)**
Rotabins

Frontier Mfg. Co.
11200 Harry Hines
Dallas TX 75220 **(M)**

Hallowell
Div. Standard Pressed Steel
Township Line Rd.
Hatfield, PA 19440

Hertz Furniture Systems Co.
220 Fifth Ave.
New York, NY 10001 **(W)**

Interlake, Inc.
135 St. & Perry Ave.
Chicago, IL 60627 **(M)**

Lear Siegler, Inc.
Borroughs Div.
3002 N. Burdick St.
Kalamazoo, MI 49007 **(M)**

Lyon Metal Products, Inc.
P.O. Box 671
Aurora, IL 60504 **(M)**

Republic Steel Corp.
Ind. Products Div.
1038 Belden Ave. N.E.
Canton, OH 44705 **(M)**

SSI Fix Equipment Ltd.
Kingsclere Rd.,
Basingstoke, Hampshire
RG21 2UJ
Great Britain **(M)**

Baskets, Boxes and Bins

Abaco Steel Products, Inc.
1560 Locust Ave.
Bohemia, NY 11716 **(M)**

Abbott & Abbott Box Corp.
28-31 Borden Ave.
Long Island City, NY 11101 **(M)**

Abbott Wire Products, Inc.
95-29 149 St.
Jamaica, NY 11435 **(M)**

Advance Speciality Co., Inc.
22 S. Union Ave.
Lansdowne, PA 19050 **(M)**

Alfredo
Centrol Ind. Europea
22078 Turate, Italy **(M)**

Allsteel Scale Co., Inc.
80 Spring St.
New York, NY 10012 **(W)**

Art et Industrie
132 Thompson St.
New York, NY 10013 **(R)**

Ascot Steel Equipment Co.
45-35 39 St.
Long Island City, NY 11104 **(W)**

Banner Mat & Products Co.
17 Mercer St.
Cincinnati, OH 45210 **(W)**

Bloomfield Ind.
4546 W. 47 St.
Chicago, IL 60632 **(M)**

Brookstone Co.
127 Vose Farm Rd.
Peterborough, NH 03458
(M.O.)

Butler Ind.
637 Central Ave.
Newark, NJ 07107 **(M)**

Cambro
P.O. Box 2000
Huntington Beach, CA 92647 **(M)**

C & H Distr., Inc.
401 S. 5 St.
Milwaukee, WI 53204 **(M.O.)**

Cole-Parmer Instrument Co.
7425 N. Oak Park Ave.
Chicago, IL 60648 **(M.O.)**

Continental Mfg. Co.
Div. of Contico Intl., Inc.
1101 Warson Rd.
St. Louis, MO 63132 **(M)**

Cook's Supply Corp.
151 Varick St.
New York, NY 10013 **(W)**

The Crate and Barrel
190 Northfield Rd.
Northfield, IL 60093 **(R)**

Dallek, Inc.
534 Broadway
New York, NY 10012

  287 Madison Ave.
  New York, NY 10016 **(W/R)**

De Feo Wire
Brookside & Penn Sts.
Yeadon, PA 19050 **(M)**

Deluxe Systems, Inc.
10 S. Commercial Ave.
Carlstadt, NJ 07072 **(W)**

Dunning Corp.
North Walpole, NH 05101 **(M)**

Ekco
1949 N. Cicero Ave.
Chicago, IL 60639 **(M)**
Food service equipment

Federal Fibre Corp.
100 E. 9 Ave.
Runnemede, NJ 08078 **(M)**

Fibre Case & Novelty Co., Inc.
708 Broadway
New York, NY 10003 **(M)**

Fidelity Products, Co.
705 Pennsylvania Ave. S.
Minneapolis, MN 55426 **(M.O.)**

Sam Flax
55 E. 55 St.
New York, NY 10022 **(R)**

Fort Steuben Metal Products Co.
P.O. Box 268
Weirton, WV 26062 **(M)**

  1532 S. California Ave.
  Monrovia, CA 91016

Bernard Franklin Co.
4424 Paul St.
Philadelphia, PA 19124 **(M)**

Frontier Mfg. Co.
11200 Harry Hines
Dallas, TX 75220 **(M)**

Fuller Stationers
45 E. 57 St.
New York, NY 10022 **(R)**

Garcy Corp.
2501 N. Elston
Chicago, IL 60647 **(M)**

C & H DISTRIBUTORS, INC.

General Home Products Corp.
745 Salem Rd.
Burlington, NJ 08016 **(M)**

Harloff Mfg. Co., Inc.
750 Garden of the Gods Rd.
Colorado Springs, CO 80907
  (M)

Helit
Friedrich Hefendehl
5883 Kierspe 1
Postfach 1146 Germany **(M)**

Hertz Furniture Systems
220 Fifth Ave.
New York, NY 10001 **(W)**

William Hodges & Co.
Div. of Falcon Products, Inc.
3031 Red Lion Rd.
Philadelphia, PA 19114 **(M)**

Homak Mfg. Co., Inc.
4433 S. Springfield Ave.
Chicago, IL 60632 **(M)**

Horchow Collection
4435 Simonton
Dallas, TX 75240

Hunt Mfg. Co.
1405 Locust St.
Philadelphia, PA 19102 **(M)**

Ikelheimer-Ernst, Inc.
601 W. 26 St.
New York, NY 10001 **(M)**
Fiberboard bins

Jimenez Wire Products Corp.
177 Cook St.
Brooklyn, NY 11206 **(M)**

Karp Assoc.
54-54 43 St.
Maspeth, NY 11378 **(M)**

Klein Tools, Inc.
7200 McCormick Rd.
Chicago, IL 60645 **(M)**

M. J. Knoud, Inc.
716 Madison Ave.
New York, NY 10021 **(R)**

Lakeside Mfg. Co.
1977 S. Allis St.
Milwaukee, WI 53207 **(M)**

Lion Office Products, Inc.
401 W. Alondra Blvd.
Gardena, CA 90248 **(M)**

A. Liss & Co.
35-03 Bradley Ave.
Long Island City, NY 11101 **(W/M.O.)**

Loumac Supply Corp.
900 Passaic Ave.
Harrison, NJ 07029 **(M)**

Lyon Metal Products, Inc.
1933 Montgomery St.
Aurora, IL 60507 **(M)**

Macaple
66, avenue Marc Dormoy
94500 Champigny
Sur Marne, France **(M)**

Mail Order Plastics
56 Lispenard St.
New York, NY 10013 **(W/R)**

Manhattan Ad Hoc Housewares
842 Lexington Ave.
New York, NY 10021 **(R)**

Manhattan Wire Goods Co.,
  Inc.
34-24 Hunters Point Ave.
Long Island City, NY 11101 **(M)**

Manutan
32 Bis, boulevard de Picpus
75012 Paris, France **(W)**

Merchandise Presentation, Inc.
2191 Third Ave.
New York, NY 10035 **(M)**

Metropolitan Wire Corp.
Wilkes-Barre, PA 18705 **(M)**

Molded Fiber Glass Tray Co.
E. Erie St.
Linesville, PA 16424 **(M)**

NVF Co.
Lafayette & Mulberry Sts.
Kennett Square, PA 19348 **(M)**

William Page & Co.
87-91 Shaftesbury Ave.
London W1V 8AJ England **(M)**

Peterboro Basket Co.
Peterborough, NH 03458 **(M)**

Peter Pepper Products
Pacific Design Ctr.
Los Angeles, CA 90069 **(W)**

Plastech
Div. of Pennsylvania Pacific
  Corp.
John Fitch Industrial Pk.
P.O. Box C-70
Warminster, PA 18974 **(M)**

Pompanette, Inc.
Sales Office & Showroom
326 First St.
Annapolis, MD 21403 **(R)**

The Professional Kitchen
18 Cooper Sq.
New York, NY 10003 **(R)**

Raburn Products
Div. of Economics Laboratory, Inc.
4 Corporate Pk. Dr.
White Plains, NY 10604 **(M)**

Result Mfg., Inc.
350 W. 31 St.
New York, NY 10001 **(M)**
Plastic boxes

Royal Wire Products, Inc.
13172 York Rd.
North Royalton, OH 44133 **(M)**

Rubbermaid Commercial
  Products, Inc.
Winchester, VA 22601 **(M)**

G. Rushbrooke (Smithfield) Ltd.
67/77 Charterhouse St.
London EC1M 6HL England
  (R)

Safco Products Co.
H.P. Div.
7425 Laurel Ave. S.
Golden Valley, MN 55426 **(M)**

SGA Scientific Corp.
735 Brand St.
Bloomfield, NJ 07003 **(M/W)**

Silite, Inc.
2600 N. Pulaski Rd.
Chicago, IL 60639 **(M)**

Sommer Metalcraft Corp.
500 Poston Dr.
Crawfordsville, IN 47933 **(M)**

The Steele Canvas Basket
  Co., Inc.
199 Concord Turnpike
Cambridge, MA 02140 **(M)**

SSI Fix Equipment Ltd.
Kingsclere Rd.
Basingstoke, Hampshire
  RG21 2UJ
Great Britain **(M)**

THE HIGH-TECH DIRECTORY

Storage Concepts Group
892 Broad St.
Newark, NJ 07102 **(W)**

Tedruth Plastics Corp.
Tedruth Plaza
P.O. Box 607
Farmingdale, NJ 07727 **(M)**

Arthur H. Thomas Co.
Vine St. at Third
P.O. Box 779
Philadelphia, PA 19105 **(M.O.)**

Thorpe Mfg. Co.
1801 Gulf St.
Lamar, MO 64759 **(M)**

Trylon Wire & Metal Works, Inc.
526 Tiffany St.
Bronx, NY 10474 **(M)**

Samuel Underberg
620 Atlantic Ave.
Brooklyn, NY 11217 **(W/R)**

United Steel and Wire
Div. of Roblin Ind., Inc.
Battle Creek, MI 49016 **(M)**
Azusa, CA 91702

Wald Mfg. Co., Inc.
Fifth & Center Sts.
P.O. Box 10
Maysville, KY 41056 **(M)**

Waldner's
22 Old Country Rd.
Mineola, NY 11501 **(R)**

  920 Conklin St.
  New York, NY 11735

Waterloo Ind., Inc.
300 Ansborough Ave.
Waterloo, IA 50704 **(M)**

Yorkville Ind., Inc.
55 Motor Ave.
Farmingdale, NY 11735 **(M)**

Rolling Storage

Able Steel Equip. Co., Inc.
50-02 23 St.
Long Island City, NY 11101
  (R/W)

Adirondack Direct
276 Park Ave. S.
New York, NY 10010 **(M.O.)**

Allsteel Scale Co., Inc.
80 Spring St.
New York, NY 10012 **(W/R)**

Amsco American Sterilizer Co.
2424 W. 23 St.
Erie, PA 16512 **(M)**

Ascot Steel Equip. Co., Inc.
45-35 39 St.
Long Island City, NY 11104 **(R)**

Blickman Health Ind., Inc.
20-21 Wagaraw Rd.
Fair Lawn, NJ 07410 **(M)**

Bloomfield Ind.
4546 W. 47 St.
Chicago, IL 60632 **(M)**

Bretford Mfg., Inc.
9715 Soreng Ave.
Schiller Park, IL 60176 **(M)**

Bucksco
Quakertown, PA 18951 **(M)**

Cambro
P.O. Box 2000
Huntington Beach, CA 92647
  (M)

C & H Distr., Inc.
401 S. 5 St.
Milwaukee, WI 53204 **(M.O.)**

Champion Chest Co.
4433 S. Springfield Ave.
Chicago, IL 60632 **(M)**

Cole-Parmer Instrument Co.
7425 N. Oak Park Ave.
Chicago, IL 60648 **(M.O.)**

Cook's Supply Corp.
151 Varick St.
New York, NY 10013 **(W)**

Crescent Metal Products, Inc.
12711 Taft Ave.
Cleveland, OH 44108 **(M)**

Deluxe Systems, Inc.
10 S. Commercial Ave.
Carlstadt, NJ 07072 **(R)**

Equipment Co. of America
1075 Hialeah Dr.
Hialeah, FL 33010 **(M/W)**

Equipto
225 S. Highland Ave.
Aurora, IL 60507 **(M)**

Fidelity Products Co.
705 Pennsylvania Ave. S.
Minneapolis, MN 55426 **(M.O.)**

Sam Flax
55 E. 55 St.
New York, NY 10022 **(R)**

Fort Steuben Metal Products
  Co.
P.O. Box 268
Weirton, WV 26062 **(M)**

  1532 S. California Ave.
  Monrovia, Calif. 91016 **(M)**

Bernard Franklin Co.
4424 Paul St.
Philadelphia, PA 19124 **(M/W)**

Fuller Stationers
45 E. 57 St.
New York, NY 10022 **(R)**

Gleason Corp.
P.O. Box 343
Milwaukee, WI 53201 **(M)**

Hallowell
Div. of Standard Pressed
  Steel Co.
Hatfield, PA 19440 **(M)**

Hardman
1668 22 St.
Santa Monica, CA 90404 **(M)**

Harloff Mfg. Co., Inc.
750 Garden of the Gods Rd.
Colorado Springs, CO 80907 **(M)**

Helit
Friedrich Hefendehl
5883 Kierspe 1
Postfach 1146 Germany **(M)**

Hertz Furniture Systems Co.
220 Fifth Ave.
New York, NY 10001 **(R)**

William Hodges & Co.
Div. of Falcon Products, Inc.
3031 Red Lion Rd.
Philadelphia, PA 19114 **(M)**

Homak
4433 S. Springfield Ave.
Chicago, IL 60632 **(M)**

Ikelheimer-Ernst, Inc.
601 W. 26 St.
New York, NY 10001 **(W/R)**

Inter-Graph
979 Third Ave.
New York, NY 10022 **(W)**

InterRoyal Corp.
Library Div.
One Park Ave.
New York, NY 10016 **(M)**

Lakeside Mfg., Inc.
1977 S. Allis St.
Milwaukee, WI 53207 **(M)**

A. Liss & Co.
35-03 Bradley Ave.
Long Island City, NY 11101 **(W/M.O.)**

Manhattan Ad Hoc House-
  wares
842 Lexington Ave.
New York, NY 10021 **(R)**

Manutan
32 Bis, boulevard de Picpus
75012 Paris, France **(W)**

Market Forge
35 Garvey St.
Everett, MA 02149

Marlo Mfg. Co., Inc.
140 Fifth Ave.
Hawthorne, NJ 07506 **(M)**

MEG Merchandising
  Equip. Group, Inc.
100 Bidwell Rd.
South Windsor, CT 06074 **(M)**

Metropolitan Wire Corp.
Wilkes-Barre, PA 18705 **(M)**

M.O.R.A.
13 et 15 rue Montmartre
75001 Paris, France **(W/R)**

Nestier
Material Handling Div.
Midland-Ross Corp.
10605 Chester Rd.
Cincinnati, OH 45215 **(M)**

NVF
Lafayette & Mulberry Sts.
Kennett Square, PA 19348 **(R)**

Orangeville Mfg. Co., Inc.
Orangeville, PA 17859 **(M)**

Peerless Ind., Inc.
4200 W. Chicago Ave.
Chicago, IL 60651 **(M)**

Plastech Div. of Penn. Pacific Corp.
John Fitch Industrial Pk.
P.O. Box C-70
Warminster, PA 18974 **(M)**

Pollard Bros. Mfg. Co., Inc.
5504-08 N.W. Hwy.
Chicago, IL 60630 **(M)**

Poly-trux
Div. Tingue, Brown & Co.
491 S. Dean St.
Englewood, NJ 07631 **(M)**

J. A. Preston Corp.
71 Fifth Ave.
New York, NY 10003 **(M.O.)**

The Professional Kitchen
18 Cooper Sq.
New York, NY 10003 **(R)**

Raburn Products
Div. of Economics Labora-
tory, Inc.
4 Corporate Pk. Dr.
White Plains, NY 10604 **(M)**

Railex Corp.
89-02 Atlantic Ave.
New York, NY 11416 **(M)**

R & W Speciality Mfg. Corp.
504 Metropolitan Ave.
Brooklyn, NY 11211 **(R)**

Shelley Mfg. Co.
P.O. Box 44038
Miami, FL 33144 **(M)**

Shure Mfg. Corp.
1601 S. Hanley Rd.
St. Louis, MO 63144 **(M)**

Spiral Steel Products Corp.
32-15 58 St.
Woodside, NY 11377 **(R)**

The Steele Canvas Basket Co., Inc.
199 Concord Turnpike
Cambridge, MA 02140 **(M)**

Super-Sturdy, Inc.
175 Liberty St.
Copiague, NY 11726 **(M)**

Supreme Steel Equip. Corp.
170 53 St.
Brooklyn, NY 11232 **(M)**

Tedruth Plastics Corp.
Tedruth Plaza
P.O. Box 607
Farmingdale, NJ 07727 **(M)**

Arthur H. Thomas Co.
Vine St. at Third
P.O. Box 779
Philadelphia, PA 19105 **(M.O.)**

Samuel Underberg, Inc.
620 Atlantic Ave.
Brooklyn, NY 11217 **(W/R)**

United Hospital Supply
Box 247
Riverton, NJ 08077 **(M)**

N. Wasserman and Sons, Inc.
2300 Lockbourne Rd.
Columbus, OH 43207 **(M)**

Waterloo Ind., Inc.
300 Ansborough Ave.
Waterloo, IA 50704 **(M)**

Wilcox Intl.
564 W. Randolph St.
Chicago, IL 60606 **(M)**

FURNITURE

Table Bases

Access Equip. Ltd.
Maylands Ave.
Hemel Hempstead
Hertfordshire, England **(M)**

Belmont Beauty and Barber
Equip.
17 W. 56 St.
New York, NY 10019 **(M)**

Business Equip., Inc.
2 Park Ave.
New York, NY 10016 **(W/R)**

Paul Dodds Co.
P.O. Box 342
Montvale, NJ 07645 **(M)**

Durkin Co., Inc.
222 Summer St.
Stamford, CT 06901 **(R)**
Restaurant bases

Falcon Products, Inc.
9387 Dielman Industrial Dr.
St. Louis, MO 63132 **(M)**

Sam Flax
55 E. 55 St.
New York, NY 10022 **(R)**

Bernard Franklin Co.
4424 Paul St.
Philadelphia, PA 19124 **(M)**

Hafele KG
P.O. Box 160
7270 Nagold, West Germany
   (M)

Intl. Contract Furnishings, Inc.
145 E. 57 St.
New York, NY 10022 **(W)**

Johnson Ind., Inc.
Elgin, IL 60120 **(M)**
Restaurant bases

L & B Products Corp.
3232 Lurting Ave.
Bronx, NY 10469 **(M)**
Restaurant bases

FALCON PRODUCTS, INC.

Kenneth Lynch and Sons
177 Factory Rd.
Wilton, CT 06897 **(M)**

J. A. Preston Corp.
71 Fifth Ave.
New York, NY 10003 **(M.O.)**
Hydraulic worktables

Thonet
491 E. Princess St.
York, PA 17405 **(M)**

Work & Dining Tables

Abaco Steel Products, Inc.
1560 Locust Ave.
Bohemia, NY 11716 **(W)**

Abitare
212 E. 57 St.
New York, NY 10022 **(R)**

Able Steel Equip. Co., Inc.
50-02 23 St.
Long Island City, NY 11101 **(W)**

Abstracta Structures, Inc.
101 Park Ave.
New York, NY 10017 **(M)**

Advance Seating & Equip. Co.
166 Fifth Ave.
New York, NY 10010 **(M)**

ADWE Hair Supply
141 20 St.
Brooklyn, NY 11232 **(M)**

Alden Systems Co., Inc.
P.O. Box A
Rte. 9 at 495
Westborough, MA 01581 **(M)**

Anthonsen & Kimmel
440 Park Ave. S.
New York, NY 10016 **(W)**

Architectural Supplements, Inc.
150 E. 58 St.
New York, NY 10022 **(W)**

August Froscher KG
Postfach 20
D-7141 Steinheim, Germany
   (M)

Bay Products Div.
American Metal Works, Inc.
8701 Torresdale Ave.
Philadelphia, PA 19136 **(M)**
Work benches in stock

Belmont Beauty and Barber
Equip.
17 W. 56 St.
New York, NY 10019 **(M)**

Belson Mfg. Co., Inc.
P.O. Box 207
North Aurora, IL 60542 **(M)**

Berc Antoine
10 et 12 boulevard
   Richard-Lenoir
Paris-Bastille, France **(M)**

Bieffeplast
P.O. Box 406
Padova, Italy **(M)**

Blickman Health Ind., Inc.
20-21 Wagaraw Rd.
Fair Lawn, NJ 07410 **(M)**

Walter A. Braun Co., Inc.
23 Mackay Ave.
P.O. Box 287
Paramus, NJ 07652 **(W)**

Bretford Mfg., Inc.
9715 Soreng Ave.
Schiller Park, IL 60176 **(M)**

C & H Distr., Inc.
401 S. 5 St.
Milwaukee, WI 53204 **(M.O.)**

POLLARD BROS. MFG. CO.

Charette Drafting Supply
Corp.
212 E. 54 St.
New York, NY 10021 (R)

31 Olympia Ave.
Woburn, MA 01801

1 Winthrop Sq.
Boston, MA 02110

44Brattle St.
Cambridge, MA 02138

Heinrich Wilhelm Dreyer
4515 Bad Essen
1/Wittlage, Germany (M)

Distributor: Vandermolen Corp.
119 Dorsa Ave.
Livingston, NJ 07039

Evans Metal Products, Inc.
432 Park Ave. S.
New York, NY 10016 (M)

Falcon Products, Inc.
9387 Dielman Industrial Dr.
St. Louis, MO 63132 (M)

Sam Flax
55 E. 55 St.
New York, NY 10022

Fort Steuben Metal Products Co.
P.O. Box 268
Weirton, WV 26062 (M)

Fuller Office Furniture Corp.
330 E. 59 St.
New York, NY 10022 (R)

J. L. Hammett Co.
Hammett Pl.
Braintree, MA 02184 (W)

Harvard Interiors Mfg. Co.
4321 Semple Ave.
St. Louis, MO 63120 (M)

Hertz Furniture Systems Co.
220 Fifth Ave.
New York, NY 10001 (R)

Homak Mfg. Co., Inc.
4433 S. Springfield Ave.
Chicago, IL 60632 (M)

ICF Intl. Contract Furnishings, Inc.
145 E. 57 St.
New York, NY 10022 (W)

Inter-Graph, Ltd.
979 Third Ave.
New York, NY 10022 (W)

Jasper Desk Co.
P.O. Box 111
Jasper, IN 47546 (M)

L & B PRODUCTS CORP./PHOTO TOM YEE

Johnson Ind., Inc.
Elgin, IL 60120 (M)

Krueger
P.O. Box 8100
Green Bay, WI 54308 (M)

H. Krug Furniture Co. Ltd.
111 Ahrens St. W.
Kitchener, Ontario
N2H 4C2 Canada (M)

L & B Products Corp.
3232 Lurting Ave.
Bronx, NY 10469 (M)

Lee's Art Shop
220 W. 57 St.
New York, NY 10019 (R)

A. Liss & Co.
35-03 Bradley Ave.
Long Island City, NY 11101 (W/M.O.)

Lister Park and Garden
Furniture
R.A. Lister Farm Equip. Ltd.
Dursley, Gloucestershire
GL11 4HS England (M)

Lyon Metal Products, Inc.
1933 Montgomery St.
Aurora, IL 60507 (M)

Manhattan Marine & Electric
Co., Inc.
116-118-120 Chambers St.
New York, NY 10007 (R)

Manutan
32 Bis, boulevard de Picpus
75012 Paris, France (W)

Marlo Mfg. Co., Inc.
140 Fifth Ave.
Hawthorne, NJ 07506 (M)

Mayline Co., Inc.
619 N. Commerce St.
Sheboygan, WI 53081 (M)

Mitchell Mfg. Co.
2778 S. 34 St.
Milwaukee, WI 53246 (M)

Plan Hold
17621 Von Karman Ave.
Irvine, CA 92714 (M)

Plasta-Flex, Inc.
105 Vance St.
P.O. Box 1004
Taylor, TX 76574 (M)

Pompanette, Inc.
1515 S.E. 16 St.
Fort Lauderdale, FL 33316 (R/W)

J. A. Preston Corp.
71 Fifth Ave.
New York, NY 10003 (M.O.)

3220 Wharton Way
Mississauga, Ontario
L4V 2C1 Canada

The Professional Kitchen
18 Cooper Sq.
New York, NY 10003 (R)

R & W Specialty Mfg. Corp.
502-512 Metropolitan Ave.
Brooklyn, NY 11211 (M)

Shelley Mfg. Co.
P.O. Box 440308
Miami, FL 33144 (M)

Shop-Vac Corp.
2323 Reach Rd.
Williamsport, PA 17701 (M)

SICO Inc.
7525 Cahill Rd.
Minneapolis, MN 55435 (M)

Spiral Steel Products Corp.
32-15 58 St.
Woodside, NY 11377 (W)

Steele Canvas Basket Co.,
Inc.
199 Concord Turnpike
Cambridge, MA 02140 (M)

Takara Belmont
1 Belmont Dr.
Somerset, NJ 08873 (M)
Adjustable-height bases

Thonet Ind., Inc.
491 E. Princess St.
York, PA 17405 (M)

Vandermolen Corp.
119 Dorsa Ave.
Livingston, NJ 07039 (W)

N. Wasserstrom and Sons,
Inc.
2300 Lockbourne Rd.
Columbus, OH 43207 (M)

Wilcox Intl.
564 W. Randolph
Chicago, IL 60606 (M)

Paul Zell Designs, Inc.
151 Union St.
San Francisco, CA 94111 (M)

Sitting Up

Abitare
212 E. 57 St.
New York, NY 10022 (R)

Advance Seating & Equip. Co.
166 Fifth Ave.
New York, NY 10010 (M)

A & E Restaurant and Bar
Mfg. Co.
379 Suydam St.
Brooklyn, NY 11237 (M)

Ajusto Equip. Co.
20163 Harkins Rd.
Bowling Green, OH 43402 (M)

Alfredo
Centrol Ind. Europeo
22078 Turate, Italy (M)

Maurice Drucker
Ameublement en Rotin
166 rue Gerard-de-Seroux
60320 Bethisy, St. Martin,
France (M)
Rattan café chairs

Anthonsen & Kimmel
440 Park Ave. S.
New York, NY 10016 (W)

Architectural Supplements,
Inc.
150 E. 58 St.
New York, NY 10022 (W)

Macy's
Herald Square
New York, NY 10001 (R)
Tractor seats

L. L. Bean, Inc.
Freeport, ME 04033 **(M.O.)**

Berc Antoine
10 et 12 boulevard
 Richard-Lenoir
Paris-Bastille, France **(M)**

Brady
5921 W. Dickens Ave.
Chicago, IL 60639 **(M)**

Walter A. Braun Co., Inc.
23 Mackay Ave.
P.O. Box 287
Paramus, NJ 07652 **(W)**

Britt Ind.
420 W. Florida St.
Milwaukee, WI 53204 **(M)**
Tractor seats

Browne-Morse Co.
Muskegon, MI 49443 **(M)**

C & H Distr. Inc.
401 S. Fifth St.
Milwaukee, WI 53204 **(M.O.)**

Chairmasters
200 E. 146 St.
Bronx, NY 10451 **(M)**

Charette Drafting Supply
 Corp.
212 E. 54 St.
New York, NY 10021 **(R)**

 44 Brattle St.
 Cambridge, MA 02138

 1 Winthrop Sq.
 Boston, MA 02110

 31 Olympia Ave.
 Woburn, MA 01801

Conran's
160 E. 54 St.
New York, NY 10022 **(R)**

Cosco Business Furniture
Gallatin, TN 37066 **(M)**

Defender Ind., Inc.
255 Main St.
New Rochelle, NY 10801
 (M.O.)

D/R
Design Research
53 E. 57 St.
New York, NY 10022 **(R)**

Paul Dodds Co.
P.O. Box 342
Montvale, NJ 07645 **(M)**

Heinrich Wilhelm Dreyer
4515 Bad Essen
1/Wittlage, Germany **(M)**

 Distributor: Vandermolen Corp.
 119 Dorsa Ave.
 Livingston, NJ 07039 **(W)**

Evans Metal Products, Inc.
432 Park Ave. S.
New York, NY 10016 **(M)**

Falcon Products, Inc.
9387 Dielman Industrial Dr.
St. Louis, MO 63132 **(M)**

Sam Flax
55 E. 55 St.
New York, NY 10022 **(R)**

August Froscher KG
Postfach 20
D-7141 Steinheim, Germany **(M)**

Fuller
45 E. 57 St.
New York, NY 10022 **(R)**

GF Business Equip., Inc.
200 Park Ave.
New York, NY 10017 **(M)**

Gruppos Industriale
Via C. Colombo 53
35043 Monselice, Italy **(M)**

G. S. Assoc.
150 E. 58 St.
New York, NY 10022 **(M/W)**
Tractor seat stools

Hafele KG
P.O. Box 160
7270 Nagold, West Germany **(M)**

Harvard Interiors Mfg. Co.
4321 Semple Ave.
St. Louis, MO 63120 **(M)**

Hertz Furniture Systems Co.
220 Fifth Ave.
New York, NY 10001 **(W)**

Hussey Mfg. Co.
593 Railroad Ave.
North Berwick, ME 03906 **(M)**

Jasper Seating Co.
Jasper, IN 47546 **(M)**

Krueger
P.O. Box 8100
Green Bay, WI 54308 **(M)**

H. Krug Furniture Co. Ltd.
111 Ahrens St. W.
Kitchener, Ontario
N2H 4C2 Canada **(M)**

AJUSTO EQUIPMENT CO.

L & B Products Corp.
3232 Lurting Ave.
Bronx, NY 10469 **(M)**

Hank Loewenstein, Inc.
3105 S.W. Second Ave.
Fort Lauderdale, FL 33315
 (W)

Lyon Metal Products
1933 Montgomery St.
Aurora, IL 60507 **(M)**

Manhattan Marine & Electric
 Co., Inc.
116-118-120 Chambers St.
New York, NY 10007 **(R)**

Manutan
32 Bis, boulevard de Picpus
75012 Paris, France **(W)**

Mitchell Mfg. Co.
2778 S. 34 St.
Milwaukee, WI 53215 **(M)**

Northwest Mfg. & Supply Co.
315 N. Leavitt St.
Chicago, IL 60612 **(R)**
Folding aluminum stool

Pallet Sales
132 DuPont St.
Plainview, NY 11803 **(W)**

Penco Products, Inc.
Oaks, PA 19456 **(M)**

W. G. Phillis
144 Vonachen Ct.
East Peoria, IL 61611 **(R)**
New and used tractor seats

Planula
Agliana,
Pistoia, Italy **(M)**

Pompanette, Inc.
1515 S.E. 16 St.
Fort Lauderdale, FL 33316 **(R)**

J. A. Preston Corp.
71 Fifth Ave.
New York, NY 10003 **(M.O.)**

Prince Castle, Inc.
426 Westgate Dr.
Addison, IL 60101 **(M)**

R & G Affiliates
205 Lexington Ave.
New York, NY 10016 **(M)**

Shure Mfg. Corp.
1601 S. Hanley Rd.
St. Louis, MO 63144 **(M)**

SICO, Inc.
7525 Cahill Rd.
Minneapolis, MN 55435 **(M)**

Simpson Bosworth Co.
2531 N. Ashland Ave.
Chicago, IL 60614 **(M)**

Waldner's
222 Old Country Rd.
Mineola, NY 11501 **(R)**

 920 Conklin St.
 Farmingdale, NY 11735

Wilkhahn
3252 Bad Munder 2
Postfach 2070
Germany **(M)**

Workbench
470 Park Ave. S.
New York, NY 10016 **(R)**
Bank of England chairs

Benches

Able Steel Equip. Co., Inc.
50-02 23 St.
Long Island City, NY 11101
 (M)

Ascot Steel Equip. Co., Inc.
45-35 39 St.
Long Island City, NY 11104
 (W)

Belson Mfg. Co., Inc.
P.O. Box 207
North Aurora, IL 60542 **(M)**

Walter A. Braun Co., Inc.
23 Mackay Ave.
P.O. Box 287
Paramus, NJ 07652 **(W)**

C & H Distr., Inc.
401 S. Fifth St.
Milwaukee, WI 53204 **(M.O.)**

Bernard Franklin Co.
4424 Paul St.
Philadelphia, PA 19124 (M)

Gargoyles, Ltd.
512 S. Third St.
Philadelphia, PA 19147 (W/R)

Hertz Furniture Systems Co.
220 Fifth Ave.
New York, NY 10001 (W)

Howmet Corp.
P.O. Box 40
Magnolia, AR 71753 (M)
Stadium park-benches

Hussey Mfg. Co.
593 Railroad Ave.
North Berwick, ME 03906 (M)

Lister Park and Garden
  Furniture
R.A. Lister Farm Equip. Ltd.
Dursley, Gloucestershire,
GL11 4HS England (M)

Lyon Metal Products, Inc.
1933 Montgomery St.
Aurora, IL 60507 (M)

Medart
9701 Higgins Rd.
Suite 216
Rosemont, IL 60018 (M)

Miracle & Jamison
Miracle Recreation Equip. Co.
P.O. Box 275
Grinnell, IA 50112 (M)

Mitchell Mfg. Co.
2778 S. 34 St.
Milwaukee, WI 53246 (M)

William Page & Co. Ltd.
87-91 Shaftesbury Ave.
London W1V 8AJ England (M)

VERTEBRA CHAIR, KRUEGER

Rosenwach, Inc.
96 N. 9 St.
Brooklyn, NY 11211 (M)
Redwood benches

R & W Specialty Mfg. Corp.
502-512 Metropolitan Ave.
Brooklyn, NY 11211 (M)

SICO, Inc.
7525 Cahill Rd.
Minneapolis, MN 55435 (M)

Standard Steel Ind., Inc.
Three Rivers, MI 49093 (M)

Steele Canvas Basket Co.
199 Concord Turnpike
Cambridge, MA 02140 (M)

Sitting Down

Abacus Municipal Ltd.
Sutton-in-Ashfield
NG17 5FT England (M)

Anthonsen & Kimmel
440 Park Ave. S.
New York, NY 10016 (W)

Architectural Supplements,
  Inc.
150 E. 58 St.
New York, NY 10022 (W)

Auto World
701 N. Keyser Ave.
Scranton, PA 18508 (R)

L. L. Bean, Inc.
Freeport, ME 04033 (M.O.)
Canoe seat

Berc Antoine
10 et 12 boulevard
  Richard-Lenoir
Paris-Bastille, France (M)

Fairchild Burns Co.
1455 Fairchild Dr.
Winston-Salem, NC 27105
  (M)
Aircraft seats

Falcon Products, Inc.
9387 Dielman Industrial Dr.
St. Louis, MO 63132 (M)

Sam Flax
55 E. 55 St.
New York, NY 10022 (R)

August Froscher KG
Postfach 20
D-7141 Steinheim
Germany (M)

FALCON PRODUCTS, INC.

Harvard Interiors Mfg. Co.
4321 Semple Ave.
St. Louis, MO 63120 (M)

H.U.D.D.L.E.
3416 Wesley St.
Culver City, CA 90230 (M)

Jandy Intl.
152 W. Cypress Ave.
Burbank, CA 91502 (M)

H. Krug Furniture Co. Ltd.
111 Ahrens St. S.
Kitchener, Ontario
N2H 4C2 Canada (M)

L & B Products Corp.
3232 Lurting Ave.
Bronx, NY 10469 (M)

MacLevy Products Corp.
92-21 Corona Ave.
Elmhurst, NY 11373 (M)

Manutan
32 Bis, boulevard de Picpus
75012 Paris, France (W)

Recreation Equip. Corp.
724 W. 8 St.
Anderson, IN 46011 (M)

Scheel California Ltd, Inc.
1007 S. Fremont Ave.
Alhambra, CA 91801 (M)
Bucket seats

Seats Inc.
350 N. Dewey Ave.
Reedsburg, WI 53959 (M)
Bucket seats

Shure Mfg. Corp.
1601 S. Hanley Rd.
St. Louis, MO 63144 (M)

Takara Belmont
1 Belmont Dr.
Somerset, NJ 08873 (M)
Beauty salon chairs

Uniroyal Ltd.
General Products Div.
Kitchener, Ontario
N2H 5G5 Canada (M)

J. C. Whitney & Co.
1917-19 Archer Ave.
P.O. Box 8410
Chicago, IL 60680 (R)

Wilkhahn
3252 Bad Munder 2
Postfach 2070
Germany (M)

Rolling Tables

Bloomfield Ind.
4546 W. 47 St.
Chicago, IL 60632 (M)

Bonus-Bilt, Inc.
1096 Air Way
Glendale, CA 91201 (M)

Institutional Industries
5500 Muddy Creek Rd.
Cincinnati, OH 45238 (M)

Lakeside Mfg., Inc.
1977 S. Allis St.
Milwaukee, WI 53207 (M)

Manhattan Ad Hoc House-
  wares
842 Lexington Ave.
New York, NY 10021 (R)

Manutan
32 bis, boulevard de Picpus
75012 Paris, France (W)

Marlo Mfg. Co., Inc.
140 Fifth Ave.
Hawthorne, NJ 07506 (M)

William Page & Co. Ltd.
87-91 Shaftesbury Ave.
London W1V 8AJ England (M)

Professional Mortuary Supply
  Co.
49B W. Merrick Rd.
Freeport, NY 11520 (M)

G. Rushbrooke (Smithfield)
  Ltd.
67/77 Charterhouse St.
London EC1M 6HL England
  (R)

Shelley Mfg. Co.
P.O. Box 440308
Miami, FL 33144 (M)

Arthur H. Thomas Co.
Vine St. at Third
P.O. Box 779
Philadelphia, PA 19105 (M.O.)

LAKESIDE MFG., INC.

N. Wasserstrom and Sons,
Inc.
2300 Lockbourne Rd.
Columbus, OH 43207 **(M)**

H. Wilson Corp.
555 W. Taft Dr.
South Holland, IL 60473 **(M)**

Beds and Linens

AMF
American Athletic Equip.
200 American Ave.
Jefferson, IA 50129 **(M)**
*Landing mats and skill
cushions*

Art et Industrie
132 Thompson St.
New York, NY 10013 **(R)**

The Astrup Co.
2937 W. 25 St.
Cleveland, OH 44113 **(M)**

L. L. Bean, Inc.
Freeport, ME 04033 **(R)**

Best Hosp. Supply
Div. of Best Mfg., Inc.
32-01 57 St.
Woodside, NY 11377 **(M)**

Childcraft Inc.
Kilmer Road
Edison, NJ 08817 **(M)**

Childcraft Center
150 E. 58 St.
New York, NY 10022 **(R)**

Chris-Craft
Algonac, MI 48001 **(M.O.)**

Comfort Ind., Inc.
39-35 21 St.
Long Island City, NY 11101
(M/W)

Crest-Foam Corp.
100 Carol Pl.
Moonachie, NJ **(M/W)**

Defender Ind., Inc.
255 Main St.
New Rochelle, NY 10801
(M.O.)

Dixie Foam
20 E. 20 St.
New York, NY 10003 **(M)**

Economy Foam Center
173 E. Houston St.
New York, NY 10002 **(M/W)**

Foam-Tex
51 E. 21 St.
New York, NY 10010 **(M/W)**

Frank A. Hall & Sons
969 Third Ave.
New York, NY 10022 **(W)**
Electric beds

Herman's World of Sporting
Goods
1114 Ave. of the Americas
New York, NY 10036 **(R)**

H.U.D.D.L.E.
3416 Wesley St.
Culver City, CA 90230 **(M)**

Inner Space Foam Center
34 Ave. A
New York, NY 10009 **(M/W)**

Karoll's, Inc.
32 N. State St.
Chicago, IL 60602 **(M)**

M. J. Knoud, Inc.
716 Madison Ave.
New York, NY 10021 **(R)**
Horse blankets

Leisure-Matic Bed
58 Garrett Rd.
Upper Darby, PA 19082 **(M)**

MacLevy Products Corp.
92-21 Corona Ave.
Elmhurst, NY 11373 **(W/R)**
*Exercise mats and massage
tables*

Manhattan Ad Hoc House-
wares
842 Lexington Ave.
New York, NY 10021 **(R)**

Mason Rubber Co.
115 W. 27 St.
New York, NY 10001 **(M/W)**

Mellor Gym Supply Corp.
9 E. 40 St.
New York, NY 10016 **(W)**
Exercise mats

Oxford Metal Products Co.,
Inc.
2629-33 Belgrade St.
Philadelphia, PA 19125 **(M)**

J. A. Preston Corp.
71 Fifth Ave.
New York, NY 10003 **(M.O.)**

3220 Wharton Way
Mississauga, Ontario
L4V 2C1 Canada
*Pediatric resting cots and
hospital beds*

Simmons Commercial Prod.
Thonet
491 E. Princess St.
York, PA 17405 **(M)**

L. W. Sleepwell Warehouse
456 Johnson Ave.
Brooklyn, NY 11237 **(W)**
*New and used hospital
furniture*

A. Wittenberg
1400 Madison Ave.
New York, NY 10029 **(R)**
Electric beds

Outdoor Furniture

B. Altman & Co.
Fifth Ave. & 34 St.
New York, NY 10001 **(R)**
French park furniture

American Playground Device Co.
Drawer 2599
Anderson, IN 46011 **(M)**

Bailey-Huebner
Henri Bendel
10 W. 57 St.
New York, NY 10019 **(R)**

Belson Mfg. Co., Inc.
P.O. Box 207
North Aurora, IL 60542 **(M)**

Carefree of Colorado
2760 Industrial La.
Broomfield, CO 80020 **(M)**

Defender Ind., Inc.
255 Main St.
New Rochelle, NY 10801 **(M.O.)**

D/R
Design Research
53 E. 57 St.
New York, NY 10022 **(R)**

Georgia Marble Co.
2575 Cumberland Pkwy.
Northwest Atlanta, GA 30339
(M)

Hertz Furniture Systems, Co.
220 Fifth Ave.
New York, NY 10001 **(W)**

Howmet Corp.
P.O. Box 40
Magnolia, AR 71753 **(M)**
Stadium and park furniture

Ingo Maurer GmbH
Kaiserstrasse 47
8 Munich
Germany **(M)**

R. A. Lister Farm Equip. Ltd.
Dursle, Gloucestershire
GL 11 4HS England **(M)**

Kenneth Lynch and Sons
177 Factory Rd.
Wilton, CT 06897 **(M)**

William Page & Co. Ltd.
87-91 Shaftesbury Ave.
London W1V 8AJ England **(M)**

Recreation Equip. Corp.
724 W. 8 St.
Anderson, IN 46011 **(M)**

Stapo Ind., Inc.
10 W. 33 St.
New York, NY 10001 **(M)**

Sun & Leisure
200 Lexington Ave.
New York, NY 10016 **(W)**
Fiber-glass chaises

Williams-Sonoma
P.O. Box 3792
San Francisco, CA 94119 **(M.O.)**

Zip-Jack Umbrella Co.
703 E. Tremont Ave.
Bronx, NY 10457 **(M)**
Advertising umbrellas

BRADLEY CORP.

Conversions

Abbott & Abbott Box Corp.
28-31 Borden Ave.
Long Island City, NY 11101
(M)

American Racing
2500 A. Hamilton Blvd.
South Plainfield, NJ 07080 **(M)**
Wheels

Bretford Mfg., Inc.
9715 Soreng Ave.
Schiller Park, IL 60176 **(M)**
Cassette storage bases

Bob Calimer Carriage and
  Wheel Shop
30 E. North St.
Waynesboro, PA 17268 **(R)**
Wood wheels

Fuller Stationers
45 E. 57 St.
New York, NY 10022 **(R)**

Harbor Pallet Co.
1516 W. Embassy St.
Anaheim, CA 92803 **(M)**

Hinchcliff Products Co.
20600 Westwood Dr.
Cleveland, OH 44136 **(M)**
Pallets

Lehner and Putz
Rohrbach
Lafnitz, Austria **(M)**
Pallets

Manustock
LeTeich, France **(M)**
Pallets

Masonville Garage
Box 57-OC
Masonville, IA 50654 **(R)**
Wheels

Orangeville Mfg. Co., Inc.
Orangeville, PA 17859 **(M)**

Pennsylvania Pacific Corp.
Pennpac & Pennbox Divs.
John Fitch Industrial Pk.
Warminster, PA 18974 **(M)**
Pallets

Tilgate Pallets Ltd.
Crawley
West Sussex, England **(M)**

Unit Pallets Ltd.
Manchester, England **(M)**

Wheel Repair Service, Inc.
Dept. H.
176 Grove St.
Paxton, MA 01612 **(R)**

J. C. Whitney & Co.
1917-19 Archer Ave.
P.O. Box 8410
Chicago, IL 60680 **(R)**
Automotive catalog

MATERIALS

Sonotubes

Sonoco Products Co.
Main Office
Hartsville, SC 29550 **(M)**

  Distributors:
  Black Brollier Bldg. Material Co.
  P.O. Box 20069
  Houston, TX 77025

  Blue Diamond Co.
  2722 Logan St.
  Dallas, TX 75215

  Burke Co.
  P.O. Box 5818
  San Mateo, CA 94402

  Forms Equip. Corp.
  1585 Sycamore Ave.
  Bohemia, NY 11716

  Gateway Bldg. Products
  3233 W. Grand
  Chicago, IL 60651

  Gateway Bldg. Products
  9734 Gravois
  St. Louis, MO 63123

  A. H. Harris & Sons, Inc. of N.Y.
  55 Sicker Rd.
  Latham, NY 12110

  Keystone Bldrs. Supply
  85 Palm St.
  Rochester, NY 14615

  Lance Construction Supplies
  4225 W. Ogden Ave.
  Chicago, IL 60623

  Natl. Construction
    Specialities
  P.O. Box 570
  Dearborn, MI 48121

Raw Equip. Co.
Box 271
Bayside, NY 11361

TOOBLINE System
H.U.D.D.L.E.
3416 Wesley St.
Culver City, CA 90230 **(M)**

Waldo Brothers
202 Southampton St.
Boston, MA 02118

Tops

A & E Restaurant and Bar
  Mfg. Co.
379 Suydam St.
Brooklyn, NY 11237 **(M)**
Stainless steel tops

Art et Industrie
132 Thompson St.
New York, NY 10013 **(R)**
Wire-glass tabletops

Asbeka Ind. of N.Y., Inc.
2324 McDonald Ave.
Brooklyn, NY 11223 **(M)**

David Fabricators of N.Y., Inc.
595 Berriman St.
Brooklyn, NY 11208 **(M)**
Laboratory surfaces

Du Pont Co.
Room 25380
Wilmington, DE 19898 **(M)**
Manufacturers of Corian

Duralab Equip. Corp.
10723 Farragut Rd.
Brooklyn, NY 11236 **(M)**
Laboratory furniture

Falcon Products, Inc.
9387 Dielman Industrial Dr.
St. Louis, MO 63132 **(M)**

Sam Flax
55 E. 55 St.
New York, NY 10022 **(R)**

Johns-Manville
Greenwood Plaza
Denver, CO 80217 **(M)**
Colorlith and Colorceran

Johnson Industries
Distributer
Durkin Co. Inc.
222 Summer St.
Stamford, CT 06901 **(R)**

L & B Products Corp.
3232 Lurting Ave.
Bronx, NY 10469 **(M)**
Restaurant tables

Fabrics

Acme Stayput Pad Co.
295 Fifth Ave.
New York, NY 10016 **(M)**
Furniture pads

Accurate Flannel Bag Co.
109 W. 26 St.
New York, NY 10001 **(M)**
Makes "Silverpak"

Alan-Clarke Sailmakers, Inc.
220 Rte. 25A
Northport, NY 11768 **(M)**

B. Altman & Co.
Fifth Ave. & 34 St.
New York, NY 10001 **(R)**
Carries Pacific Silvercloth

Aquino Sailcloth, Inc.
225 Fordham St.
City Island, NY 10464 **(M)**

Belleville Wire Cloth Co., Inc.
137 Little St.
Belleville, NJ 07109 **(M)**

Joel Berman Assoc., Inc.
102 Prince St.
New York, NY 10012 **(M/W)**
Makers of "Stretchwall"

John Boyle & Co., Inc.
112-114 Duane St.
New York, NY 10007 **(M)**

  70-72 Reade St.
  New York, NY 10007

  7455 Washington St.
  Pittsburgh, PA 15218

  2007-2009 Locust St.
  St. Louis, MO 63103

Canvas Specialty Co., Inc.
54 W. 21 St.
New York, NY 10010 **(M)**

C & H Distr., Inc.
201 S. 5 St.
Milwaukee, WI 53204 **(M.O.)**
Canvas tarps

Duracote Corp.
350 N. Diamond St.
Ravenna, OH 44266 **(M)**
*Makes foil-laminated,
  reinforced fabrics*

FYREPEL

Elkay Products Co., Inc.
35 Brown Ave.
Springfield, NJ 07081 **(M)**
Movers pads

Etalage Fabrics, Inc.
979 Third Ave.
New York, NY 10022 **(W)**
Quilting in "industrial" patterns

Fogh Sails East, Inc.
1001 Roosevelt Ave.
Carteret, NJ 07008 **(M)**

Fyrepel
Box 518
Newark, OH 43055 **(M)**
Aluminized fabric

Gioia Sails, Inc.
459 City Island Ave.
Bronx, NY 10464 **(M)**

Hild Sails, Inc.
225 Fordham St.
City Island, NY 10464 **(M)**

IDEN
7520 W. Central Ave.
River Forest, IL 60305 **(M)**
Furniture pads

Ind. Plastic Supply Co.
309 Canal St.
New York, NY 10013 **(M)**
Carries fiber-glass screenings

Island Nautical, Inc.
225 Fordham St.
City Island, NY 10464 **(M)**

Janos Ind. Insulation Corp.
80 W. Commercial Ave.
Moonachie, NJ 07074 **(M)**
Asbestos substitutes

La Lame, Inc.
1170 Broadway
New York, NY 10001 **(M)**

Lawrence Piller, Inc.
2351 Bedford Ave.
Brooklyn, NY 11226 **(M)**
Furniture pads and covers

New Haven Moving Equip. Corp.
37 Washington
East Haven, CT 06512 **(M)**
Furniture pads

Nollet et Fils
33, rue de la Vigne
Roubaix 59100 France **(M)**
Blankets, upholstery fabrics

Owens-Corning Fiberglas Corp.
717 Fifth Ave.
New York, NY 10022 **(M)**

Pellon Corp.
Consumer Products Div.
491 Dutton St.
Lowell, MA 01852 **(M)**
Artist's canvas

Ratsey & Lapthorn, Inc.
Schofield St.
Bronx, NY 10464 **(M)**
Sailmaker

Rennert Intl. Corp.
93-99 Greene St.
New York, NY 10012 **(M)**
Furniture pads

Rinascente Dept. Store
Milan, Italy **(R)**
Silver polishing cloth

Ben Rose
Space 11-123 Merchandise Mart
Chicago, IL 60654 **(W)**

 D & D Bldg.
 979 Third Ave.
 New York, NY 10022

 Space 211 Pacific Design Ctr.
 Los Angeles, CA 90069

 2010 Winrock
 Houston, TX 77027

Isabel Scott
979 Third Ave.
New York, NY 10022 **(W)**
Fiber-glass screening

Shore Sails
645 New York Ave.
Huntington, NY 11743

J. P. Stevens & Co.
Ind. Glass Fabrics Dept.
1460 Broadway
New York, NY 10036 **(M)**

Tetko Wire Cloth
Elmsford, NY 10523 **(M)**

Ulmer Chas Inc.
175 City Island Ave.
Bronx, NY 10464 **(M)**
Sailmaker

United Textile Corp.
20 Universal Pl.
Carlstadt, NJ 07072 **(M)**

Vallentine G. W. & Son
135 City Island Ave.
Bronx, NY 10464 **(M)**
Sailmaker

Village Stripper
519 Hudson St.
New York, NY 10014 **(R)**
Movers pads

Wamsutta Specialty Products
 Group
1430 Broadway
New York, NY 10018 **(M)**
Pacific Silvercloth

"Industrial" Carpet

Allied Mat & Matting Inc.
476 Broome St.
New York, NY 10013 **(W)**
Sisal

American Cyanamid Co.
Berdam Ave.
Wayne, NJ 07470 **(M)**

Bigelow
330 Madison Ave.
New York, NY 10017 **(M)**

The Carpet Loft
161 Ave. of the Americas
New York, NY 10014 **(R)**

Century Carpet
68 E. 56 St.
New York, NY 10022 **(W)**

Chevron Chemical Co.
Fibers Div.
Glen Burnie, MD 21061 **(M)**
Synthetic grass

Conran's
160 E. 54 St.
New York, NY 10022 **(R)**
Sisal by the yard

Deering Milliken, Inc.
Floor Covering Business
LaGrange, GA 30240 **(M)**

Dow Badische Co.
P.O. Drawer D
Williamsburg, VA 23185 **(M)**

General Felt Ind., Inc.
Park 80 Plaza W. One
Saddle Brook, NJ 07662 **(M)**

Heuga U.S.A., Inc.
185 Summer Ave.
Kenilworth, NJ 07033 **(M)**

ICF Int'l. Inc.
145 E. 57 St.
New York, NY 10022 **(W)**

Import Specialists, Inc.
82 Wall St.
New York, NY 10005 **(M/W)**
Cocoa matting importers

Koffler Sales Corp.
4501 Lincoln Ave.
Chicago, IL 60625 **(W/M.O.)**
*Importer of cocoa mats and
 matting*

Jack Lenor Larsen
232 E. 58 St.
New York, NY 10022 **(W)**

Lasher Carpet Co.
444 Madison Ave.
New York, NY 10022 **(W)**

Lees Carpet
Burlington Ind., Inc.
Bridgeport, PA 19405 **(M)**

Ozite Corp.
1755 Butterfield Rd.
Libertyville, IL 60048 **(M)**

Patterson Flynn & Martin
979 Third Ave.
New York, NY 10022 **(W)**

Rittenhouse Carpets, Inc.
1712 Walnut St.
Philadelphia, PA 19103 **(W/R)**
Tretford carpet

West Point Pepperell
Carpet and Rug Div.
Dalton, GA 30720 **(M)**

THE HIGH-TECH DIRECTORY

Window Dressing

Abingdon Mfg. Co.
232 7th Ave.
New York, NY 10011 **(M/W)**
Transparent shades

Ambienti Design
792 Madison Ave.
New York, NY 10021 **(R)**
Telos curtain system

Amelco Window Corp.
Box 32 *(516) 759-1049*
Glen Cove, NY 11542 **(M)**

Joel Berman Assoc., Inc.
102 Prince St.
New York, NY 10012 **(M)**

Bronx Window Shade Co.
372 E. 162 St.
Bronx, NY 10451 **(M)**
Pleated shades and awnings

Castelli Furniture
950 Third Ave.
New York, NY 10022 **(W)**
Telos curtain system

Clear View Shade Co.
6124-26 N. Broadway
Chicago, IL 60660 **(M/R)**
Transparent shades

Dillon Construction Co.
125 N. Lafayette Ave.
Ventnor, NJ 08046 **(M)**
Roll-a-way shutters

Faber Blinds Ltd.
Viking House
Kangley Bridge Rd.
Sydenham Kent SE26
England **(M)**
Venetian blinds

Flexalum Decor Blinds
Hunter Douglas, Inc.
20 Campus Rd.
Totowa, NJ 07512 **(M)**

Graber
Executive Offices
Middleton, WI 53562 **(M)**
Drapery hardware

Holland Shade Co., Inc.
306 E. 61 St.
New York, NY 10021 **(M)**

Liken Home Furniture
7411 Lorge Cir.
P.O. Box 2450
Huntington Beach, CA 92647 **(W)**
Verosol SunScreen

LouverDrape, Inc.
P.O. Box 1685
1100 Colorado Ave.
Santa Monica, CA 90401 **(M)**

W. B. McGuire Co., Inc.
1 Hudson Ave.
Hudson, NY 12534 **(M)**

Manutan
32 bis, boulevard de Picpus
75012, Paris, France **(W)**

Melrose Shade Co.
6614 Melrose Ave.
Los Angeles, CA 90038 **(W/R)**
Transparent shades

National Temp-Trol Prod. Corp.
2405-11 N. Milwaukee
Chicago, IL 60647 **(M/R)**
Transparent shades

Nissen & Co.
5312 E. Beverly Blvd.
Los Angeles, CA 90022 **(M)**
Divider curtains

Owens-Corning Fiberglas Corp.
Fiberglas Tower
Toledo, OH 43659 **(M)**

Owens-Corning Fiberglas Corp.
Decorative & Home
  Furnishings
717 Fifth Ave.
New York, NY 10022 **(M)**

The Peelle Co.
50 Inez Pathway
Bay Shore, NY 11706 **(M)**

The Peelle Company Ltd.
7415 Torbram Rd.
Mississauga Ontario
L4T 1G8 Canada

The Richmond Fireproof
  Door Div. of the
  Peelle Co.
P.O. Box 1265
Richmond, IN 47374

PPG Ind., Inc.
Fiber Glass Div.
1 Gateway Ctr.
Pittsburgh, PA 15222 **(M)**

Isabel Scott Fabrics
125 Newtown Rd.
Plainview, NY 11803 **(W)**

Solar Screen
53-11 105 St.
Corona, NY 11201 **(M/W)**
Transparent shades

Tetko Wire Cloth Co.
420 Sawmill River Rd.
Elmsford, NY 10523 **(M/W)**

Transparent Shade Co.
501 N. Figeros St.
Los Angeles, CA 90012 **(R)**
Transparent shades

Verosol U.S.A., Inc.
252 Nassau St.
Princeton, NJ 08540 **(W)**
Pleated shades

Verosol
P.O. Box 34
Enschede, Holland **(M)**
Pleated shades

Verticals, Inc.
704 E. 133 St.
New York, NY 10454 **(M)**
Vertical blinds

Metals

Abbingdon Ceiling Co., Inc.
2149 Utica Ave.
Brooklyn, NY 11234 **(W)**

Adam Metal Supply
625 Evans St.
Elizabeth, NJ 07072 **(M)**

Alan Wood Steel Co.
Wood Rd.
Conshohocken, PA 19428 **(M)**
Super Diamond Floor Plate

Alloy Steel-Tool Steel
Orient Way
Lyndhurst, NJ 07071 **(M)**

Alpro Acoustics Div.
Structural Systems Corp.
P.O. Box 30460
New Orleans, LA 70190 **(M)**

American Metal Restaurant
  Equip. Co.
43-04 19 Ave.
Long Island City, NY 11105
  (M)
Quilted metal

Architectural Bronze &
  Aluminum Corp.
3638 W. Oakton St.
Skokie, IL 60076 **(M)**

Arrow Metal Ceiling Co.
303 E. 119th St.
New York, NY 10035 **(R)**

Athos Steel & Aluminum, Inc.
Grand Ave. & Rome St.
Farmingdale, NY 11735 **(W)**

Barney Brainum-Shanker
  Steel
70-32 83 St.
Glendale, NY 11227 **(M)**
Pressed-tin ceilings

Beckley Perforating
Garwood, NJ 07027 **(M)**
Perforated metals

Bethlehem Steel
Martin Tower
Bethlehem, PA 18016 **(M)**

Bushwick Iron & Steel
Borden Ave. & 31 St.
Long Island City, NY 11101
  (W)

Central Metal Ceiling Co.
1200 Gates Ave.
Brooklyn, NY 11221 **(W)**

Colonial Moulding & Frame
  Co., Inc.
37 E. 18 St.
New York, NY 10003 **(M)**

Colorguard Corp.
1 Johnson Dr.
Raritan, NJ 08869 **(M)**

Corrugated Metals, Inc.
P.O. Box 465
First & Washington Sts.
Jersey City, NJ 07303 **(M)**

Dominion Fence, Ltd.
2400 Stone Mountain Rd.
Lithonia, GA 30058
Cyclone fencing

Dominion Fence & Wire, Ltd.
P.O. Box 43
Plainfield, IL 60544

Dominion Fence & Wire
  Products Ltd.
40 Glidden Rd.
Bramalea, Ontario L6T 2H7
  Canada **(M)**

Hunter Douglas
400 W. Main St.
Durham, NC 27701 **(M)**
Aluminum siding

Dynaflair Corp.
555 Broad Hollow Rd.
Suite 104
Melville, NY 11746

Dynaflair Corp. Ltd.
108 Nordic Ave.
Pointe Clair, Quebec
H9R 3Y2 Canada

Dynaflair Corp. Ltd.
Suite 214, 159 Bay St.
Toronto, Ontario M5J 1J7
 Canada

Eastern Stainless Steel Co.
Div. of Eastmet Corp.
P.O. Box 1975
Baltimore, MD 21203 **(M)**
Dock plate

District Sales Offices:
Suite 136-2971 Flowers Rd.
Atlanta, GA 30341

4100 Executive Pk. Dr.
Cincinnati, OH 45241

5959 W. Loop South—Suite
 500
Houston, TX 77401

Suite 820-6055 E. Wash-
 ington Blvd.
Los Angeles, CA 90040

Executive Towers
1301 W. 22 St.
Oakbrook, IL 60521

SVC Bldg. 14 Washington Rd.
Princeton, NJ 08550

Suite 103-940 W. Port Plaza
St. Louis, MO 63141

ECOA, Equip. Co. of America
4077 Hialeah Dr.
Hialeah, FL 33010 **(M)**
Dock plate

Equipto
225 S. Highland Ave.
Aurora, IL 60507 **(M)**

Fisher Bros. Steel Corp.
502 Nordhoff Pl.
Englewood, NJ 07631 **(M)**

Forms & Surfaces
Box 5215
Santa Barbara, CA 93108 **(M)**

Theodore J. Fuchs, Inc.
205 E. 78 St.
New York, NY 10021 **(M)**

Gargoyles, Ltd.
Sharpstown Ctr.
Houston, TX 77036 **(R/W)**
Tin ceilings

General Wire & Cable Co. Ltd.
609 William St.
Cobourg, Ontario, Canada **(M)**
Vinylink fencing

Ideal Stainless Supply Co., Inc.
1860 Midtown Rd.
Ronkonkoma, NY 11779 **(M)**

Inland Steel Co.
30 W. Monroe St.
Chicago, IL 60603 **(M)**
Component building systems

Inryco
Inland Steel Co.
Bldg. Panels Div.
P.O. Box 393
Milwaukee, WI 53201 **(M)**

Jessop Specialty Steels
Executive Mall
Wayne, PA 19087 **(M)**

Keycolor Fence Corp.
581 Rivermede Rd.
Concord, Ontario
L4K 1B6 Canada **(M)**
Coated fences

Lewisohn Sales Co., Inc.
4001 Dell Ave.
North Bergen, NJ 07047 **(W)**

J. C. MacElroy Co., Inc.
74 Trinity Pl.
New York, NY 10006 **(W)**
Safety gratings

Manutan
32 Bis, boulevard de Picpus
75012 Paris, France

Metal Purchasing Co., Inc.
501 W. 30 St.
New York, NY **(W)**

Bob Michaels Surplus Corp.
324 Canal St.
New York, NY 10013 **(W)**

Norbotten Steel Ltd.
11th Fl., Berkshire House
Queen St. Maidenhead
Berkshire SL6 1NF England **(M)**

North Atlantic Steel Corp.
777 Third Ave.
New York, NY 10021 **(W)**

The October Co., Inc.
Easthampton, MA 01027 **(M)**

Republic Steel Corp.
P.O. Box 6778 C
Cleveland, OH 44101 **(M)**
Roofing and siding

Reynolds Metals Co.
Richmond, VA 23261 **(M)**
*Quilted/embossed aluminum
 sheeting*

Simplex Ceiling Corp.
50 Harrison St.
Hoboken, NJ 07030 **(M)**
Metal ceilings

The Professional Kitchen
18 Cooper Sq.
New York, NY 10003 **(R)**

Thypin Steel Co., Inc.
49-49 30 St.
Long Island City, NY 11104 **(M)**

Titus
12820 Hillcrest Rd.
Suite 209
Dallas, TX 75230 **(M)**
Subway grating

TubeSales
Prospect Plains Rd.
Cranbury, NJ 08512 **(M)**
Pipe & tubing

Tuttle & Baily
Div. of Allied Thermal Corp.
P.O. Box 1313
New Britain, CT 06050 **(M)**
Grills, registers, etc.

Union Steel Corp.
Strip Div.
2150 Stanley Terr.
P.O. Box 156
Union, NJ 07083 **(M)**

United Interlock Grating
Columbus, OH 43216 **(M)**
Metal grating

U.S. Steel
Pittsburgh, PA 15230 **(M)**

Albert Weiss Air Conditioning
 Products, Inc.
270 Madison Ave.
New York, NY 10016 **(M)**

White Metal Rolling &
 Stamping Corp.
80 Moultrie St.
Brooklyn, NY 11222 **(M)**

Rubber

Aborn Rubber Co., Inc.
20 Greene St.
New York, NY 10013 **(W)**

Allstate Rubber Corp.
105-12 101 Ave.
Ozone Park, NY 11416 **(W)**

American Biltrite, Inc.
Consumer Products Div.
P.O. Box 1039
Boston, MA 02103 **(M)**

American Floor Products Co.
5010 Boiling Brook Pkwy.
Rockville, MD 20852 **(M)**

Banner Mat & Products Co.
17 Mercer St.
Cincinnati, OH 45210 **(M)**

Beam Supply
712 Broadway
New York, NY 10012 **(W/R)**
Mats

Belting Assoc., Inc.
Commercial Floor Matting
 Div.
148 Lauman La.
Hicksville, NY 11801 **(M)**

A. N. Brabrook, Inc.
548 W. 53 St.
New York, NY 10019 **(M/W)**

Cactus Mat Mfg. Co.
P.O. Box 3164
10740 Weaver St.
South El Monte, CA 91733 **(M)**

Flexco
Div. of Textile Rubber Co., Inc.
P.O. Box 553
Tuscumbia, AL 35674 **(M)**

Carl Freudenberg Ltd.
Lutterworth
Leicestershire LE17 4DU
 England **(M)**

Samuel Furiness Mat Co., Inc.
Inman Ave.
Edison, NJ 08817 **(M)**

Fuso Gomu Ind. Co. Ltd.
Head Office 11-25 Hasune 3
 Chome
Itabishiku, Tokyo 174 **(M)**

Jason Ind. Inc.
340 Kaplan Dr.
Box 365
Fairfield, NJ 07006 **(M/W)**
Pirelli tile

Jason Ind. of California, Inc.
2481 Porter St.
Los Angeles, CA 90021 **(M/W)**

Jason Ind. (Canada) Ltd.
9733 Cote De Liesse
Box 2097
Dorval 780 P.Q., Canada
(M/W)

The Johnson Rubber Co.
Flooring Accessories Div.
Middlefield, OH 44062 (M)

Koffler Sales Corp.
4501 Lincoln Ave.
Chicago, IL 60625 (M.O.)

Charles Luria
128 Autumn Ave.
Brooklyn, NY 11208
Studs floor tiles

Mondo Rubber Canada Ltd.
2655, Francis Hughes, Parc
  Industriel,
Chomedey Laval
Quebec H7L 3S8 Canada

The R. C. Musson Rubber Co.
1320 Archwood Ave.
Akron, OH 44306 (M)

Pawling Rubber Corp.
Standard Products Div.
157 Maple Blvd.
Pawling, NY 12564 (M)

Plastic Extruders Ltd.
Heron Ave.
Wickford, Essex SS11 8DN
  England (M)

Roblan Mfg. Co.
310 Richardson St.
Brooklyn, NY 11222 (M)
Tile studding

Roblin Ind.
Div. of United Steel & Wire
Battle Creek, MI 49016 (M)

  Azusa, CA 91702

Roppe Rubber Corp.
1602 N. Union St.
Box 309
Fostoria, OH 44830 (M)

Stiles Rubber Co.
P.O. Box 273
Landing, NJ 07850 (M)
Rubber pads

Tenex Corp.
1850 E. Estes Ave.
Elk Grove Village, IL 60007 (M)

Tepromark Intl. Inc.
206 Mosher Ave.
Woodmere, NY 11598 (M)

Arthur H. Thomas Co.
Vine St. at Third
P.O. Box 779
Philadelphia, PA 19105 (M)

Trans-Continental Distr.
300 W. Hubbard St.
Chicago, IL 60610 (W)

U.S. Mat & Rubber Co.
P.O. Box 152
Brocton, MA 02403 (M)

Vinyl Plastics, Inc.
3123 S. 9 St.
Sheboygan, WI 53081 (M)

Vydel Corp. of America
1660 Old Deerfield Rd.
Highland Park, IL 60035

Wallcoverings

Acoustic Standards
1227 W. Trenton Ave.
Orange, CA 92667 (M)
Acoustic panels

DecoGard Products
  Div. of Construction
  Specialties, Inc.
P.O. Box 400
Route 405
Muncy, PA 17756 (M)
Protective wallcoverings

Pawling Rubber Corp.
Standard Products Div.
157 Maple Blvd.
Pawling, NY 12564 (M)
Wall bumpers and guards

Sears Farm and Ranch
  Catalog
Sears Roebuck and Co.
Sears Tower
Chicago, IL 60684
Corrugated aluminum paneling

Ceramic Tiles

Agency Tile, Inc.
499 Old Nyack Turnpike
Spring Valley, NY 10977 (W)

  Showrooms:
  1444 Oaklawn Ave.
  Suite 556
  Dallas, TX 75207

  61 N. Saw Mill River Rd.
  Elmsford, NY 10523

4242 N.E. Second Ave.
Miami, FL 33137

D & D Bldg.
Suite 1716
979 Third Ave.
New York, NY 10022

  430 E. Westfield Ave.
  Roselle Park, NJ 07203

American Olean Tile Co.
Executive Offices
Lansdale, PA 19446 (M)

Franciscan Tile
Interpace Corp.
2901 Los Feliz Blvd.
Los Angeles, CA 90039 (M)

Gail Intl. Corp.
1201 Douglas St.
Redwood City, CA 94063 (M)

U.S. Ceramic Tile Co.
Subsidiary of Spartec, Inc.
1375 Raff Rd. S.W.
Canton, OH 44711 (M)

Mats and Slats

Aborn Rubber Co., Inc.
20 Greene St.
New York, NY 10013 (W)

Alfredo
Centrol Ind. Europeo
22078 Turate, Italy (M)

American Biltrite Inc.
Consumer Products Div.
P.O. Box 1039
Boston, MA 02103 (M)

American Floor Products Co.
5010 Boiling Brook Pkwy.
Rockville, MD 20852 (M)

Art et Industrie
132 Thompson St.
New York, NY 10013 (R)
Vinyl duckboard

Auto World
701 N. Keyser Ave.
Scranton, PA 18508 (R)

Banner Mat & Products Co.
17 Mercer St.
Cincinnati, OH 45210 (M)

Beam Supply
712 Broadway
New York, NY 10012 (W/R)

Belting Assoc., Inc.
148 Lauman La.
Hicksville, NY 11801 (M)

A. N. Brabrook, Inc.
548 W. 53 St.
New York, NY 10019 (W/R)

Brookstone Co.
Vose Farm Rd.
Peterborough, NH 03458
(M.O.)

Cactus Mat Mfg. Co.
P.O. Box 3164
10740 Weaver St.
South El Monte, CA 91733 (M)

DecoGard Products
Div. of Construction
  Specialties, Inc.
P.O. Box 400
Rte. 405
Muncy, PA 17756 (M)

Flexco Products
Div. of Textile Rubber Co.,
  Inc.
P.O. Box 553
Tuscumbia, AL 35674 (M)

Samuel Furiness Mat Co.,
  Inc.
Inman Ave.
Edison, NJ 08817 (M)

Harbor Pallet Co.
1516 W. Embassy St.
Anaheim, CA 92803 (M)

Hinchcliff Products Co.
20600 Westwood Dr.
Cleveland, OH 44136 (M)

The Johnson Rubber Co.
Flooring Accessories Div.
Middlefield, OH 44062 (M)

Koffler Sales Corp.
4501 Lincoln Ave.
Chicago, IL 60625 (M.O)

Le Beau Products
715 Lynn Ave.
Baraboo, WI 53913 (M)

Lehner and Putz
Rohrbach
Lafnitz, Austria (M)

Manustock
LeTeich, France (M)

Manutan
32 Bis, boulevard de Picpus
75012 Paris, France (W)

The R. C. Musson Rubber Co.
1320 Archwood Ave.
Akron, OH 44306 **(M)**

Pawling Rubber Corp.
Standard Products Div.
157 Maple Blvd.
Pawling, NY 12564 **(M)**

Pennsylvania Pacific Corp.
John Fitch Industrial Pk.
Warminster, PA 18974 **(M)**

Perko, Inc.
16490 N.W. 13 Ave.
P.O. Box 64000-D
Miami, FL 33164 **(W/R)**

Rubbermaid Commercial
   Products, Inc.
Winchester, VA 22601 **(M)**

Rosenwach, Inc.
96 N. 9 St.
Brooklyn, NY 11211 **(M)**
Redwood decking

Tedruth Plastics Corp.
747 E. Green St.
Pasadena, CA 91101 **(M)**

Tenex Corp.
1850 E. Estes Ave.
Elk Grove Village, IL 60007
   (M)

Tepromark Intl., Inc.
206 Mosher Ave.
Woodmere, NY 11598 **(W)**

Tilgate Pallets Ltd.
Crawley
West Sussex, England **(M)**

Unit Pallets Ltd.
Manchester, England **(M)**

Vanguard Patio Products
P.O. Box 1569
Riverside, CA 92502 **(M)**

Vydel Corp. of America
1660 Old Deerfield Rd.
Highland Park, IL 60035 **(M)**

J. C. Whitney & Co.
1917-19 Archer Ave.
P.O. Box 8410
Chicago, IL 60680 **(R)**

More Materials

Amplast, Inc.
3020 Jerome Ave.
New York, NY 10468 **(M)**

359 Canal St.
New York, NY 10013
Acrylic sheets, cubes, rods

Anthonsen & Kimmel
440 Park Ave. S.
New York, NY 10016 **(W)**
Plexiglass panels

Bangor Cork Co., Inc.
William & D Sts.
Pen Argyl, PA 18072 **(M)**

Claridge Products & Equip.,
   Inc.
P.O. Box 910
Harrison, AR 72601 **(M)**
Chalkboards

Coating Products
101 W. Forest Ave.
Englewood, NJ 07632 **(M)**
Metalized plastics

Cobon Plastics Corp.
44 Lafayette St.
Newark, NJ 07102 **(M)**

Cole-Parmer Instrument Co.
7425 N. Oak Pk. Ave.
Chicago, IL 60648 **(M.O.)**
Plastic tubing

Coyne & Paddock
100 Ave. of the Americas
New York, NY 10013 **(M)**
   Chalkboards
   Bulletin boards

Crystal-X Plastics
Second & Pine Sts.
Darby, PA 19023 **(M)**

Dynaflair Corp.
555 Broad Hollow Rd.
Suite 104
Melville, NY 11746 **(M)**
Lexan panels

Dynaflair Corp. Ltd.
108 Nordic Ave.
Pointe Claire, Quebec
H9R 3Y2 Canada

Dynaflair Corp. Ltd.
Suite 214
159 Bay St.
Toronto, Ontario
M5J 1J7 Canada

Fibergrate Corp.
13604 Midway Rd.
Dallas, TX 75234 **(M)**
Reinforced plastic grating

Filon Div. of Vistron Corp.
12333 S. Van Ness Ave.
Hawthorne, CA 90250 **(M)**
Reinforced plastic panels

Sam Flax
55 E. 55 St.
New York, NY 10022 **(R)**

Forms & Surfaces, Inc.
Box 5215
Santa Barbara, CA 93108 **(M)**
Wood panels

Fourco Glass Co.
P.O. Box 2230
Clarksburg, WV 26301 **(M)**

General Electric
Plastics Div.
1 Plastics Ave.
Pittsfield, MA 01201 **(M)**

Insta-Foam Products, Inc.
2050 N. Broadway
Joliet, IL 60435 **(M)**
Urethane foam

Libbey-Owens-Ford Co.
222 S. Marginal Rd.
Fort Lee, NJ 07024 **(M)**

Mirro-Brite
101 W. Forest Ave.
Englewood, NJ 07631 **(M)**
Metallized plastics

Monad Plastics, Inc.
3960 Merritt Ave.
Bronx, NY 10466 **(M)**

Plastech
Div. of Pennsylvania Pacific Corp.
John Fitch Industrial Pk.
P.O. Box C-70
Warminster, PA 18974 **(M)**
Plastic pallets

Plastics of Philadelphia
N.E. Cor. 12 & Arch Sts.
Philadelphia, PA 19107 **(M)**

Rohm and Haas
Philadelphia, PA 19105 **(M)**
Plastics

Rohm and Haas Canada Ltd.
2 Manse Rd.
West Hill, Ontario
M1E 3T9 Canada **(M)**

Saint Gobain Vitrage
62 boulevard Victor-Hugo
92209 Neuilly-sur-Seine,
   France **(M)**
Glass

U.S. Plywood
1 Landmark Sq.
Stamford, CN 06921 **(M)**

Stanwood Corp.
715 N. Broadway
Stanley, WI 54768 **(M)**
Wood frame grills

Glass Block

Fidenza Vetraria
Via Felice Casati, 32
20124 Milano, Italy **(M)**

Pittsburgh Corning Corp.
800 Presque Isle Dr.
Pittsburgh, PA 15239 **(M)**

Saint Gobain Vitrage
Une Division de Saint-Gobain
   Industries
62 boulevard Victor-Hugo
B.P. 122
92201 Neuilly-sur-Seine,
   France **(M)**

Supro Bldg. Products Corp.
48-16 70 St.
Woodside, NY 11377 **(W)**

LIGHTING

Factory Lights

Abolite Lighting, Inc.
West Lafayette, OH 43845 **(M)**

Appleton Electric Co.
1701 Wellington Ave.
Chicago, IL 60657 **(M)**

Art et Industrie
132 Thompson St.
New York, NY 10013 **(R)**
Carries complete Abolite line

Benjamin Electric Mfg. Co.
Subsidiary of Thomas Ind.
P.O. Box 180
Sparta, TN 38583 **(M)**

Conran's
160 E. 54 St.
New York, NY 10022 **(R)**

Crouse-Hinds Co.
1347 Wolf St.
Syracuse, NY 13201 **(M)**

Erco Leuchten GmbH
Postfach 2460
5880 Ludenscheid, West
 Germany **(M)**

Femi
Viale Certosa 1
20149, Milan, Italy **(M)**

Harry Gitlin Lighting, Inc.
305 E. 50 St.
New York, NY 10022 **(M/W)**

Habitat
206-222 King's Rd.
London SW 35 XP England **(R)**

Habitat
Centre Commercial de la Tour
Tour-Montparnasse
11 rue de l'Arrivee
Boite Cidex 1001 Paris, France **(R)**

Hobb Electrical Supply
Div. of Holt Electrical Distr., Corp.
541 W. 34 St.
New York, NY 10001 **(W)**

Harvey Hubbell, Inc.
Electric Way
Christiansburg, VA 24073 **(M)**

The Lighting Center, Ltd.
1097 Second Ave.
New York, NY 10022 **(R)**
Carries Appleton

Omega Lighting
Melville, NY **(R)**
Carries Erco

Rosetta Electric
79 Chambers St.
New York, NY 10007 **(R)**

 73 Murray St.
 New York, NY 10007

 21 W. 46 St.
 New York, NY 10036

The Spero Electric Corp.
18222 Lanken Ave.
Cleveland, OH 44119 **(M)**

Sylvania
Sylvania Outdoor Lighting
21 Penn St.
Fall River, MA 02724 **(M)**

Westinghouse Electric Corp.
Lighting Div.
Vicksburg, MI 39180 **(M)**

HOLOPHANE DIV., JOHNS-MANVILLE CORP.

Holophane and Vaportight

Abolite Lighting, Inc.
West Lafayette, OH 43845 **(M)**

Appleton Electric Co.
1701 Wellington Ave.
Chicago, IL 60657 **(M)**

Crouse-Hinds Co.
1347 Wolf St.
Syracuse, NY 13201 **(M)**

Hobb Electrical Supply
Div. of Holt Electrical Distr. Corp.
541 W. 34 St.
New York, NY 10001 **(W)**

Holophane Div.
Johns Manville
Greenwood Plaza
Denver, CO 80217 **(M)**

 Holophane Australia
 16 Langridge St.
 Collingwood, Melbourne
 Victoria 3066 Australia

 The Holophane Co. Ltd.
 Bramalea, Ontario, Canada

 The Holophane Co. Ltd.
 St. Hyacinthe, Quebec, Canada

 Holophane Europe Ltd.
 Bond Ave.
 Milton Keynes MK1 1JG
  England

 Holophane S.A. de C.V.
 Apartado Postal 75-415
 Mexico 14 D.F. Mexico

Harvey Hubbell, Inc.
Lighting Div.
Electric Way
Christiansburg, VA 24073 **(M)**

The Lighting Center, Ltd.
1097 Second Ave.
New York, NY 10022 **(R)**

Rab Electric Mfg. Co. Inc.
321 Rider Ave.
Bronx, NY 10451 **(M)**

Russell & Stoll
Div. of Midland-Ross Corp.
P.O. Box 1348
Pittsburgh, PA 15230 **(M)**

Sylvania, Inc.
Outdoor Lighting
21 Penn St.
Fall River, MA 02724 **(M)**

Westinghouse Electric Corp.
Lighting Div.
Vicksburg, MS 39180 **(M)**

Alternative Lights

Anthes Div.
Gleason Corp.
Box 343
Milwaukee, WI 53201 **(M)**

Appleton Electric Co.
1701 Wellington Ave.
Chicago, IL 60657 **(M)**

Art de Industrie
132 Thompson St.
New York, NY 10013 **(R)**
Warning/construction lights

Benjamin Electric Mfg. Co.
Subsidiary of Thomas Ind., Inc.
P.O. Box 180
Sparta, TN 38583 **(M)**

Brookstone Co.
Vose Farm Rd.
Peterborough, NH 03458 **(M.O.)**

C & H Distr., Inc.
401 S. 5 St.
Milwaukee, WI 53204 **(M.O.)**

Columbia Lighting, Inc.
3808 Sullivan Rd.
Spokane, WA 99216 **(M)**

Cordomatic Reels, Inc.
Div. of Vacuum Cleaner Corp.
 of America
1730 W. Indiana Ave.
Philadelphia, PA 19132 **(M)**

Crouse-Hinds Co.
1347 Wolf St.
Syracuse, NY 13201 **(M)**

Defender Ind., Inc.
255 Main St.
New Rochelle, NY 10801 **(M.O.)**

Fidelity Products Co.
705 Pennsylvania Ave. S.
Minneapolis, MN 55426
 (M.O.)

Four Star Stage Lighting
3935 N. Mission Rd.
Los Angeles, CA 90031 **(R)**
Theatrical lighting

GAF Corp.
140 W. 51 St.
New York, NY 10020 **(M)**
X-ray viewers

Harwood Mfg. Co.
1800 W. Fullerton Ave.
Chicago, IL 60614 **(M)**

Harvey Hubbell, Inc.
Lighting Div.
Electric Way
Christiansburg, VA 24073 **(M)**

McGill Mfg. Co., Inc.
Electrical Div.
Valparaiso, IN 46383 **(M)**

Manhattan Marine & Electric
 Co., Inc.
116-118-120 Chambers St.
New York, NY 10007 **(R)**

Modern Supply Co.
19 Murray St.
New York, NY 10007 **(R/W)**
Ceiling fan w/light

Morsa
182 Hester St.
New York, NY 10002 **(M)**

CROUSE-HINDS CO.

Nicro Fico
Nicro Corp.
2065 West Ave. 140
San Leandro, CA 94577 (M)

Olesen
1535 Ivar Ave.
Hollywood, CA 90028 (R)
Theatrical lighting

Perkins Marine Lamp &
  Hardware Corp.
16490 N.W. 13 Ave.
Miami, FL 33164 (M)

Perko, Inc.
16490 N.W. 13 Ave.
P.O. Box 64000-D
Miami, FL 33164 (M)

Phoenix Products Co., Inc.
4715 N. 27 St.
Milwaukee, WI 53209 (M)

Russell & Stoll Div.
Midland-Ross Corp.
P.O. Box 1348
Pittsburgh, PA 15230 (R)

Russell Uniform Co.
44 E. 20 St.
New York, NY 10003 (W)
Flashlight signal wand

Sears Farm and Ranch Catalog
Sears Roebuck and Co.
Sears Tower
Chicago, IL 60684 (M.O.)
Mercury vapor lamp

The Simes Co., Inc.
College Point, NY 11356 (M)
Traffic lights

Sylvania, Inc.
Sylvania Outdoor Lighting
21 Penn St.
Fall River, MA 02724 (M)

Theatre Vision, Inc.
15211 Blakeslee Ave.
North Hollywood, CA 91605 (R)
Theatrical lighting

J. C. Whitney & Co.
1917-19 Archer Ave.
P.O. Box 8410
Chicago, IL 60680 (W/R)
Warning lights

Daniel Woodhead Co.
3411 Woodhead Dr.
Northbrook, IL 60062 (M)

Yankee Metal Products Corp.
Norwalk, CT 06852 (M)

Big Lights

Abolite Lighting Co., Inc.
West Lafayette, OH 43845 (M)

Appleton Electric Co.
1701 Wellington Ave.
Chicago, IL 60657 (M)

Benjamin Electric Mfg. Co.
Subsidiary of Thomas Ind., Inc.
P.O. Box 180
Sparta, TN 38583 (M)

Hobb Electrical Supply
Div. of Holt Electrical Distr. Corp.
541 W. 34 St.
New York, NY 10001 (W)

Holophane Div.
Johns Manville
Greenwood Plaza
Denver, CO 80217 (M)

Harvey Hubbell, Inc.
Lighting Div.
Electric Way
Christiansburg, VA 24073 (M)

Koppers Co.
Forest Products Div.
750 Koppers Bldg.
Pittsburgh, PA 15219 (M)

The Lighting Center, Ltd.
1097 Second Ave.
New York, NY 10022 (R)

The Simes Co., Inc.
College Point, NY 11356 (M)

The Spero Electric Corp.
18222 Lanken Ave.
Cleveland, OH 44119 (M)

Sylvania Corp.
Outdoor Lighting
21 Penn St.
Fall River, MA 02724 (M)

Westinghouse Electric Div.
Vicksburg, MS 39180 (M)

Sources of Illusion

Acousticolor
100 Decker Rd.
Walled Lake, MI 48088 (M)
Audio Kaleidoscopes

Erco Leuchten GmbH
Postfach 2460
5880 Ludenscheid, West
  Germany (M)

SWIVELIER

Harwood Mfg. Co.
Subsidiary of Elgin Natl. Ind.
1802 W. Fullerton Ave.
Chicago, IL 60614 (M)

Kliegl Bros. Univ. Elec. Stage
  Lighting Co.
32-32 48 Ave.
Long Island City, NY 11101 (M)

The Lighting Center, Ltd.
1097 Second Ave.
New York, NY 10022 (R)
Barn door spot lights

Lowel-Light Mfg., Inc.
421 W. 54 St.
New York, NY 10019 (M)
Photo umbrellas

Olesen Co.
1535 Ivar
Los Angeles, CA 90028 (W)

Omega Lighting
Melville, NY 11746 (W)

Photax
Hampden Park
Eastbourne, East Sussex,
  England (M)

Strand Century, Inc.
20 Bushes La.
Elmwood, NJ 07407 (M/W)

Swivelier Lighting Products Div.
Nanuet, NY 10954 (M)

Times Square Theatrical &
  Studio Supply Corp.
318 W. 47 St.
New York, NY 10036 (M)

Willoughby-Peerless Ind. Sales Div.
115 W. 31 St.
New York, NY 10001 (R)
Photo umbrellas

Yorkville Ind., Inc.
55 Motor Ave.
Farmingdale, NY 11735 (M)

Neon

A & B Art
412 E. 176 St.
Bronx, NY 10457 (M)

Ad Art
Luminart Div.
4550 E. Olympic Blvd.
Los Angeles, CA 90022 (M)

Advance Neon Signs, Inc.
2055 W. Walnut St.
Chicago, IL 60612 (M)

Artistic Neon by Gasper
76-19 60 La.
Glendale, NY 11227 (M)

Arthur Blum Signs, Inc.
146 W. 28 St.
New York, NY 10001 (M)

Glo Plastic Signs
39-08 Janet Pl.
Flushing, NY 11351 (M)

Jo-Ran Neon
North Haven, CT 06473 (M)

Let There Be Neon
451 W. Broadway
New York, NY 10012 (M/R)

Midtown Neon Sign Corp.
550 W. 30 St.
New York, NY 10001 (M)

Midway Sign Corp.
646 Gerard Ave.
Bronx, NY 10451 (M)

Neon Rami
83 Bis, r. R, Rolland
93 Les Lilas, Paris, France (M)

Neon Roby
6 Bis, rue du Docteur Emile Roux
92110 Clichy, Paris, France (M)

Power Neon Signs Ltd.
121-143 Bow Rd.
London E3 England (M)

THE HIGH-TECH DIRECTORY

The Sign Makers
Chase Products (neon) Ltd.
31 Colville Rd.
Acton, London W3 8BT
England **(M)**

Track & Spot

Abolite Lighting, Inc.
West Lafayette, OH 43845 **(M)**

Auto World
701 N. Keyser Ave.
Scranton, PA 18508 **(R)**

Candle Lighting Co.
via Ariberto 24
20123 Milano Italia

Concorde Lighting Intl. Ltd.
241 City Rd.
London EC1 England **(M)**

Erco Leuchten GmbH
Postfach 2460
5880 Ludenscheid, West
Germany **(M)**

Fuller
45 E. 57 St.
New York, NY 10022 **(R)**

Harry Gitlin Lighting
305 E. 60 St.
New York, NY 10022 **(W)**

Gould, Inc.
Electrical Products Group
Spring House, PA 19477 **(M)**

Halo Lighting
Div. of McGraw Edison Co.
333 W. River
Elgin, IL 60120 **(M)**

Hobb Electrical Supply
Div. of Holt Electrical Distr. Corp.
541 W. 34 St.
New York, NY 10001 **(W)**

Holophane Co., Inc.
Montvale, NJ 07645 **(M)**

Harvey Hubbell, Inc.
Lighting Div.
Electric Way
Christiansburg, VA 24073 **(M)**

Koch & Lowy
940 Third Ave.
New York, NY 10022 **(M/W)**

   1245 Merchandise Mart
   Chicago, IL 60654

   639 Pacific Design Ctr.
   Los Angeles, CA 90096

The Lighting Center, Ltd.
1097 Second Ave.
New York, NY 10022 **(R)**

Lighting Services, Inc.
150 E. 58 St.
New York, NY 10022 **(M/W)**

Lightolier
11 E. 36 St.
New York, NY 10016 **(M/W)**

   300 Loyola Dr.
   Atlanta, GA 30336

   1266 Merchandise Mart
   Chicago, IL 60654

   501 W. Walnut St.
   Compton, CA 90220

   2650 Nova Dr.
   Dallas, TX 75229

   1910 Fairview Ave. E.
   Seattle, WA 98102

Lightolier-Canada Ltd.
4935 Bourg St.
Ville St. Laurent
Montreal, P.Q. H4T1J1
Canada **(M/W)**

   20 Torbay Rd.
   Markham, Ontario L3R1G6
   Canada

   2736 S.E. Marine Dr.
   Vancouver, B.C. V5S2H1
   Canada

The Christopher Lloyd
Collection
2015 Bridgeway
Sausalito, CA 94965 **(M)**

Luxo Lamp Corp.
Monument Pk.
Port Chester, NY 10573 **(M)**

Manhattan Ad Hoc House-
wares
842 Lexington Ave.
New York, NY 10021 **(R)**

Manhattan Marine & Electric
Co., Inc.
116-118-120 Chambers St.
New York, NY 10007 **(R)**

Meteor Light and Sound Co.
Div. of Hammond Ind., Inc.
155 Michael Dr.
Syosset, NY 11791 **(M)**

580 Orly Ave.
Dorval
Quebec H9P 1E9 Canada

105-109 Oyster La.
Byfleet Surrey
KT 14 7 LA England

Mole-Richardson Co.
937 N. Sycamore Ave.
Hollywood, CA 90038 **(M)**

Omega Lighting
Melville, NY 11746 **(W/R)**
Erco dealer

Perkins Marine Lamp &
Hardware Corp.
16490 N.W. 13 Ave.
Miami, FL 33164 **(M)**

Phoenix Products Co., Inc.
4715 N. 27 St.
Milwaukee, WI 53209 **(M)**
Pogolites

Robart-Green, Inc.
17 Newark Way
Maplewood, NJ 07040 **(W)**
Pogolites

Swivelier Co., Inc.
33 Rte. 304
Nanuet, NY 10954 **(M)**

Sylvania, Inc.
Outdoor Lighting
21 Penn St.
Fall River, MA 02724 **(M)**

Thomas Ind., Inc.
207 E. Broadway
Louisville, KY 40202 **(M)**

Mood Lighting

American Cyanamid Co.
Berdam Ave.
Wayne, NJ 07470 **(M)**

Crouse-Hinds Co.
1347 Wolf St.
Syracuse, NY 13201 **(M)**

Erco Leuchten GmbH
Postfach 2460
5880 Ludenscheid, West
Germany **(M)**

Harry Gitlin Lighting
305 E. 60 St.
New York, NY 10022 **(M/W)**

Harvey Hubbell, Inc.
Electric Way
Christiansburg, VA 24073 **(M)**

McGill Mfg. Co., Inc.
Electrical Div.
Valparaiso, IN 46383 **(M)**

Meteor Light and Sound Co.
Div. of Hammond Ind., Inc.
155 Michael Dr.
Syosset, NY 11791 **(M)**

   580 Orly Ave.
   Dorval
   Quebec H9P 1E9 Canada

   105-109 Oyster La.
   Byfleet Surrey
   KT 14 7LA England

Times Sq. Stage Lighting
318 W. 47 St.
New York, NY 10036 **(W/R)**

Daniel Woodhead Co.
3411 Woodhead Dr.
Northbrook, IL 60062 **(M)**

Yorkville Ind., Inc.
55 Motor Ave.
Farmingdale, NY 11735 **(M)**

Fluorescent Lighting

Abolite Lighting, Inc.
West Lafayette, OH 43845 **(M)**

Benjamin Electric Mfg. Co.
Subsidiary of Thomas Ind.,
Inc.
P.O. Box 180
Sparta, TN 38583 **(M)**

Day-Brite Lighting
Div. of Emerson Electric Co.
8100 W. Florissant
St. Louis, MO 63136 **(M)**

Erco Leuchten GmbH
Postfach 2460
5880 Ludenscheid, West
Germany **(M)**

Hobb Electrical Supply
Div. of Holt Electrical Distr. Corp.
541 W. 34 St.
New York, NY 10001 **(W)**

Harvey Hubbell, Inc.
Lighting Div.
Electric Way
Christiansburg, VA 24073 **(M)**

McGill Mfg. Co., Inc.
Electrical Div.
Valparaiso, IN 46383 **(M)**

Radionic Ind.
411 S. Sangamon St.
Chicago, IL 60607 **(M)**
Aircraft cleaning light

The Simes Co., Inc.
College Point, NY 11356 **(M)**

Sun-Lite Mfg. Co.
575 Bellevue
Detroit, MI 48207 **(M)**

Swivelier Co., Inc.
33 Rte. 304
Nanuet, NY 10954 **(M)**

Sylvania Corp.
Outdoor Lighting
21 Penn St.
Fall River, MA 02724 **(M)**

Westinghouse Electric Co.
Vicksburg, MS 39180 **(M)**

Task Lighting

Abaco Steel Products, Inc.
1560 Locust Ave.
Bohemia, NY 11716 **(W)**
Docklights

Andrews/Mantner, Inc.
2040 W. Wisconsin Ave.
Suite 565
Milwaukee, WI 53233
Docklight with flex-arm joint

William Bloom and Son, Inc.
25 Almeida Ave.
East Providence, RI 02914 **(M)**

Bloomingdale's
1000 Third Ave.
New York, NY 10021 **(R)**

Charette Drafting Supply Corp.
212 E. 54 St.
New York, NY 10021 **(R)**

Erco Leuchten GmbH
Postfach 2460
5880 Ludenscheid, West
  Germany **(M)**

Fidelity Products Co.
705 Pennsylvania Ave. S.
Minneapolis, MN 55426 **(M.O.)**

Sam Flax
55 E. 55 St.
New York, NY 10022 **(R)**

Fuller Stationers
45 E. 57 St.
New York, NY 10022 **(R)**

Harry Gitlin Lighting
305 E. 60 St.
New York, NY 10022 **(M/W)**

Grimes Mfg. Co.
515 N. Russel
Urbana, OH 43078 **(M)**
747 airplane lights

Hammacher Schlemmer
147 E. 57 St.
New York, NY 10022 **(R)**
*Battery-operated portable
  lanterns*

Hobb Electrical Supply
Div. of Holt Electrical Distr.
  Corp.
541 W. 34 St.
New York, NY 10001 **(W)**

Hoffritz for Cutlery
Executive Offices
20 Cooper Sq.
New York, NY 10003 **(R)**
*Portable battery-operated
  lamps*

Harvey Hubbell, Inc.
Electric Way
Christiansburg, VA 24073 **(M)**

Invento
205 E. Post Rd.
White Plains, NY 10601 **(R)**

Lewis & Conger
39-25 Skillman Ave.
Long Island City, NY 11104 **(R)**
*Portable battery-operated
  lamps*

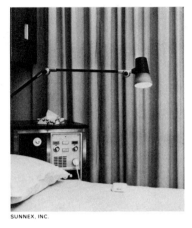

SUNNEX, INC.

The Lighting Center, Ltd.
1097 Second Ave.
New York, NY 10022 **(R)**

Lighting Services, Inc.
150 E. 58 St.
New York, NY 10022 **(W)**

Lucas Ind. North America
30 Van Nostrand Ave.
Englewood, NJ 07632 **(M)**
Flexilight

Luxo Lamp Corp.
Monument Pk.
Port Chester, NY 10573 **(M)**

McGill Mfg. Co., Inc.
Electrical Div.
Valparaiso, IN 46383 **(M)**

Macy's
Herald Square
New York, NY 10001 **(R)**

SUNNEX, INC.

Omega Lighting
Melville, NY 11746 **(W/R)**

Perko, Inc.
Factory and Main Office
16490 N.W. 13 Ave.
P.O. Box 64000D
Miami, FL 33164 **(M)**
Marine lights

Phoenix Products Co., Inc.
4715 N. 27 St.
Milwaukee, WI 53209 **(W)**
Pogolite

Photax
Hampden Park
Eastbourne, E. Sussex,
England

J. A. Preston of Canada Ltd.
3220 Wharton Way
Mississauga, Ontario
L4X 2C1 Canada **(M.O.)**

J. A. Preston Corp.
71 Fifth Ave.
New York, NY 10003 **(M.O.)**

*Scandinavian Design
127 E. 59 St.
New York, NY 10022* **(W/R)**

Sunnex, Inc.
87 Crescent Rd.
Needham, MA 02194 **(M)**
Hospital bed lamp

Swivelier Co., Inc.
33 Rte. 304
Nanuet, NY 10954 **(M)**

Arthur H. Thomas Co.
Vine St. at Third
P.O. Box 779
Philadelphia, PA 19105 **(M.O.)**
Medical luxo lamps

Vimco Mfg. Co., Inc.
Holland, NY 14080 **(M)**

Wasomark, Inc.
Ledu Lamp Div.
1 Willard Rd.
Norwalk, CT 06856 **(M)**
Architects lamps

Wemac
18475 Pacific St.
Fountain Valley, CA 92708 **(M)**

Yorkville Ind., Inc.
55 Motor Ave.
Farmingdale, NY 11735 **(M)**

THE WORKS

Moving Air

Beckley Perforating Co.
Garwood, NJ 07027 **(M)**

Blaw-Knox Equip., Inc.
Blawnox, PA 15238 **(M)**
Steel grating

Borden Metal Products Co.
Box 172
Elizabeth, NJ 07207 **(M)**

Chris-Craft
Algonac, MI 48001 **(M.O.)**
Fans

Defender Ind., Inc.
255 Main St.
New Rochelle, NY 10801 **(M.O.)**

The Flexaust Co.
Div. of Callahan Mining Corp.
277 Park Ave.
New York, NY 10017 **(M)**

New England Office
Amesbury, MA 01913

3700 Longview Dr.
Chamblee, GA 30341

300 Windsor Dr.
Oak Brook, IL 60521

199 Thousand Oaks Blvd.
Thousand Oaks, CA 91360

Forms & Surfaces
Box 5215
Santa Barbara, CA 93108 **(W)**
Grills

Gargoyles, Ltd.
512 S. Third St.
Philadelphia, PA 19147 **(M)**
Ceiling fans

General Electric
Housewares and Audio
Business Div.
Bridgeport, CT 06602 **(M)**

Hafele KG
P.O. Box 160
7270 Nagold/West Germany **(M)**
Grills

Hunter
Div. of Robbins & Myers, Inc.
2500 Frisco Ave.
Memphis, TN 38114 **(M)**
Fans

Import Specialists, Inc.
82 Wall St.
New York, NY 10005 **(M/W)**
Ceiling fans

Ind. Utilities Corp.
1426 Atlantic Ave.
Brooklyn, NY 11216 **(W)**

133 Milbar Blvd.
Farmingdale, NY 11736

147 Rte. 36
Port Monmouth, NJ 07758

Irving Grating
IKG Ind.
50-09 27 St.
Long Island City, NY 11101
(M)

Lomanco, Inc.
P.O. Box 519
2101 W. Main St.
Jacksonville, AR 72076 **(M)**

Manhattan Marine & Electric
Co., Inc.
116-118-120 Chambers St.
New York, NY 10007 **)R)**

Modern Supply Co.
19 Murray St.
New York, NY 10007 **(R/W)**
Fans

Nicro Fico
2065 W. Ave. 140
San Leandro, CA 94577 **(M)**
Boat ventilators

Patton Electric Co., Inc.
P.O. Box 9340
Fort Wayne, IN 46809 **(M)**
Ceiling fans

Perko, Inc.
16490 N.W. 13 Ave.
P.O. Box 64000-D
Miami, FL 33164 **(R)**
Boat ventilators

Register and Grill Mfg. Co.
202 Norman Ave.
Brooklyn, NY 11222 **(M)**

Seco Products
McGraw-Edison Co.
P.O. Box 7116
St. Louis, MO 63177 **(M)**

Titus
12820 Hillcrest Rd.
Suite 209
Dallas, TX 75230 **(M)**

PATTON ELECTRIC CO., INC.

Tuttle & Bailey
Div. of Allied Thermal Corp.
Box 1313
New Britain, CT 06050 **(M)**

Albert Weiss Air Conditioning
Prod. Inc.
270 Madison Ave.
New York, NY 10016 **(W/R)**

J. C. Whitney & Co.
1917-19 Archer Ave.
P.O. Box 8410
Chicago, IL 60680 **(R)**
Car heaters

Willoughby-Peerless
115 W. 31 St.
New York, NY 10001 **(R)**

The Bathroom

Accessory Specialties, Inc.
1335 E. Bay Ave.
New York, NY 10474 **(M)**

Agnew Assoc., Inc.
10-50 50 Ave.
Long Island City, NY 11101
(W)
Faucets

American Athletic Corp.
P.O. Box 2422
3425 S. Federal Hwy.
Fort Lauderdale, FL 33316
(M)
Whirlpools

American Metal Restaurant
Equipment Co.
43-04 19 Ave.
Long Island City, NY 11105
(M)

American Standard
40 W. 40 St.
New York, NY 10018 **(M)**

AMSCO
American Sterilizer Co.
Erie, PA 16501 **(M)**

Aqua Plunge
Div. of Wiedemann Ind., Inc.
P.O. Box 677
Muscatine, IA 52761 **(M)**
Whirlpools

Architectural Complements
P.O. Box 168
Lincoln, MA 01773 **(W)**
Vola

Blickman Health Ind., Inc.
20-21 Wagaraw Rd.
Fair Lawn, NJ 07410 **(M)**

Bobrick Washroom Equip.
Inc.
Northway 10 Industrial Pk.
Ballston Lake, NY 12019 **(M)**

11611 Hart St.
North Hollywood, CA 91605

Bradley Washroom Access-
ories
P.O. Box 309
Menomonee Falls, WI 53051 **(M)**

Bradley Corp.:

Aristocrat Mfg. Co. Ltd.
4500 Dixie Rd.
Mississauga, Ontario L4W 1V
7 Canada

Barnett & Co.
P.O. Box 25005
Albuquerque, NM 87125

B.K.A. Sales
33051 Breckenridge
Sterling Heights, MI 48077

B.K.A. Sales
10803 N. 19 St.
Plainwell, MI 49080

Bradley-Engstrom Sales Co.
W142 N9041 Fountain Blvd.
P.O. Box 716
Menomonee Falls, WI 53051

Bradley Washfountain Co. of
  S. Africa Ltd.
P.O. Box 2863
Johannesburg, 2000 South
  Africa

Bradley Washfountain Co.
  Pty. Ltd.
P.O. Box 7
Lakemba, N.S.W. 2195
  Australia

H. Ben Brown, Jr.
1200 S. 20 St.
Birmingham, AL 35205

Jim Burch & Assoc.
4548 McEwen Rd.
Dallas, TX 75240

Jim Burch & Assoc.
6654 Gulf Freeway
Houston, TX 77017

Ken Cameron & Assoc.
P.O. Box 524
Blair, NB 68008

Carroll/Oliver & Assoc.
819 A St.
San Rafael, CA 94901

Carroll/Oliver & Assoc.
1400 S Street
Sacramento, CA 95814

Jack Y. Carruth
2347 S. Garrison Ct.
Lakewood, CO 80227

Walter E. Cathell Assoc.
1206 Goucher Blvd.
Towson, MD 21204

Central States Sales
7502 W. Madison St.
Forest Park, IL 60130

Clapper Co., Inc.
2102 Second Ave. N.
Billings, MT 59101

Christopher C. Cotton &
  Assoc.
1385 Martina Dr.
Atlanta, GA 30339

Walter C. Dollinger
1276 St. Cyr Rd.
St. Louis, MO 63137

Esposito Sales
46 King St.
Port Jefferson Station, NY
  11776

KOHLER

Faucet & Special Products
  Div.
P.O. Box 348
Menomonee Falls, WI 53051
  (M)

George H. Giesler Co.
5410 Homberg Dr.
Knoxville, TN 37919

George H. Giesler Co.
1040 Murfreesboro Rd.
Nashville, TN 37217

D. J. Gillis Corp.
343 Neponset St.
Canton, MA 02021

Great Western Sales, Inc.
17000 S. Vermont Ave.
Gardena. CA 90247

E. S. Hensley, Jr.
1200 Madison St.
Metairie, LA 70001

JM Sales Co.
570 Auahi St. Suite 214
Honolulu, HI 96804

Harry Kleppner
1697 Citation Dr.
Library, PA 15129

Kolstad Assoc., Inc.
422 Niagara Falls Blvd.
Buffalo, NY 14223

Kolstad Assoc., Inc.
16 Hillcrest Rd.
Latham, NY 12110

Kolstad Assoc., Inc.
875 Atlantic Ave.
Rochester, NY 14609

L. Lake Co.
3723 Meadowbrook Blvd.
Cleveland, OH 44118

W. G. Lesemann & Son
4905 Radford Ave.
Richmond, VA 23230

Ernest J. Maron Co.
P.O. Box 8688
Greensboro, NC 27410

Mid-States Sales Co.
5052 Norman Dr.
Minnetonka, MN 55343

Mitchell-Gordon & Assoc.
49 S.E. Clay St.
Portland, OR 97214

Morrical Sales Co.
1602 W. Villa Maria
Phoenix, AZ 85023

Don Regan Sales Corp.
Woodfield Dr.
Middlebury, CT 06762

Don Regan Sales Corp.
21 Powder Mill Rd.
Southwick, MA 01077

Frank Riddle & Assoc.
1852 16 St.
Moline, IL 61265

Frank Riddle & Assoc.
4609 Prospect Rd.
Peoria Heights, IL 61614

Rivard & Assoc. Inc.
4501 Merriam Dr.
Overland Park, KS 66203

Robco Specialties, Inc.
103 N. Lake Ave.
Albany, NY 12206

SES Agency, Inc.
134 N. Main St.
Milltown, NJ 08850

S & H Sales Co., Inc.
1520 Edgewater Dr. Suite F
Orlando, FL 32804

Steck Sales Co., Inc.
4890 Battery La. 125
Bethesda, MD 20014

Rex Williams & Sons
976 Fourth Ave.
Salt Lake City, UT 84103

Gib Wilson Enterprises
5608 N. Locust
North Little Rock, AR 72116

Leonard Woldoff
1600 Pennypack Rd.
Huntingdon Valley, PA 19006

Jack Zinser
223 Brierley Way
Carmel, IN 46032

Briggs, a Jim Walter Co.
P.O. Box 22622
Tampa, FL 33622 (M)

Cole-Parmer Instrument Co.
7425 N. Oak Park Ave.
Chicago, IL 60648 (M.O.)

Continental Mfg. Co.
Div. of Continco Intl., Inc.
1101 Warson Rd.
St. Louis, MO 63132 (M)

Continental Mfg. (U.K.) Ltd.
Beaconsfield Rd.
Hayes, Middlesex
UB4 ONW England (M)

David Fabricators of N.Y., Inc.
595 Berriman St.
Brooklyn, NY 11208 (M)
Laboratory sinks and tops

Defender Ind., Inc.
255 Main St.
New Rochelle, NY 10801 (M.O.)

Duralab Laboratory Furniture
10723 Farragut Rd.
Brooklyn, NY 11236 (M)
Laboratory sinks

Duricon Co., Inc.
Dayton, OH 45401 (M)

Elkay Mfg. Co.
2700 S. 17 Ave.
Broadview, IL 60153 (M)

Encon
Div. of Vallen Co.
4914 Dickson St.
P.O. Box 3826
Houston, TX 77001 (M)
Showers, face/eye washes

Esposito Sales
46 King St.
Port Jefferson Station, NY
  11776 (W)
Washroom railings etc.

Franklin Specialities
67 Chrystie St.
New York, NY 10002 (W)
Surgeon's sink

Friedrich Grohe
587 Hermer/Westf
Postfach 260 West Germany
  (M)
Faucets

Hafele KG
P.O. Box 160
7270 Nagold, West Germany (M)

THE HIGH-TECH DIRECTORY

Halbrand, Inc.
4413 Hamann Pkwy.
Willoughby, OH 44094
*"Toothette" disposable
toothbrushes*

Hospital Ware
Div. of APFC
778 Burlway Rd.
Burlingame, CA 94010 **(M)**

Kenco Products Corp.
P.O. Box 630
153 S. Dean St.
Englewood, NJ 07631 **(M)**
Plumbing fixtures

G. M. Ketcham Co., Inc.
132-06 89 Ave.
Richmond Hill, NY 11418 **(M)**

Kohler Co.
Kohler, WI 53044 **(M)**

Lawson
Div. of Tappan
801 Evans St.
Cincinnati, OH 45204 **(M)**
Medicine cabinets

Manhattan Ad Hoc House-
wares
842 Lexington Ave.
New York, NY 10021 **(R)**

Manhattan Marine & Electric
Co., Inc.
116-118-120 Chambers St.
New York, NY 10007 **(R)**

Marble Products
2049 Wassall
Wichita, KS 67216 **(M)**
Shampoo bowls

Market Forge
35 Garvey St.
Everett, MA 02149 **(M)**
Scrub stations

Marlo Mfg. Co., Inc.
140 Fifth Ave.
Hawthorne, NJ 07506 **(M)**

Miami-Carey
203 Garver Rd.
Monroe, OH 45050 **(M)**

Multinational Ind.
2221 Vista Dr.
Manhattan Beach, CA 90266 **(M)**
Hairdryers

William Page & Co. Ltd.
87-91 Shaftesbury Ave.
London W1V 8AJ England **(M)**

Charles Parker
290 Pratt St.
Meriden, CT 06450 **(M)**

Representatives:

The Anderson Co.
P.O. Box 358
Park Ridge, IL 60068

Donald L. Benz
3822 S.W. Corbett Ave.
Portland, OR 97201

J. L. Brasher
533 Highland Forest Dr.
Matthews, NC 28105

Bldg. Products, Inc.
3947 Excelsior Blvd.
Minneapolis, MN 55416

Robert A. Burton
4333 Windemere Pl.
Sarasota, FL 33579

Butler Sales
P.O. Box 5464
Pearl, MS 39208

B.W.A. Co., Inc.
1951 Waverly Ave.
Norwood, OH 45212

Leonard Carr
P.O. Box 11414
Philadelphia, PA 19111

Dixon Chubbuck & Assoc.
11815 E. Slauson Ave.
Santa Fe Springs, CA 90670

Corrigan Co.
5100 Poplar Ave.
Memphis, TN 38117

The Dages Co.
1910 Byrd Ave.
Richmond, VA 23230

Jack F. Dale & Assoc., Inc.
P.O. Box 864
Mountain Grove, MO 65711

Douglass Co.
13034 W. 102 St.
Shawnee Mission, KS 66215

Dana Drosby
Rt. 4 Box 162A
Salem, MA 65560

Fassett Sales Co.
P.O. Box 578
Bloomington, IL 61701

Ed French Assoc.
P.O. Box 301
Rochester, MI 48063

Interstate Sales Corp.
3244 Oakcliff Industrial St.
Atlanta, GA 30340

Harry Laudig
145 E. 6 Ave.
Mount Dora, FL 32757

A. Mitchell Assoc.
Clark Terr.
Marcellus, NY 13108

Edward C. Oldach
5555 Main St.
Williamsville, NY 14221

G. C. Ratcliff
1738 E. Orange Dr.
Phoenix, AZ 85016

Marty Reilly Co., Inc.
P.O. Box 298
Kensington, MD 20795

John Roth
1251 97 St.
Miami Beach, FL 33154

Sales Direction, Inc.
101 Park Ave.
New York, NY 10017

Fred Smith Co.
P.O. Box 877
North Little Rock, AR 72115

Gary N. Smith
293 Ludlow Pl.
San Ramon, CA 94583

Specification Sales Co.
1818 Westlake Ave.
Seattle, WA 98109

Specification Sales, Inc.
3814 Marquis Dr.
Garland, TX 75042

Spohn Assoc., Inc.
2400 W. 42 St.
Indianapolis, IN 46208

Stammer & Associates
666 Washington Rd.
Pittsburgh, PA 15228

L. J. Sweeney
518 35 St.
Des Moines, IA 50312

Joseph Tanet & Son
312 E. Park Blvd.
Braithewaite, LA 70040

R. L. Tucker Co., Inc.
217 Thorndike St.
Cambridge, MA 02141

J. J. Venable Jr.
1200 S. 20 St.
Birmingham, AL 35205

Jerry Vinck, A.H.C.
2409 N. 22 St.
Boise, ID 83702

Williamsport Bldg. Spec. Inc.
P.O. Box 863
Williamsport, PA 17701

John N. Yauger & Co.
P.O. Box 8232
Roanoke, VA 24014

Perko, Inc.
16490 N.W. 13 Ave.
P.O. Box 64000-D
Miami, FL 33164 **(M)**

The Perlick Co., Inc.
P.O. Box 8128
Milwaukee, WI 53223 **(M)**
Workboards

Plasta-Flex, Inc.
105 Vance
P.O. Box 1004
Taylor, TX 76574 **(M)**

J. A. Preston of Canada Ltd.
3220 Wharton Way
Mississauga, Ontario
L4X 2C1 Canada **(M.O.)**

J. A. Preston Corp.
71 Fifth Ave.
New York, NY 10003 **(M.O.)**

Speakman Co.
299 E. 30 St.
Wilmington, DE 19899 **(M)**
Hospital faucets

Frederick U. Sylvester &
Assoc., Inc.
101 Park Ave.
New York, NY 10017 **(W)**

Takara-Belmont
17 W. 56 St.
New York, NY 10019 **(W)**
Beauty parlor supply

T & S Brass and Bronze
Works, Inc.
128 Magnolia Ave.
Westbury, NY 11590 **(M)**

N. Wasserstrom and Sons, Inc.
2300 Lockbourne Rd.
Columbus, OH 43207 **(M)**

WhirlSpa
5320 N.W. 10th Terr.
Fort Lauderdale, FL 33309 **(M)**

Wiedemann Ind., Inc.
P.O. Box 677
Muscatine, IA 52761 (M)
Fiber-glass baptistries

Support Hardware

Architectural Supplements,
Inc.
150 E. 58 St.
New York, NY 10022 (W)
Umbrella stands

Automatic Devices Co.
2121 S. 12 St.
Allentown, PA 18103 (M)
*Overhead light suspension
systems*

Auto World
701 N. Keyser Ave.
Scranton, PA 18508 (R)
Luggage racks

Berc Antoine
10 et 12 boulevard
Richard-Lenoir
Paris-Bastille, France (M)

Blickman Health Ind., Inc.
20-21 Wagaraw Rd.
Fair Lawn, NJ 07401 (M)
Plant stands

Julius Blum & Co., Inc.
P.O. Box 292
Carlstadt, NJ 07072
Connectorail system

Bradley Corp.
P.O. Box 348
Menomonee Falls, WI 53051
Grab bars

Brey-Krause Mfg. Co.
Front & Chews Sts.
Allentown, PA 18102 (M)
Grab bars

Chesebro-Whitman Co.
Div. of Patent
Scaffolding-Harsco Corp.
38-21 12 St.
Long Island City, NY 11101
(M)
Shoring poles

Claridge Products and Equip.,
Inc.
P.O. Box 910
Harrison, AR 72601 (M)
Dismountable wall system

40 N. Old Rand Rd.
Lake Zurich, IL 60047

14736 Wicks Blvd.
San Leandro, CA 94577

Comyn Ching & Co. Ltd.
13-21 Shelton St.
Upper St. Martin's La.
London WC2H 9JP England
(M)
Pulls

Crosby Europe
Leuvensebaan 49-51
2870 Putte
(Mechelen) Belgium

The Crosby Group
Div. of Amhoist
P.O. Box 3128
Tulsa, OK 74101 (M)

145 Heart Lake Rd.
Brampton, Ontario, Canada

Crosby-Laughlin
Carlton Chambers
Station Rd. Shortlands
Bromley BR 2 OEY England

Dean and Deluca
121 Prince St.
New York, NY 10012 (R)

DecoGard Products
Div. of Construction
Specialties, Inc.
P.O. Box 400
Rte. 405
Muncy, PA 17756 (M)

725 Twin Oaks Valley Rd.
San Marcos, CA 92069 (M)

Defender Ind., Inc.
255 Main St.
New Rochelle, NY 10801
(M.O.)

Sid Diamond Display Corp.
964 Third Ave.
New York, NY 10022 (W)
Wall rack grill

Esposito Sales
46 King St.
Port Jefferson Sta.
New York, NY 11776 (W)

Fairfield Medical Products
Corp.
2777 Summer St.
Stamford, CT 06905 (M)
Aluminum track system

Sam Flax
55 E. 55 St.
New York, NY 10022 (R)

1515 Spring St. N.W.
Atlanta, GA 30309 (R)

2606 Oaklawn Ave.
Dallas, TX 75219 (R)

Forms & Surfaces
Box 5215
Santa Barbara, CA 93108 (M/W)

Garelick Mfg. Co.
St. Paul Park, MN 55071 (M)

Hafele KG
P.O. Box 160
7270 Nagold, West Germany (M)
Towel and wardrobe racks

Hamilton Caster & Mfg. Co.
1637 Dixie Hwy.
Hamilton, OH 45011 (M)

Hammacher Schlemmer
147 E. 57 St.
New York, NY 10022 (R)

J. L. Hammett Co.
Hammett Pl.
Braintree, MA 02184 (M)
Easels

U.S. Rte. 29 S.
Lynchburg, VA 24502

165 Water St.
Lyons, NY 14489

2393 Vauxhall Rd.
Union, NJ 07083

Hardman Ind.
1668 22 St.
Santa Monica, CA 90404 (M)

Inter-Graph
979 Third Ave.
New York, NY 10022 (W)

The Ironmonger
446 N. Wells St.
Chicago, IL 60610 (W)

G. M. Ketcham Co., Inc.
132-06 89 Ave.
Richmond Hill, NY 11418 (M)
Bathroom equip.

Lawrence Metal Products, Inc.
P.O. Box 400-M
Bay Shore, NY 11706 (M)

The F. M. Lawson Co.
Bldg. Products Div.
Cincinnati, OH 45204 (M)

Manhattan Marine & Electric
Co., Inc.
116-118-120 Chambers St.
New York, NY 10007 (R)

Miami-Carey
203 Garver Rd.
Monroe, OH 45050 (M)

M.O.R.A.
13 et 15 rue Montmartre
75001 Paris, France (M)

Nicro Fico
2065 West Ave. 140
San Leandro, CA 94577 (M)

Charles Parker
290 Pratt St.
Meriden, CT 06450 (M)

Peerless Ind., Inc.
4200 W. Chicago Ave.
Chicago, IL 60651 (M)

Perko, Inc.
16490 N.W. 13 Ave.
P.O. Box 64000-D
Miami, FL 33164 (M)

Plaza Towel Holder Co., Inc.
2016 N. Broadway
Wichita, KS 67214 (M)

G. Rushbrooke (Smithfield)
Ltd.
67/77 Charterhouse St.
London EC1M 6HL England (R)

Schaffer Metal Products
117-04 93 Ave.
Jamaica, NY 11433 (M)
Con Ed guardrails

Southeastern Bolt & Screw
Div.
U.S. Pipe and Foundry Co.
Birmingham, AL 35203 (M)

Stewart-Warner Corp.
Bassick Div.
960 Atlantic St.
Bridgeport, CT 06602 (M)

Stimpson Co., Inc.
Bayport, NY 11705 **(M)**

  Pompano Beach, FL 33060

Taylor & NG
P.O. Box 200
400 Valley Dr.
Brisbane, CA 94005 **(M)**

Tri State Ind., Ltd.
1436 Williamsbridge Rd.
Bronx, NY 10461 **(M)**
Display stands

Tubular Specialties
8119 S. Beach St.
P.O. Box 71527 Florence
  Branch
Los Angeles, CA 90001 **(M)**

B. Walter & Co., Inc.
Wabash, IN 46992 **(M)**
Ajusta-leaf supports

N. Wasserstrom and Sons, Inc.
2300 Lockbourne Rd.
Columbus, OH 43207 **(M)**
Pot racks

F. Weber Co.
Wayne & Windrim Aves.
Philadelphia, PA 19144 **(M)**
Easels

J. C. Whitney & Co.
1917-19 Archer Ave.
P.O. Box 8410
Chicago, IL 60680 **(R)**
Luggage racks

D. G. Williams, Inc.
498 Seventh Ave.
New York, NY 10018 **(M)**
Display fixture, racks

Willoughby-Peerless
115 W. 31 St.
New York, NY 10001 **(R)**

Yorkville Ind., Inc.
55 Motor Ave.
Farmingdale, NY 11735 **(M)**

Drapery Hardware

ADC Hospital Equip.
Div. of Automatic Devices Co.
2121 S. 12 St.
Allentown, PA 18103 **(M)**

Julius Blum & Co., Inc.
P.O. Box 292
Carlstadt, NJ 07072 **(M)**

Defender Ind., Inc.
255 Main St.
New Rochelle, NY 10801
  (M.O.)

Fairfield Medical Products
  Corp.
2777 Summer St.
Stamford, CT 06905 **(M)**
Aluminum track system

Graber
Executive Offices
Middleton, WI 53562 **(M)**

Graber
80 Galaxy Blvd.
Unit 8, Rexdale 605
Ontario, Canada

Hild Sails
225 Fordham St.
City Island, NY 10464 **(M)**

Imperial Fastener Corp.
1400 S.W. 8 St.
Pompano Beach, FL 33060
  (M)

Ka-Lor Cubicle & Supply Co.
P.O. Box 804
Fair Lawn, NJ 07410 **(M/W/R)**

Kirsch Co., Inc.
261 Fifth Ave.
New York, NY 10016 **(M)**

Manhattan Marine & Electric
  Co., Inc.
116-118-120 Chambers St.
New York, NY 10007 **(R)**

Mr. Cubicle
3802 14 Ave.
Brooklyn, NY 11218 **(W/R)**

OB/MASCO Drapery
  Hardware Co.
2930 Maria St.
P.O. Box 5643
Compton, CA 90221 **(M)**

Small Appliances

AAA Restaurant Equip.
284 Bowery
New York, NY 10012 **(W)**

Aikenwood Corp.
2151 Park Blvd/Box 26
Palo Alto, CA 94302 **(W)**

ALH, Inc.
Subsidiary of Aladdin Ind., Inc.

WARING PRODUCTS DIV., DYNAMICS CORP. OF AMERICA

P.O. Box 7235
703 Murfreesboro Rd.
Nashville, TN 37210 **(M)**
Heaters

Anets
Anetsberger Bros., Inc.
158 N. Anets Dr.
Northbrook, IL 60062 **(M)**

Bazaar De La Cuisine, Inc.
1003 Second Ave.
New York, NY 10022 **(R)**

G. S. Blakeslee & Co.
1844 S. Laramie Ave.
Chicago, IL 60650 **(M)**

Chris Craft
Algonac, MI 48001 **(M.O.)**

Cook's Supply Corp.
151 Varick St.
New York, NY 10013 **(W)**

The Crate and Barrel
190 Northfield Rd.
Northfield, IL 60093 **(R)**

Crescent Metal Products, Inc.
12711 Taft Ave.
Cleveland, OH 44108 **(M)**

Daroma Restaurant Equip.
  Corp.
196 Bowery
New York, NY 10012 **(W)**
Soda fountains

Dean & Deluca, Inc.
121 Prince St.
New York, NY 10012 **(R)**

Eastern Mountain Sports
725 Saw Mill River Rd.
Ardsley, NY 10502 **(R)**

Faema Sales Corp.
450 W. 44 St.
New York, NY 10036 **(W)**
Espresso machines

Federal Restaurant Supply
  Co., Inc.
202 Bowery
New York, NY 10012 **(W)**

The Frymaster Corp.
5000 Hollywood Ave.
P.O. Box 8618
Shreveport, LA 71108 **(M)**

Garland Commercial Ranges
185 E. South St.
Freeland, PA 18224 **(M)**

Garland Commercial Ranges
  Ltd.
41 Medulla Ave.
Toronto, 18, Ontario Canada

General Electric
Housewares and Audio
  Business Div.
Bridgeport, CT 06602 **(M)**

Gideco
4-8 rue Louis Desavis
78570 Andresy, France **(M)**
Automatic crepe machines

Groen
Div. of Dover Corp.
1900 Pratt Blvd.
Elk Grove Village, IL 60007 **(M)**
Steam kettles, braising pans

Hobart Mfg. Co.
Troy, OH 45373 **(M)**

Hollywood Refrigeration Co.
6100 Melrose Ave.
Los Angeles, CA 90038 **(M)**

Imperial Equip. Corp.
107 E. 31 St.
New York, NY 10016 **(W)**
Soda fountains

Innovec Marketing Systems
P.O. Box 1382
Huntington Beach, CA 92647
  (W)
Soda fountains

Keating of Chicago, Inc.
715 S. 25 Ave.
Bellwood, IL 60104 **(M)**
Food warmers

Lion Office Products, Inc.
401 W. Alondra Blvd.
Gardena, CA 90248 **(M)**
Electric pencil sharpeners

Manhattan Ad Hoc House-
wares
842 Lexington Ave.
New York, NY 10021 **(R)**

Matas Restaurant Supply
Corp.
186 Bowery
New York, NY 10012 **(W)**

Mazer Store Equip. Co., Inc.
207 Bowery
New York, NY 10012 **(W)**

M.O.R.A.
13 et 15 rue Montmartre
75001 Paris, France **(M)**

New York Soda Fountain Co.
1401 Park Ave.
New York, NY 10029 **(M)**

NuTone Housing Products
Div. of Scovill
Madison & Red Bank Rds.
Cincinnati, OH 45227 **(M)**

William Page & Co. Ltd.
87-91 Shaftesbury Ave.
London W1V 8AJ England
(M)

J. A. Preston Corp.
71 Fifth Ave.
New York, NY 10003 **(M.O.)**

3220 Wharton Way
Mississauga, Ontario
L4X 2C1 Canada
Medical stove

Prince Castle Inc.
426 Westgate Dr.
Addison, IL 60101 **(M)**

The Professional Kitchen
18 Cooper Sq.
New York, NY 10003 **(R)**

Raburn Products
Div. of Economics Laboratory
Inc.
4 Corporate Pk. Dr.
White Plains, NY 10604 **(M)**
Dishmachine, splash curtains

KEATING OF CHICAGO, INC.

Recon Corp.
P.O. Box 98
Park Ridge, IL 60068 **(M)**
Flatware recovery equip.

Salton Ind., Inc.
519 E. 72 St.
New York, NY 10021 **(M)**

Seco Products
Div. of McGraw Edison Co.
P.O. Box 7116
St. Louis, MO 63177 **(M)**
Slicers, cutters

Shelley Mfg. Co.
P.O. Box 440308
Miami, FL 33144 **(M)**

Sunkist Growers, Inc.
P.O. Box 7888
Van Nuys, CA 91409 **(M)**

Taylor Freezer
Rockton, IL 61072 **(M)**

Temprite Products Corp.
E. Maple Rd.
Birmingham, MI 48012 **(M)**
Soda fountains

Arthur H. Thomas Co.
Vine St. at Third
P.O. Box 779
Philadelphia, PA 19105 **(M.O.)**

Toastmaster
Div. of McGraw-Edison Co.
Algonquin, IL 60102 **(M)**

Waring Products
Div. of Dynamics Corp. of
America
New Hartford, CT 06057 **(M)**

Wells Mfg. Corp.
Harbor Way & Littlefield Ave.
South San Francisco, CA 94080
(M)
Griddles

Kitchen Appliances

AAA Restaurant Equip.
284 Bowery
New York, NY 10012 **(W)**

AMSCO
American Sterilizer Co. **(M)**

Regional Offices USA:

12990 Branford St.
Arleta, CA 91331

1-3 De Angelo Dr.
Bedford, MA 01730

P.O. Box 4126
833 Mahler Rd.
Burlingame, CA 94010

2270 Wilson St.
Cincinnati, OH 45231

7835 W. 16 Ave.
Denver, CO 80215

10 S. Clinton St.
Doylestown, PA 18901

7907 212 St. S.W.
Edmonds, WA 98020

20853 Farmington Rd.
Farmington, MI 48024

5754 Nicollet Ave. S.
Minneapolis, MN 55419

5534 Canal Blvd.
New Orleans, LA 70124

6398 Interstate 85
Norcross, GA 30071

1752 N. Highland Rd.
Pittsburgh, PA 15241

88 Sunnyside Blvd.
Plainview, NY 11803

1002 Central Expwy.
Richardson, TX 75080

701 Research Rd.
Richmond, VA 23235

6738 Chippewa St.
St. Louis, MO 63109

4424 N. Dale Mabry
Tampa, FL 33614

9930 Derby La.
Westchester, IL 60153

Amsco Canada Div.
20 Bond Ave.
Don Mills, Ontario M3B 1L9
Canada

Anets
Anetsberger Bros., Inc.
158 N. Anets Dr.
Northbrook, IL 60062 **(M)**

Bally Case & Cooler, Inc.
Bally, PA 19503
*Prefab walk-in coolers and
freezers*

Basic Leasing Corp.
509 W. 38 St.
New York, NY 10018 **(W)**
"Energy Mizer" dishwashers

G. S. Blakslee & Co.
1844 S. Laramie Ave.
Chicago, IL 60650 **(M)**

Challenge-Cook Bros., Inc.
15421 E. Gale Ave.
Industry, CA 91745 **(M)**
Large laundry systems

Cook's Supply Corp.
151 Varick St.
New York, NY 10013 **(W)**

Crescent Metal Products, Inc.
12711 Taft Ave.
Cleveland, OH 44108 **(M)**
*Restaurant ranges, ovens,
warmers*

Davis Kitchen Div.
Vacu-Master Corp. of America
233 Ferris Ave.
White Plains, NY 10603 **(W)**

Dean & Deluca, Inc.
121 Prince St.
New York, NY 10012 **(R)**

Defender Ind., Inc.
255 Main St.
New Rochelle, NY 10801 **(M.O.)**
*Refrigerators and stoves for
boats*

Evans Metal Products, Inc.
435 Park Ave. S.
New York, NY 10016 **(M)**
Glass-door refrigerators

The Frymaster Corp.
5000 Hollywood Ave.
P.O. Box 8618
Shreveport, LA 71108 **(M)**
Deep fat fryers

Garland
Div. of Welbilt Corp.
Welbilt Sq.
Maspeth, NY 11378 **(M)**
Ranges

Garland Commercial Ranges
Ltd.
41 Medulla Ave.
Toronto, 18, Ontario

Glenco Refrigeration Co.
Div. of J. P. Heilweil Ind.,
Ltd.
8000 Penrose Ave.
Philadelphia, PA 19153 **(M)**

Hafele KG
P.O. Box 160
7270 Nagold, West Germany **(M)**
Refrigerators

Hobart Mfg. Co.
Troy, OH 45373 **(M)**

Hollywood Refrigeration Co.
6100 Melrose Ave.
Los Angeles, CA 90038

Hot Food Boxes, Inc.
4107 W. Lake St.
Chicago, IL 60624 **(M)**

King Refrigerator Corp.
7602 Woodhaven Blvd.
Glendale, NY 11227 **(M)**

Koch
Subsidiary of Hobart Mfg. Co.
Troy, OH 45373 **(M)**

Manhattan Marine & Electric
Co.
116-118-120 Chambers St.
New York, NY 10007 **(R)**

Market Forge
35 Garvey St.
Everett, MA 02149 **(M)**

Mazer Store Equip. Co., Inc.
207 Bowery
New York, NY 10012 **(W)**

William Page & Co. Ltd.
87-91 Shaftesbury Ave.
London, W1V 8AJ England **(M)**
*Restaurant and kitchen
equipment*

Pompanette, Inc.
1515 S.E. 16 St.
Ft. Lauderdale, FL 33316 **(M)**

The Professional Kitchen
18 Cooper Sq.
New York, NY 10003 **(R)**

Raetone
Victory Mfg. Co.
200 W. Germantown Pike
Plymouth Meeting, PA 19462 **(M)**

Roper
1905 W. Court St.
Kankakee, IL 60901 **(M)**

Seco Products
Div. of McGraw Edison Co.
P.O. Box 7116
St. Louis, MO 63177 **(M)**
Ranges, ovens, dishwashers

Sharp Electronics Corp.
10 Keystone Pl.
Paramus, NJ 07652 **(M)**
Microwave ovens

Shelley Mfg. Co.
P.O. Box 440308
Miami, FL 33144 **(M)**
Fiber-glass food service equip.

Representatives:

Bill Edwards
Restaurant Equip. Pacific,
Inc.
51-529 Kam Hwy.
Kaawaa, HI 96730

Ken Thomson
928 Fresno Pl.
Coquitiam, B.C., Canada

Southbend
201 S. Cherry St.
South Bend, IN 46627 **(M)**
Ranges

Thermador
5119 District Blvd.
Los Angeles, CA 90040 **(M)**

Toastmaster Commercial Div.
McGraw Edison Co.
Algonquin, IL 60102 **(M)**
Ovens and dishwashers

Town Food Service Equip. Co.
351 Bowery
New York, NY 10003 **(W)**
*Specializes in restaurant
equipment for Chinatown*

UniMac Co., Inc.
2002 Dresden Dr., N.E.
Atlanta, GA 30005 **(M)**
Large laundry systems

Vollrath Co.
1236 N. 18 St.
Sheboygan, WI 53081 **(M)**
Buffet service

Vulcan-Hart
3600 N. Point Blvd.
Baltimore, MD 21222 **(M)**
Ranges

N. Wasserstrom and Sons,
Inc.
2300 Lackbourne Rd.
Columbus, OH 43207 **(M)**
Hot-food tables

Wells Mfg. Co.
202 Littlefield Ave.
San Francisco, CA 94080 **(M)**

Pulls

Allen-Stevens Corp.
33-53 62 St.
Woodside, NY 11377 **(M)**

Alvarado Mfg. Co., Inc.
10626 E. Rush St.
South El Monte, CA 91733
(M)

Architectural Supplements,
Inc.
150 E. 58 St.
New York, NY 10022 **(W)**

Julius Blum & Co., Inc.
P.O. Box 292
Carlstadt, NJ 07072

Bradley Corp.
P.O. Box 348
Menomonee Falls, WI 53051
(M)
Grab bars

Brey-Krause Mfg. Co.
Front & Chews Sts.
Allentown, PA 18102
Grab bars

Comyn Ching and Co. Ltd.
13-21 Shelton St.
Upper St. Martin's La.
London WC2H 9Jp England **(M)**

Crompton Nettlefold Stenman
Ltd.
Ashton-in-Market
Wigan, Lancashire WN4
9AN England **(M)**

Defender Ind., Inc.
255 Main St.
New Rochelle, NY 10801
(M.O.)

Emhart Ind., Inc.
Hardware Div.
Berlin, CT 06037 **(M)**

Forms & Surfaces
Box 5215
Santa Barbara, CA 93108 **(M/W)**

Fuso Gomu Ind. Co. Ltd.
Head Office 11-25 Hasune
3 Chome
Itabashi-Ku, Tokyo 174 **(M)**

Hafele KG
P.O. Box 160
7270 Nagold, West Germany **(M)**

The Ironmonger
446 N. Wells St.
Chicago, IL 60610 **(W)**

Manhattan Marine & Electric
Co., Inc.
116-118-120 Chambers St.
New York, NY 10007 **(R)**

Metos Sauna
13000 Bellevue Redmond Rd.
Bellevue, WA 98005 **(M)**
Sauna door pulls

Charles Parker
290 Pratt St.
Meriden, CT 06450 **(M)**

H. Pfanstiel Hardware Co.,
Inc.
Jeffersonville, NY 12748 **(M)**

Plastech
Div. of Pennsylvania Pacific
Corp.
John Fitch Industrial Pk.
P.O. Box C-70
Warminster, PA 18974 **(M)**

Sentronic Intl.
Div. of General Nucleonics,
Inc.
P.O. Box 116TR
Brunswick, OH 44212 **(W)**
Turnstiles

Simon's Hardware
421 Third Ave.
New York, NY 10016 **(R)**

Yorkville Ind., Inc.
55 Motor Ave.
Farmingdale, NY 11735 **(M)**

Ladders

American LaFrance
Div. of A-T-O, Inc.
P.O. Box 6159
Charlottesville, VA 22906 **(M)**
Fire-escape ladders

Blickman Health Ind., Inc.
20-21 Wagaraw Rd.
Fair Lawn, NJ 07410 **(M)**

Defender Ind., Inc.
255 Main St.
New Rochelle, NY 10801
(M.O.)

Equip. Co. of America
1075 Hialeah Dr.
Hialeah, FL 33010 **(M)**
Rolling ladders

Fidelity Products Co.
705 Penn Ave. S.
Minneapolis, MN 55426
(M.O.)

Sam Flax
55 E. 55 St.
New York, NY 10022 **(R)**

Fuller
45 E. 57 St.
New York, NY 10022 **(R)**

Garelick Mfg. Co.
644 2 St.
St. Paul Park, MN 55071 **(M)**
Marine supplies

Hardman Ind.
1668 22 St.
Santa Monica, CA 90404 **(M)**

A. Liss & Co.
35-03 Bradley Ave.
Long Island City, NY 11101
(W/R)

Little Giant Ind., Inc.
31 S. 100 W.
American Fork, Utah 84003
(M)

Manhattan Marine & Electric
Co., Inc.
116-118-120 Chambers St.
New York, NY 10007 **(R)**

Manutan
32 Bis, boulevard de Picpus
75012 Paris, France **(W)**

Peerless Ind., Inc.
4200 W. Chicago Ave.
Chicago, IL 60651 **(M)**

Pompanette, Inc.
1515 S.E. 16 St.
Fort Lauderdale, FL 33316
(M)

326 First St.
Annapolis, MD 21403

Putnam Rolling Ladder Co.,
Inc.
32 Howard St.
New York, NY 10013 **(M)**

Recreation Equip. Corp.
724 W. 8 St.
Anderson, IN 46011 **(M)**

Rubbermaid Commercial
Products, Inc.
Winchester, VA 22601 **(M)**

Spiral Steel Products
35-15 58 St.
Woodside, NY 11377 **(M)**

R. D. Werner Co., Inc.
P.O. Box 580
Greenville, PA 16125 **(M)**

P.O. Box 448
Franklin Park, IL 60131

White Metal Rolling and
Stamping Corp.
80 Moultrie St.
Brooklyn, NY 11222 **(M)**

EQUIPTO

Electrical

Air-Ways Distr., Inc.
1456 Middle Country Rd.
Centereach, NY 11720 **(W)**

Bally Manufacturing
2640 W. Belmont
Chicago, IL 60618 **(M)**
Pin-ball Machines

Briarwood
Div. of Brunswick Co.
Skokie, IL **(M)**
Pin-ball Machines

Briscoe Mfg. Co.
P.O. Box 628
1055 Gibbard Ave.
Columbus, OH 43216 **(M)**

Brookstone Co.
Vose Farm Rd.
Peterborough, NH 03458
(M.O.)

Bunting SteriSystems, Inc.
46 Beatrice St.
P.O. Box 4114
Bridgeport, CT 06607 **(M)**

Cole-Parmer Instrument Co.
7425 N. Oak Park Ave.
Chicago, IL 60648 **(M.O.)**

Cordomatic Reels
17 & Indiana Ave.
Philadelphia, PA 19132 **(M)**

Daburn Electronics & Cable
Corp.
2360 Hoffman St.
Bronx, NY 10458 **(M)**
Coiled cords

Defender Ind., Inc.
255 Main St.
New Rochelle, NY 10801
(M.O.)

Electro-Systems, Inc.
25141 Fremont Rd.
Los Altos, CA 94022 **(M)**

Sam Flax
55 E. 55 St.
New York, NY 10022 **(R)**

Manhattan Marine & Electric
Co., Inc.
116-118-120 Chambers St.
New York, NY 10007 **(R)**

Morsa
182 Hester St.
New York, NY 10002 **(R)**

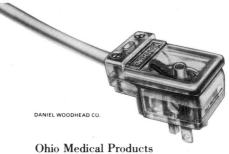

DANIEL WOODHEAD CO.

Ohio Medical Products
3030 Airco Dr.
P.O. Box 7550
Dept. 353
Madison, WI 53707 **(M)**

Perko, Inc.
16490 N.W. 13 Ave.
P.O. Box 64000-D
Miami, FL 33164 **(M)**

Scovill
NuTone Div.
Madison & Red Bank Rds.
Cincinnati, OH 45227 **(M)**
Fire intruder alarm systems

Square D Co.
3300 Medalist Dr.
Oshkosh, WI 54901 **(M)**
Modular medicalware

Stanley Door Operating Equip
Div. of The Stanley Works
Farmington, CT 06032 **(M)**
Automatic door opening

Wainland's Inc.
1108 First Ave.
New York, NY 10021
(M/R)

Daniel Woodhead Co.
3411 Woodhead Dr.
Northbrook, IL 60062 **(M)**

Yorkville Ind., Inc.
55 Motor Ave.
Farmingdale, NY 11735 **(M)**
Lamp hardware

Broom Closet

Allsteel Scale Co., Inc.
80 Spring St.
New York, NY 10012 **(W)**
Hampers

Artwire Creations, Inc.
41 Wayne Ave.
Suffern, NY 10901 **(M)**

Banner Mat & Products
17 Mercer St.
Cincinnati, OH 45210 **(W)**

Beacon Products Corp.
Newton Highlands, MA 02161
(M)

Beam Supply
Ind. Maintenance Supplies &
 Equip.
712 Broadway
New York, NY 10003 **(W/R)**

Boss Mfg. Co.
Consumer Div.
221 W. 1 St.
Kewanee, IL 61443 **(M)**
Work gloves

Brookstone Co.
Vose Farm Rd.
Peterborough, NH 03458 **(M.O.)**
Brooms

Cardinal Glove Co., Inc.
902 Passaic Ave.
East Newark, NJ 07029 **(M)**
Work gloves

Continental Mfg. Co.
Div. of Contico Intl., Inc.
1101 Warson Rd.
St. Louis, MO 63132 **(M)**

Continental Mfg. (U.K.) Ltd.
Teaconsfield Rd.
Hayes, Middlesex
UB4 ONW England

Cordomatic
17 & Indiana Ave.
Philadelphia, PA 19132 **(M)**
*Automatic retracting
 clotheslines*

Craftsman Brush Co., Inc.
39 Pearl St.
Brooklyn, NY 11201 **(M)**

Crystal Lake Mfg.
P.O. Box 159
Autaugaville, AL 36003 **(M)**
Mops and brooms

Dahnz Ind., Inc.
2 Park Ave.
New York, NY 10016 **(W)**
Galvanized cans

 1051 Clinton St.
 Buffalo, NY 14206

Elkay Mfg. Co.
2700 S. 17 Ave.
Broadview, IL 60153 **(M)**

F. H. LAWSON CO.

Emsco, Inc.
P.O. Box 151
Girard, PA 16417 **(M)**
Mop pails

Eureka Co.
Div. of Natl. Union Electric
 Corp.
Bloomington, IL 61701 **(M)**

Federal Restaurant Supply
 Co., Inc.
202 Bowery
New York, NY 10012 **(W)**

Howard Metalcraft
14 & Laurel Sts.
Pottsville, PA 17901 **(M)**

ICF
International Contract
 Furnishings, Inc.
145 E. 57 St.
New York, NY 10022 **(W)**

Iron-A-Way, Inc.
220 W. Jackson
Morton; IL 61550 **(M)**
Built-in ironing centers

Lawson
A Tappan Div.
801 Evans St.
Cincinnati, OH 45204 **(M)**
Pails

Loroman Co., Inc.
230 Fifth Ave.
New York, NY 10001 **(M)**
Clothes-drying racks

Lustro-Ware
Div. of Borden Chemical
Columbus, OH 43223 **(M)**
Heavy-duty pails

Macy's
Herald Square
New York, NY 10001 **(R)**

Manhattan Ad Hoc Housewares
842 Lexington Ave.
New York, NY 10021 **(R)**

Manutan
32 Bis, boulevard de Picpus
75012 Paris, France **(M)**

Medalist Canvas Products
19 E. McWilliams St.
Fond du Lac, WI 54935 **(M)**
Canvas hampers

Mery, Inc.
Box 728
San Juan, Puerto Rico 00902 **(M)**
Cleaning equipment

Metropolitan Wire Corp.
Wilkes-Barre, Pa 18705 **(M)**

 16, avenue des Courses
 1050 Brussels, Belgium

Morrell Brush Mfg. Co., Inc.
33 Mulberry St.
Middletown, NY 10940 **(M)**

Naco Fabrics
145 Plant Ave.
Hauppauge, NY 11787 **(W/R)**
*Jiffy Steamer for rugs,
 upholstery, and drapery*

Oxwall Tool Co.
Consolidated Foods Co.
133-10 32 Ave.
Flushing, NY 11352 **(M)**

Prince Castle, Inc.
426 Westgate Dr.
Addison, IL 60101
Waste bins

The Professional Kitchen
18 Cooper Sq.
New York, NY 10003 **(R)**

R & W Specialty Mfg. Corp.
504 Metropolitan Ave.
Brooklyn, NY 11211 **(W)**
Built-in ironing centers

Rosenwach, Inc.
96 N. 9 St.
Brooklyn, NY 11211 **(M)**
Trash receptacles

Royal Maid, Inc.
P.O. Drawer 30
Hazlehurst, MS 39083 **(M)**
Squeegee window cleaners

Rubbermaid Commercial
 Products, Inc.
Winchester, VA 22601 **(M)**

G. Rushbrooke (Smithfield)
 Ltd.
67/77 Charterhouse St.
London EC1M 6HL England **(R)**
Aprons

Schlueter Mfg. Co.
4700 Goodfellow Blvd.
St. Louis, MO 63120 **(M)**
Mopping equipment

Southeastern Machine &
 Tool Co., Inc.
P.O. Box 31087
Raleigh, NC 27612 **(M)**
"Jetaway" water brooms

Sparkle Plenty, Inc.
625 N. Michigan Ave.
Chicago, IL 60611 **(M)**
Chandelier cleaner

Steele Canvas Basket Co.
199 Concord Turnpike
Cambridge, MA 02146 **(M)**
Canvas hampers

Tedruth Plastics Corp.
Tedruth Plaza
P.O. Box 607
Farmingdale, NJ 07727 **(M)**
Garbage hampers

Tucker Cosco
345 Central St.
Leominster, MA 01453 **(M)**

 1-721-111 St.
 Arlington, TX 76011

Union Fork and Hoe Co.
500 Dublin Ave.
Columbus, OH 43216 **(M)**

United Metal Receptacle
 Corp.
14 & Laurel St.
Pottsville, PA 17901 **(M)**

The Weck Corp.
1218 Third Ave.
New York, NY 10021 **(R)**
Clotheslines

White Metal Rolling &
 Stamping Corp.
80 Moultrie St.
Brooklyn, NY 11222 **(M)**
Rakes

Whiting and Davis Co.
23 W. Bacon St.
Plainville, MA 02762 **(M)**
Metal mesh protective aprons

FINISHING TOUCHES

Wall Graphics

Akins Mfg. Corp.
100 Ave. of Americas
New York, NY 10013 **(M)**

Bailey/Huebner
Henri Bendel
10 W. 57 St.
New York, NY 10019 **(R)**
Maps

Broadway, Ltd.
2768 Broadway
New York, NY 10025 **(R)**

Caddylak Systems, Inc.
201 Montrose Rd.
Westbury, NY 11590 **(M)**
Magnetic boards

Ceco Publishing Co.
30400 Van Dyke Ave.
Warren, MI 48093 **(M)**
Billboards

Coyne & Paddock
100 Ave. of the Americas
New York, NY 10013 **(M)**

Environmental Graphics, Inc.
15295 Minnetonka Blvd.
Minnetonka, MN 55343 **(M)**
Wallpaper photomurals

Foster & Kleiser
A MetroMedia Co.
49-29 Maspeth Ave.
Maspeth, NY 11378 **(M)**

Gopher Stamp & Die Co.
Prior St. & W. Minnehaha Ave.
St. Paul, MN 55104 **(M)**

J. L. Hammett Co.
Hammett Pl.
Braintree, MA 02184 **(M/R)**

U.S. Rte. 29 S.
Lynchburg, VA 24502

165 Water St.
Lyons, NY 14489

2393 Vauxhall Rd.
Union, NJ 07083

The Hammond Map Store, Inc.
12 E. 41 St.
New York, NY 10017 **(R)**

Letterama, Inc.
17 DuPont St.
Plainview, NY 11803 **(M)**

Rand McNally Map Stores
23 E. Madison
Chicago, IL 60602 **(R)**

10 E. 53 St.
New York, NY 10022 **(R)**

206 Sansome St.
San Francisco, CA 94104 **(R)**

Manutan
32 Bis, boulevard de Picpus
75012 Paris, France **(W)**

Merit Studios
250 W. 54 St.
New York, NY 10019 **(R)**
Photomurals

Mitten Designer Letters
85 Fifth Ave.
New York, NY 10003 **(M)**

Standard Signs, Inc.
3190 E. 65 St.
Cleveland, OH 44127 **(M)**

3 M Co.
Architectural Paintings Div.
3 M Ctr.
P.O. Box 33660
St. Paul, MN 55101 **(M)**
Architectural paintings

Berkey K & L Custom Lab
222 E. 44 St.
New York, NY 10017

Graetz Brothers Ltd.
715 St. Maurice St.
Montreal, Quebec H3C1L4
Canada

Imero Fiorentino Assoc., Inc.
10 W. 66 St.
New York, NY 10023

Imero Fiorentino Assoc., Inc.
7250 Franklin Ave.
Hollywood, CA 90046

K & S Photo Graphics
180 N. Wabash Ave.
Chicago, IL 60601

Metacolor
855 Sansome St.
San Francisco, CA 94111

Parkway Color Lab
57 W. Grand Ave.
Chicago, IL 60610

Portfolio Inc.
2631 Reynard Way
P.O. Box 3567
San Diego, CA 92103

Rapid Color, I.S.D.
17981 Sky Park Circle
Irvine, CA 92714

Ina Victor Assoc.
1095 Park Ave.
New York, NY 10028

Preparation

AAA Restaurant Equip.
284 Bowery
New York, NY 10012 **(W)**

Allied Metal Spinning Corp.
808 Cauldwell Ave.
Bronx, NY 10456 **(M)**

American Cutlery & Hardware Co.
184 Bowery
New York, NY 10012 **(W)**

Anchor Hocking
Lancaster, OH 43130 **(M)**

Bazaar de la Cuisine, Inc.
1003 Second Ave.
New York, NY 10022 **(R)**

Bloomfield Ind.
4536 W. 47 St.
Chicago, IL 60632 **(M)**

Bloomfield Ind. Canada Ltd.
260 Belfield Rd.
Rexdale, Ontario, Canada

Bloomingdale's
1000 Third Ave.
New York, NY 10022 **(R)**

Bromwell
Universal-Derwin Div. of
Leigh Products, Inc.
Michigan City, IN 46360 **(M)**

Brookstone Co.
127 Vose Farm Rd.
Peterborough, NH 03458
(M.O.)

Cambro
P.O. Box 2000
Huntington Beach, CA 92647 **(M)**

Chris Craft
Algonac, MI 48001 **(M.O.)**
Boating supply

Cook's Supply Corp.
151 Varick St.
New York, NY 10013 **(W)**

Co-Rect Products, Inc.
3340 Gorham Ave.
Minneapolis, MN 55426 **(M)**
Racks for water-cooker bottles

Corning Glass Works
Corning, NY 14830 **(M)**
Laboratory glass

The Crate and Barrel
190 Northfield Rd.
Northfield, IL 60093 **(R)**

Dean and Deluca
121 Prince St.
New York, NY 10012 **(R)**

EKCO Products, Inc.
Div. of GLACO Group
1949 N. Cicero Ave.
Chicago, IL 60639 **(M)**
Baking pans—special shapes

Erno
55 N. 2 St.
Philadelphia, PA **(W/R)**
Dressing jars, bottles

Federal Restaurant Supply
Co., Inc.
202 Bowery
New York, NY 10012 **(W)**

Foley Housewares Div.
Foley Mfg. Co.
3300 N.E. 5 St.
Minneapolis, MN 55418 **(M)**

General Housewares Corp.
Cookware Group
P.O. Box 4066
Terre Haute, IN 47804 **(M)**

Leyse Aluminum Co.
Kewaunee, WI 54216 **(M)**

Manhattan Ad Hoc Housewares
842 Lexington Ave.
New York, NY 10021 **(R)**

Matas Restaurant Supply
Corp.
186 Bowery
New York, NY 10012 **(W)**

Mazer Store Equip. Co., Inc.
207 Bowery
New York, NY 10002 **(W)**

Mirro Aluminum Co.
Manitowoc, WI 54220 **(M)**

M.O.R.A.
13 et 15 rue Montmartre
75001 Paris, France **(M)**

William Page & Co. Ltd.
87-91 Shaftesbury Ave.
London W1V 8AJ England
(M)

The Professional Kitchen
18 Cooper Sq.
New York, NY 10003 **(R)**

Rubbermaid Commercial
Products, Inc.
Winchester, Va 22601 **(M)**

G. Rushbrooke (Smithfield)
Ltd.
67/77 Charterhouse St.
London EC1M 6HL England
(R)

Shelley Mfg. Co.
P.O. Box 440308
Miami, FL 33144 **(M)**

Taylor & Ng
P.O. Box 200
Brisbane, CA 94005 **(M)**

Town Food Service Equip. Co.
351 Bowery
New York, NY 10002 **(W)**
*Specializes in restaurant
equipment for Chinatown*

Samuel Underberg
620 Atlantic Ave.
Brooklyn, NY 11217 **(W/R)**

Tabletop

AAA Restaurant Equip.
284 Bowery
New York, NY 10012 **(W)**

Alco Tableware, Inc.
11 E. 26 St.
New York, NY 10010 **(M)**

Alladin Synergetics, Inc.
1 Vantage Way
Box 10888
Nashville, TN 37210 **(M)**

Amoco Chemicals Corp.
Packaging and Custom
Products Div.
200 E. Randolph Dr.
Chicago, IL 60601 **(M)**

Anchor Hocking
Lancaster, OH 43130 **(M)**

KIMBERLY-CLARK TOWEL, COURTESY GRAYARC

Bailey/Huebner
Henri Bendel
10 W. 57 St.
New York, NY 10019 **(R)**

Bari Restaurant & Pizza
Equip.
244 Bowery
New York, NY 10012 **(W/R)**

Bloomfield Ind.
4546 W. 47 St.
Chicago, IL 60632 **(M)**

    Bloomfield Ind. Canada Ltd.
    260 Belfield Rd.
    Rexdale, Ontario,
    Canada

Bloomingdale's
1000 Third Ave.
New York, NY 10022 **(R)**

Bromwell
Div. of Leigh Products, Inc.
Michigan City, IN 46360 **(M)**
Camping goods

L. Brun
19, rue des Halles
Paris, 1 France **(R)**

Cambro
P.O. Box 2000
Huntington Beach, CA 92647 **(M)**

Carrieri
174-176 boulevard
Saint-Germaine
75006 Paris, France **(M)**

Chris Craft
Algonac, MI 48001 **(M.O.)**

Cokesbury
1661 N. N.W. Highway
Park Ridge, IL 60068 **(M)**
*Communion plates,
candleholders*

Cole-Parmer Instrument Co.
7425 N. Oak Park Ave.
Chicago, IL 60648 **(M.O.)**

Cook's Supply Corp.
151 Varick St.
New York, NY 10013 **(W)**

The Crate and Barrel
Administrative Offices
190 Northfield Rd.
Northfield, IL 60093 **(R)**

Cres-Cor
Crescent Metal Products, Inc.
12711 Taft Ave.
Cleveland, OH 44108 **(M)**

Dean and Deluca
121 Prince St.
New York, NY 10012 **(R)**

Defender Ind., Inc.
255 Main St.
New Rochelle, NY 10801
(M.O.)

Dripcut Corp.
Box S
400 Rutherford
Goleta, CA 93017 **(M)**

    Dripcut Corp.
    York, SC 29745

Erno
55 N. 2 St.
Philadelphia, PA **(W/R)**
Barware

Fallani & Cohn, Inc.
14 E. 38 St.
New York, NY 10016 **(M)**
Restaurant tablecloths

Federal Glassware
Div. of Federal Paper Board
Co., Inc.
555 E. Woodrow Ave.
Columbus, OH 43207 **(M)**

Federal Restaurant Supply
Corp., Inc.
202 Bowery
New York, NY 10012 **(W)**

Grayarc
Subsidiary of Dictaphone
882 Third Ave.
Brooklyn, NY 11232 **(M)**
Industrial wipes

Igloo Corp.
P.O. Box 19322
Houston, TX 77024 **(M)**

Jackson China
3 & Osborne
Falls Creek, PA 15840 **(M)**

Krown Products
120 Copeland Rd., N.E.
P.O. Box 76399
Atlanta, GA 30328 **(W)**

Leyse Aluminum Co.
Kewaunee, WI 54216 **(M)**

MacLevy Products Corp.
92-21 Corona Ave.
Elmhurst, NY 11373 **(M)**
Sauna accessories

Macy's
Herald Square
New York, NY 10001 **(R)**

Manhattan Ad Hoc House-
wares
842 Lexington Ave.
New York, NY 10021 **(R)**

Matas Restaurant Supply
Corp.
186 Bowery
New York, NY 10012 **(W)**

Mirro Aluminum Co.
Manitowoc, WI 54220 **(M)**

M.O.R.A.
13 et 15 rue Montmartre
75001 Paris, France **(M)**

Morton Quality Products
Div. of Morton-Norwich
Products, Inc.
110 N. Wacker Dr.
Chicago, IL 60606 **(M)**
Institutional salt shakers

William Page & Co. Ltd.
87-91 Shaftesbury Ave.
London W1V 8AJ England
(M)

Papeterie Moderne
12, rue de la Feronnerie
Paris, 1er France **(R)**
Cheese price signs

BAMBU SALES, INC.

HALL CHINA CO.

Pittsburgh Corning Corp.
800 Presque Isle Drive
Pittsburgh, PA 15239 **(M)**
Glass block

The Professional Kitchen
18 Cooper Sq.
New York, NY 10003 **(R)**

Rivoli
55 rue de la Verrerie
75004 Paris, France **(M)**

G. Rushbrooke (Smithfield)
  Ltd.
67/77 Charterhouse St.
London EC1M 6HL England **(M)**

Saint Gobain Ind.
Gobeleterie
Boite Postale 1925
45009 Orleans Cedex, France **(M)**

Server Products, Inc.
P.O. Box 249
Menomonee Falls, WI 53051 **(M)**

Shenango China By Interpace
P.O. Box 120
New Castle, PA 16103 **(M)**
Creamers

Siege Soial
66 rue Marx Dormoy
94500 Champigny sur Marne,
  France **(M)**

Sigma Marketing Systems,
  Inc.
615 South St.
Garden City, NY 11530 **(W)**

Supro Bldg. Products Corp.
48-16 70 St.
Woodside, NY 11377 **(W)**

Taylor & Ng
P.O. Box 200
Brisbane, CA 94005 **(M/M.O.)**

Town Food Service Equip. Co.
351 Bowery
New York, NY 10002 **(W)**
*Restaurant equipment for
  Chinatown*

Tri-State Ind., Ltd.
1436 Williamsbridge Rd.
Bronx, NY 10461 **(W)**
Votive candles

U.S. Mat & Rubber Co., Inc.
P.O. Box 152
Brockton, Mass 02403 **(M)**

Wood Brothers Glass Co. Ltd.
Borough Flint Glass Works
Pontefract Rd.
Barnsley, South Yorkshire
S71 1HL England **(M)**

Laboratory Glass

Archer Surgical Supplies, Inc.
217 E. 23 St.
New York, NY 10010 **(W/R)**

Arnel Products Co.
2701 Ave. U
Brooklyn, NY 11229 **(M)**

Bailey/Huebner
Henri Bendel
10 W. 57 St.
New York, NY 10019 **(R)**

Cole-Parmer Instrument Co.
7425 N. Oak Park Ave.
Chicago, IL 60648 **(M.O.)**

Corning Glass Works
Corning, NY 14830 **(M)**

Edmund Scientific Co.
Edscorp Bldg.
Barrington, NJ 08007 **(M.O.)**

Fisher Scientific
52 Fadem Rd.
Springfield, NJ 07081 **(W)**

Houde Glass Co.
3277 McCarter Hwy.
Newark, NJ 07104 **(M)**

Kimble Products
Div. of Owens-Illinois, Inc.
P.O. Box 1035
Toledo, OH 43666 **(M)**

Lab Glass, Inc.
11 West Blvd. & Oak Rd.
Vineland, NJ 08360 **(W)**

Loumac Supply Corp.
900 Passaic Ave.
Harrison, NJ 07029 **(M)**

Mayflower Medical Supplies Co.
25-15 85 St.
Brooklyn, NY 11214 **(W)**

Mercer Glass Works
725 Broadway
New York, NY 10012 **(W)**

N.Y. Lab Supply Co., Inc.
510 Hempstead Turnpike
West Hempstead, NY 11552
  (W)

Sarstedt, Inc.
743 Alexander Rd.
Princeton, NJ 08540 **(M)**
*Disposable plastics for
  medical labs*

SGA Scientific, Inc.
737 Broad St.
Bloomfield, NJ 07003 **(W)**
Laboratory equipment

  Park Sq. Bldg.
  Boston, MA 02116

  2375 Pratt Blvd.
  Elk Grove Village, IL 60007

  2560 E. Fender Ave.
  Fullerton, CA 92631

  109 Church St.
  New Haven, CT 06510

  1420 Walnut St.
  Philadelphia, PA 19102

  Wheaton Plaza Office Bldg.
  Silver Springs, MD 20902

  109 S. Warren St.
  Syracuse, NY 13202

Arthur H. Thomas Co.
Vine St. at Third
P.O. Box 779
Philadelphia, PA 19105 **(M.O.)**
Laboratory equipment

Ware Medics
434 Broadway
New York, NY 10012 **(W)**
Laboratory glassware

Mirrors

Accessory Specialties, Inc.
1335 E. Bay Ave.
New York, NY 10474 **(M)**

Allsteel Scale Co., Inc.
80 Spring St.
New York, NY 10012 **(W)**
Detection mirrors

Auto World
701 N. Keyser Ave.
Scranton, PA 18508 **(R)**

Bell Glass & Mirror Co.
1328 Flatbush Ave.
Brooklyn, NY 11210 **(M)**
Detection mirrors

Chic Display Co.
142 W. 14 St.
New York, NY 10011 **(W/R)**
Mirror mosaics

Defender Ind., Inc.
255 Main St.
New Rochelle, NY 10801
  (M.O.)

Edmund Scientific Co.
Edscorp Bldg.
Barrington, NJ 08007 **(M.O.)**

Eliason Corp.
Easy Swing Door Div.
P.O. Box 2128
Kalamazoo, MI 49003 **(M)**

Fuller Stationers
49 E. 57 St.
New York, NY 10022 **(R)**

Gargoyles, Ltd.
512 S. Third St.
Philadelphia, PA 19147 **(M)**

MEG-Merchandising Equip.
  Group, Inc.
100 Bidwell Rd.
S. Windsor, CT 06074 **(M)**
Three-way mirrors

Miami-Carey
203 Garver Rd.
Monroe, OH 45050 **(M)**

Saint Gobain Vitrage
Une Division de Saint-Gobain
  Industries
62 boulevard Victor-Hugo
B.P. 124
92209 Neuilly-sur-Seine,
  France **(M)**

Tomorrow Designs, Ltd.
979 Third Ave.
New York, NY 10022 **(W)**
Mirror mosaics

J. C. Whitney & Co.
1917-19 Archer Ave.
P.O. Box 8410
Chicago, IL 60680 **(R)**

Yankee Metal Products Corp.
Norwalk, CT 06852 **(M)**

Planters/Ash Urns

Accessory Specialties, Inc.
1335 E. Bay Ave.
New York, NY 10474 **(M)**

Akins Mfg. Corp.
100 Ave. of the Americas
New York, NY 10013 **(M)**

Architectural Supplements,
Inc.
150 E. 58 St.
New York, NY 10022 **(W)**

Broadway, Ltd.
2768 Broadway
New York, NY 10025 **(R)**
Railroad ashtrays

Century Lumber
1875 2 Ave.
New York, NY 10028 **(R)**
Cement troughs

Corning Glass Works
Corning, NY 14830 **(M)**

Fib-Con Corp.
Box 5564
4005 Wisconsin Ave., N.W.
Washington, D.C. 20016 **(M)**

Henry Molded Products, Inc.
71 N. 16 St.
P.O. Box 75
Lebanon, PA 17042 **(M)**

H.U.D.D.L.E.
3416 Wesley St.
Culver City, CA 90230 **(M)**

Lawson
A Tappan Div.
801 Evans St.
Cincinnati, OH 45204 **(M)**

A. Liss & Co.
35-03 Bradley Ave.
Long Island City, NY 11101
(W/M.O.)

Loumac Supply Corp.
900 Passaic Ave.
Harrison, NJ 07029 **(M)**
Glass cylinders

Metalweave Products Corp.
F.O.B.
New Rochelle, NY 10801 **(M)**

William Page & Co.
87-91 Shaftesbury Ave.
London W1V 8AJ England
(M)

Robots
Viale Caldara 34
20122 Milan, Italy **(M)**

Rosenwach, Inc.
40-25 Crescent St.
Long Island City, NY 11101
(M)

Sears Farm and Ranch
Catalog
Sears Roebuck & Co.
Sears Tower
Chicago, IL 60684
Animal feeding troughs

Scales and Clocks

Allsteel Scale Co., Inc.
80 Spring St.
New York, NY 10012 **(W)**

Aristo Import Co., Inc.
630 Fifth Ave.
New York, NY 10020 **(W)**
Clocks and timers

C & H Distr., Inc.
401 S. 5 St.
Milwaukee, WI 53204 **(W)**

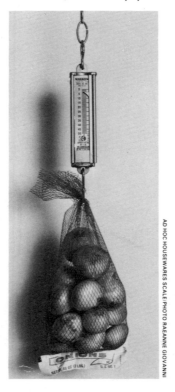

AD HOC HOUSEWARES SCALE/PHOTO RAEANNE GIOVANNI

Chris Craft
Algonac, MI 48001 **(M.O.)**

Defender Ind., Inc.
255 Main St.
New Rochelle, NY 10801
(M.O.)

Detecto Scales, Inc.
230 Fifth Ave.
New York, NY 10001 **(M)**

Fair-Play Scoreboards
Box 1847
Des Moines, IA 50306 **(M)**

Franklin Instrument Co., Inc.
Box 735
Richboro, PA 18954 **(M)**

General Electric
Housewares and Audio
Business Div.
Bridgeport, CT 06602 **(M)**

Koch
Div. of Hobart Mfg. Co.
Troy, NY 45373 **(M)**

MacLevy Products Corp.
92-21 Corona Ave.
Elmhurst, NY 11373 **(M)**

Manhattan Marine & Electric
Co., Inc.
116-118-120 Chambers St.
New York, NY 10007 **(R)**

Manutan
32 Bis, boulevard de Picpus
75012 Paris, France **(W)**

Mellor Gym Supply Corp.
9 E. 40 St.
New York, NY 10016 **(W)**

Howard Miller Clock Co.
Zeeland, MI 49464 **(M)**

M.O.R.A.
13 et 15 rue Montmartre
75001 Paris, France **(M)**

Ohio Medical Products
3030 Airco Dr.
P.O. Box 7550
Madison, WI 53707 **(M)**

Pennsylvania Scale Co.
Leola, PA 17540 **(M)**

J. A. Preston Corp.
71 Fifth Ave.
New York, NY 10003 **(M.O.)**

J. A. Preston of Canada Ltd.
3220 Wharton Way

Mississauga, Ontario
L4X 2C1 Canada **(M.O.)**

The Professional Kitchen
18 Cooper Sq.
New York, NY 10003 **(R)**

Jules Racine & Co.
85 Executive Blvd.
Elmsford, NY 10523 **(W)**

Racine
LaChaux de Fonds,
Switzerland

R & W Specialty Mfg. Corp.
504 Metropolitan Ave.
Brooklyn, NY 11211 **(M/W)**

Sears Farm and Ranch Catalog
Sears Roebuck and Co.
Sears Tower
Chicago, IL 60684 **(R)**

Solari America, Inc.
45 W. 45 St.
New York, NY 10036 **(M)**

Solari and Cie.
Via Pieri 29
33100 Udine, Italy

Sorgel Electric Corp.
Subsidiary of Square D Co.
3300 Medalist Dr.
Oshkosh, WI 54901 **(M)**
Digital Clocks and timers

Arthur H. Thomas Co.
Vine St. at Third
P.O. Box 779
Philadelphia, PA 19105 **(M.O.)**

Seth Thomas
Div. of General Time Corp.
Thomaston, CT 06787 **(M)**

Samuel Underberg
620 Atlantic Ave.
Brooklyn, NY 11217 **(W/R)**

Weigh-Tronix, Inc.
Fairmont, MN 56031 **(M)**

Antiques

Les Galeries Modernes de Paris
30, rue St. Denis
75001 Paris, France **(R)**
Antique restaurantware

Long Island Phone Co.
121 Lakeville Rd.
New Hyde Park, NY 11040 **(R)**
Vintage pay telephone

Kenneth Lynch and Sons
177 Factory Rd.
Wilton, CT 06897 (M)

Mandarin Products Corp.
37 W. 23 St.
New York, NY 10010 (M/W)
Nautical antiques

Niccolini
926 Third Ave.
New York, NY 10022 (W)
Antique drawers and cabinets

Village Stripper
519 Hudson St.
New York, NY 10014 (R)

Industrial Inspired

Abitare
212 E. 57 St.
New York, NY 10022 (R)

Acerbis Intl.
Via Brusaporto 31
24068 Seriate, Italy (M)

Lato Via Orefici
Milano, Italy

Ambienti
792 Madison
New York, NY 10021 (R)

Art et Industrie
132 Thompson St.
New York, NY 10013 (R)

Artemide
Via Brughiera
20010 Milanese, Italy (M)

Astori s.a.s.
industria per l'arrendamento
20124 Viale Restelli 5
Milano, Italy (M)

v.s. Maria Dell'anima
00186 Rome, Italy

9 E. 38 St.
New York, NY 10016

Atelier Intl.
595 Madison Ave.
New York, NY 10022 (W)

Bieffeplast
P.O. Box 406
35100 Padova, Italy (M)

Britt Ind.
420 W. Florida St.
Milwaukee, WI 53204 (M)
Tractor seats

Conran's
160 E. 54 St.
New York, NY 10022 (R)

Danese
Piazza San Fedele'2
20121 Milan, Italy (M)

D/R
Design Research Stores
53 E. 57 St.
New York, NY 10022 (R)

9630 Wilshire Blvd.
Beverly Hills, CA 90212

48 Brattle St.
Cambridge, MA 02138

S. Coast Plaza
3333 Bristol St.
Costa Mesa, CA 92626

Chestnut Hill Mall
Newton, MA 02167

1801 Walnut St.
Philadelphia, PA 19103

900 N. Point St.
Ghirardelli Sq.
San Francisco, CA 94109

1 Embarcadero Ctr.
San Francisco, CA 94111

180 Post Rd., E.
Westport, CT 06880

Erco Leuchten GmbH
Casella Postale 2460
D-5880 Ludenscheid, Italy (M)

Etalage Fabrics, Inc.
979 Third Ave.
New York, NY 10022 (W)

Flos
Via Moretto 58
25100 Brescia, Italia (M)

30 rue de Lisbonne
Paris 8, France

Riehler Strasse 21
5000 Koln 1, Germany

36, place du Bourg de Four
1204 Geneva, Switzerland

Fuso Gomu Ind. Co. Ltd
Head Office 11-25 Hasune 3
Chome
Itabashi-Ku, Tokyo 174 (M)

Giovenzana Style
Via Drivata Cascia 8
20128 Milan, Italy

G.S. Assoc., Inc.
150 E. 58 St.
New York, NY 10022 (W)
"Tractor" chairs

Habitat
Centre Commercial
de la Tour
Maine-Montparnasse
11 rue de l'Arrivée
Boite Cidex
Paris, France (R)

Intl. Harvester
401 N. Michigan Ave.
Chicago, IL 60611 (M)
Tractor seats

George Kovacs Lighting, Inc.
69-07 69 Pl.
Glendale, NY 11227 (M)

ICF
International Contract
Furnishings, Inc.
145 E. 57 St.
New York, NY 10022 (W)

Industrie Secco
C.P. 101
31100 Treviso, Italy (M)

Inter-Graph
979 Third Ave.
New York, NY 10022 (W)

Ingo Maurer
Design M
Kaiserstrasse 47
Munich, Germany (M)

Skipper
Via S. Spirito
14, Milan, Italy (M)

High-Tech does not claim personal
knowledge of all the manufacturers,
dealers, and retailers listed above.
All information was correct, to the
best of our knowledge, at the time
the book went to press; never-
theless, we cannot guarantee the
accuracy of this information. All
product inquiries should be directed
directly to these companies and not
to the authors or the publisher.

INDEX

INDEX

INDEX

JOAN KRON is a former reporter for the Home section of *The New York Times*, former senior editor and home furnishings writer for *New York* magazine, and associate editor at *Philadelphia* magazine. She has also written for the *Ladies' Home Journal*, *Esquire*, and *Town & Country*.

SUZANNE SLESIN, a senior editor at *Esquire*, writes about design and home furnishings. She is a former contributing editor of *New York* magazine, where she covered home furnishings. She has also contributed to *American Home*, *Industrial Design*, *Architecture Plus*, *Abitare*, and *Domus*.

WALTER BERNARD is the art director of *Time* magazine, which he redesigned last year, and the former art director of *New York* magazine. He is also a visiting professor at Cooper Union.